FERGUSON

CAREER
COACH
MANAGING YOUR CAREER IN THE

Music
Industry

The Ferguson Career Coach Series

FERGUSON

CAREER COACH

MANAGING YOUR CAREER IN THE

Music Industry

Shelly Field

Ferguson
An imprint of Infobase Publishing

Ferguson Career Coach: Managing Your Career in the Music Industry

Copyright © 2008 by Shelly Field

Ferguson
An imprint of Infobase Publishing, Inc.
132 West 31st Street
New York NY 10001

Library of Congress Cataloging-in-Publication Data

Field, Shelly.
    Ferguson career coach: managing your career in the music industry / by Shelly Field. — 1st ed.
        p. cm.
    Includes bibliographical references (p.   ) and index.
    ISBN-13: 978-0-8160-5350-6 (hardcover : alk. paper)
    ISBN-10: 0-8160-5350-2 (hardcover : alk. paper)
    1. Music—Vocational guidance. 2. Music—Economic aspects. I. Title.
    ML3795.F498 2008
    780.23—dc22
                            2007026795

Ferguson books are available at special discounts when purchased in bulk quantities for businesses, associations, institutions, or sales promotions. Please call our Special Sales Department in New York at (212) 967-8800 or (800) 322-8755.

You can find Ferguson on the World Wide Web at http://www.fergpubco.com

Text design by Kerry Casey
Cover design by Takeshi Takahashi

Printed in the United States of America

VB FOF 10 9 8 7 6 5 4 3 2 1

This book is printed on acid-free paper and contains 30% post-consumer recycled content.

Disclaimer: The examples and practices described in this book are based on the author's experience as a professional career coach. No guarantee of success for individuals who follow them is stated or implied. Results may vary. Readers should bear in mind that techniques described might be inappropriate in some professional settings, and that changes in industry trends, practices, and technology may affect the activities discussed here. The author and publisher bear no responsibility for the outcome of any reader's use of the information and advice provided herein.

CONTENTS

1

Introducing Your Career Coach

So you want to be in the music business? Great! You've just chosen to work in one of the most exciting industries in the world. It can be glamorous; it can be fun; and it can be financially rewarding. It can also be very competitive. Can you make it?

I'm betting you can, and if you let me, I'm going to help you get there. Whether you've just decided that you want to be in the music industry or you're in and you want to move up the career ladder, this book is for you. Whether you want to be on the business end or in the talent area, this book can be your guide to success.

What makes me such an expert? I've been where you are. For as long as I can remember, I wanted to be in the music industry, probably more than anything else in the world. I struggled to get in. Could I find anyone to help? No. Did I know anyone in the business? No. Did I live in one of the music capitals? No. The only thing I had going for me was a burning desire to be in the industry and the knowledge that I wasn't going to quit until it happened.

At the time I was trying to enter the industry, I wished there was a book to give me advice on how to move ahead, to guide me toward my goals and give me insider tips. Unfortunately there wasn't. I wished that I had a mentor or

a coach or someone who really knew what I should be doing and could tell me what it was. Unfortunately, I didn't have that either.

Did anyone ever help me? It wasn't that no one wanted to help, but most of the people in my network just didn't have a clue about the music industry. Did they know that the music industry was a multibillion dollar business? Did they know that it offered countless opportunities? It really didn't matter, because no one I knew could give me an edge on getting in anyway.

A couple of times I did run into some music industry professionals who did try to help. In one instance, a few months after I had started job hunting, I finally landed an interview at a large booking agency. I arrived for my appointment and sat waiting for the owner of the agency to meet with me. I sat and sat and sat.

A recording artist who was a client of the agency walked over to me after his meeting with the agent and asked how long I had been there. "Close to three hours," I replied. My appointment was for 1 P.M. and it was almost 4 P.M. "What are you here for?" he asked. "I want to be in the music industry," was my answer. "I want to be a tour manager."

"Someday," he said, "you'll make it and this joker [the agency owner] will want something from you and you can make *him* wait. Mark my words; it will happen." He then stuck his head inside the agency owner's door and said, "This woman has been sitting out here for hours; bring her in already." As I walked into the office I had a glimmer of hope. It was short lived, but it was hope just the same.

The agency owner was very nice. During our meeting he told me something to the effect of, if he ever needed someone with my skills and talents, he would be glad to give me a call and I should keep plugging away. In other words, thanks for coming in. I talked to you; now please leave. Don't call me; I'll call you.

He then explained in a hushed voice, "Anyway, you know how it is: Most managers don't want *girls* on the road with their acts." Not only was I being rejected because of my skills and talents, but now it was because I was a *girl*. (Because my name is Shelly, evidently many people incorrectly assumed I was male instead of female when their secretary's were setting up appointments. The good news is that this got me into a lot of places I probably wouldn't have had a chance to get in. The bad news—once I got there, they realized I was not a man.)

⭐ Tip from the Top

During that interview at the booking agency, I learned two important lessons. One, use what you have to get your foot in the door. If someone thought I was a man because of my name, well, my idea was not to correct them *until* I got in the door. At least that way I could have a chance at selling myself.

The second lesson is choose your battles wisely. Had I complained about sexual discrimination at that point, I might have won the battle, but I would have lost the war.

I smiled, thanked the agent for meeting with me, and left wondering if I would ever get a job doing what I wanted. Was it sexual discrimination? Probably, but in reality the agent was just telling me the way it was at that time. He actually believed he was being nice. Was it worth complaining about? I didn't think so. I was new to the industry and I wasn't about to make waves *before* I even got in. The problem was, I just couldn't find a way to get in.

On another occasion, I met a road manager at a concert and told him about how I wanted to be a tour manager. He told me he knew how hard it was to get into the industry so he was going to help me. "Call me on Monday," he told me Saturday. I did. "I'm working on it," he said. "Call me Wednesday." On Wednesday he said, "Call me Friday." This went on for a couple of weeks before I realized that he was trying to be nice but really wasn't going to do anything for me.

I decided that if I were ever lucky enough to break into the music industry, I would help as many people who wanted a job doing *anything* to fulfill their dream as I possibly could. I wasn't sure when I'd make it, but I knew I would get there eventually.

Although like many others I dreamed about standing on a stage in front of thousands of adoring fans singing my number one song, in reality, I knew that was not where my real talent was. I knew, however, that I did have the talent to make it on the business end of the industry.

I did all the traditional things to try to get a job. I sent my resume, I searched out employment agencies that specialized in the music industry, I made cold calls, and I read the classifieds.

And guess what? I still couldn't land a job. Imagine that. A college degree and a burning desire still couldn't get me the job I wanted. I had some offers, but the problem was that they

> ## ⭐ Tip from the Coach
>
> The music industry is small, so make sure you always leave a good impression. Remember what the recording artist at the booking agency told me? A number of years after I broke into the industry, his words actually did come true. At the time, I was working on a project booking the talent for a big music festival overseas, and the booking agent heard about it. He put in a call to me to see if I'd consider using his talent for the show. "Hi, Shelly, it's Dave. It been a long time," said the voice mail. "I heard you were booking a new show and wanted to talk to you about having some of my acts appearing on the show." As soon as I heard his name, the words of that recording artist came flooding back into my mind. This was a true "mark my words" moment.
>
> I was busy, so I couldn't call him right away. He kept calling back. He really wanted his acts on the show. I finally took his call and told him we'd get back to him. He must have called 25 times in a two-day period to see if we'd made up our mind.
>
> I then reminded him of the day I sat in his office and waited and waited for him to see me. He, of course, didn't even remember the moment, but to his credit, he apologized profusely and promised never to have me wait again. I accepted his apology and told him he'd only have to wait . . . a little bit longer.

weren't offers to work in the music industry. I had offers for jobs as a social worker, a teacher, a newspaper reporter, and a number of other positions I have since forgotten. Were any of these jobs I wanted? No! I wanted to work in the music business, period, end of story.

Like many of you might experience, I had people telling me I was pipe dreaming. "The music industry," I was told, "is for *the other people*. You know, the *lucky ones*. The ones who have connections in the industry." I was also told consistently how difficult the music industry was to get into and, once in, how difficult it was to succeed.

Want to hear the good news? I eventually did get into the industry. I'll share the story of how I did it later, but basically I had to "think outside of the box" to get there. The important thing was that I found a way to get in. Want to hear some more good news? You can too! As a matter of fact, not only can you get in, but you can succeed.

Remember when I said that if I got in, I'd help every single person who ever wanted a job

doing anything? Well, you want to be in the music industry and I want to help you get there.

I give seminars around the country on entering and succeeding in the music industry, and I'm a personal coach and stress management specialist to many acts and executives in the entertainment industry, but unfortunately I can't be there in person for each and every aspiring music industry professional. So, through the pages of this book, I'm going to be your personal coach, your cheerleader, and your inside source to getting into and succeeding in the music industry.

A Personal Coach— What's That?

The actual job title of "personal coach" is relatively new, but coaches are not. Athletes and others in the sports industry have always used coaches to help improve their game and their performance. Over the past few years, coaches have sprung up in many other fields as well.

There are those who coach people toward better fitness or nutrition; vocal coaches to help people improve their voices; acting coaches to help people with acting skills; and etiquette coaches to help people learn how to act in every situation. There are parenting coaches to help people parent better, retirement coaches to help people be successful in retirement, and time management coaches to help people better manage their time.

There are stress management coaches to help people better manage their stress; executive business coaches to help catapult people to the top; life coaches to help people attain a happier, more satisfying life; and career coaches to help people create a great career. Personal coaches often help people become more successful and satisfied in a combination of areas.

"I don't understand," you might be saying. "Exactly what does a coach do and what can he or she do for me?" Well, there are a number of things.

A coach can help you find your way to success faster. He or she can help motivate you, help you find what really makes you happy, get you on track, and help you focus your energies on what you really want to do. Unlike some family and friends, coaches aren't judgmental. You, therefore, have the ability to freely explore ideas with your coach without fear of them being rejected. Instead of accepting your self-imposed limitations, coaches encourage you to reach to your full potential and improve your performance.

Coaches are objective, and one of the important things they can do for you is point out things that you might not see yourself. Most of all, a coach helps you find the best in you and then shows you ways to bring it out. This, in turn, will make you more successful.

As your coach, what do I hope to do for you? I want to help you find your passion and

then help you go after it. If being in the music industry is what you want, I want you to get in and I want you to be successful.

If you want to be on the business end of the industry, I'm going to help you find ways to get in. If you're already in, we'll work on ways to help you climb the career ladder to your dream position. Is your career aspiration to be on the talent end of the industry? Then we'll work on finding ways to catapult you to the top there too.

Look at me as your personal cheerleader, and look at this book as your guide. I want you to succeed and will do as much as possible to make that happen. No matter what anyone tells you, it is possible to get into the industry and succeed. Thousands of people have done so, and now you can be one of them!

Did you ever notice that some people just seem to attract success? They seem to get all the breaks, are always at the right place at the right time, and have what you want? It's not that you're jealous; you just want to get a piece of the pie.

"They're so lucky," you say. Well, here's the deal. You can be that lucky too. Want to know why? While a little bit of luck is always helpful, it's not just chance. Some people work to attract success. They work to get what they want. They follow a plan, keep a positive attitude, and they know that they're worthy of the prize. Others just wait for success to come, and when all you do is wait, success often just passes you by.

The good news here is that you can be one of the lucky ones who attract success if you take the right steps. This book will give you some of the keys to control your destiny; it will hand you the keys to success in your career and your life.

Through the pages of this book, you'll find the answers to many of your questions about the music business in general, as well as both the business and talent areas. You'll get the inside scoop on how the business works, key employment issues, moving from amateur to pro, and finding opportunities.

You'll find insider tips, tricks, and techniques that worked not only for me but for others who have succeeded in the industry. You'll discover secrets to help get you get in the door and up the ladder of success, as well as the lowdown on things I wish I had known when I was first beginning my quest for success in the music industry.

If you haven't attended one of my Making It in Music seminars or any of the other music industry, stress management, or career workshops I offer, you will get the benefit of being there by simply reading this book. If you have attended one, here is the book you've been asking for!

Change Your Thinking, Change Your Life

Sometimes, the first step in getting what you want is just changing the way you think. Did you know that if you think you don't deserve something, you usually don't get it? Did you know that if you think you aren't good enough, neither will anyone else? Did you know that if you think you deserve something, you have a much better chance of getting it? Or that if you think you are good enough, your confidence will shine through?

When you have confidence in yourself, you start to find ways to get what you want, and guess what? You succeed!

And while changing your thinking can change your life, this book is not just about a positive attitude. It's a book of actions you can take.

While a positive attitude is always helpful in order to succeed in whatever part of the industry you're interested in pursuing, you need to take positive actions, too.

If all it took for you to be successful was for me to tell you what you needed to do or even do it for you, I would. I love the music industry and I want everyone interested in being part of it to live their dream. Unfortunately, that's not the way it works.

Here's the reality of the situation. I can only offer advice, suggestions, and tell you what you need to do. You have to do the rest. Talking about what you can do or should do is fine, but without your taking action, it's difficult to get where you want to go.

This is your chance to finally get what you want. You've already taken one positive step toward getting your dream career simply by picking up this book. As you read through the various sections, you'll find other actions to take that will help get you closer—whether you choose the talent or business end of the music industry.

As you read through the book, we'll talk about creating your own personal action plan. This plan can help you focus on exactly what you want and then show you the actions needed to get it.

Your personal action plan is a checklist of sorts. Done correctly, it can be one of the main keys to your career success. It will put you in the driver's seat and give you an edge over others who haven't prepared a plan themselves.

We'll also discuss putting together a number of different kinds of journals to help you be more successful in your career and life. For example, one of the problems many people experience when they're trying to get a new job, move up the career ladder, or accomplish a goal is that they often start feeling as though they aren't accomplishing anything. A career journal is a handy tool to help you track exactly what you've done to accomplish your goals. Once that is in place, you know what else needs to be done.

Is This the Right Career for Me?

Unsure about exactly what you want to do in the music industry? Not sure what your options are? As you read through the book, you'll see possibilities you might not have thought about. You might also want to check out one of my other books, *Career Opportunities in the Music Industry,* to learn more about specific careers.

"But what if I'm already working at a job in another industry?" you ask. "Is it too late? Am I stuck here forever? Is it too late to get into the music industry?" Here's the deal. It is never too late to change careers, and going after something you're passionate about can drastically improve the quality of your life.

Thousands of people stay in jobs because it's easier than going after what they want. You don't have to be one of them.

We all know people who are in jobs or careers that they don't love. They get up every day waiting for the workweek to be over. They go through the day, waiting for it to be over. They waste their life waiting and waiting. Is this the life you want to lead? Probably not. You now have the opportunity to get what you want. Are you ready to go after it? I'm hoping you are.

If the music industry is where you want to work, there are countless opportunities in both the talent and the business areas. In addition to the traditional ones most people think of, there is an array of others for you to explore. No matter what your skills or talents, you can almost always find a way to parlay them into your music business career.

"Really?" you ask. "What if I'm a nurse? What if I'm an artist? What if I work in a bank? What do any of those have to do with the music industry?"

Here's the good news. If you think in a creative manner, you probably can use any of your skills to get you into the music business.

A number of years ago I was on a radio call-in show about getting into the music industry. A woman called and said, "I really want to work in the music business."

"What do you do now?" I asked.

"I'm a nurse," she replied.

"Use your skills," I told her.

"No," she said. "You didn't hear me. I'm a nurse."

"I heard you," I said. "Here's an idea. Why don't you put a small ad in the trades? There might be some touring acts who are dealing with drug rehab or medical issues who need a nurse on the road with them."

Four months later she called me again. She had placed an ad in the trade journals and didn't get a response. She had, however, won tickets from a local radio station to a concert and "meet and greet" event for a major recording act appearing in her area. She went and enjoyed the show and met the act. In a conversation with the group's road manager, she told him how excited she was to meet the group and happened to mention that she had just placed an ad in the trades for going on the road but that it hadn't brought in any response. A couple of weeks later she got a call from the group's management asking

⭐ Tip from the Coach

Don't procrastinate. Every day you wait to get the career you are passionate about is another day you're not living your dream. Start today!

Words from the Wise

Always carry business cards with your phone number and other contact information. Make it easy for people to find you when an opportunity presents itself.

if she was interested in going on the road with the group to handle first aid and minor medical needs. They located her number by calling the local radio station that had sponsored the contest she had won. While being in the right place at the right time certainly helped, had she not "thought outside of the box," she might not have been living her dream.

During that same radio call-in show, another woman called who was a CPA. She, too, wanted to work in the music business in some capacity. "Can you tell me how to get a job as an intern?" she asked.

"An intern?" I asked. "Why would you want to be an intern?"

"I want to work at a record company," she replied. "Isn't that how you get in?"

"Well, yes, sometimes if you're in college an internship helps," I noted, "but you have skills that a record company might need. An entry-level job is probably not for you."

I suggested that she send her resume with a cover letter to a number of record companies. A few months down the line, she contacted me to tell me how happy she was in her new job in the accounting department of a large record label.

A Job versus a Career: What's the Difference?

What do you want in life? Would you rather just have a job or do you want a career? What's the difference? A job is just that. It's something you

do to earn a living. It's a means to an end. A career, on the other hand, is a series of related jobs. It's a progressive path of achievement, a long-term journey. A career is something you build using your skills, talents, and passions.

You might have many jobs in your career. You might even follow more than one career path. The question is what do you want?

If all you want is to go to work, day after day, week after week just to get paid, a job is all you need, and there is nothing wrong with that. On the other hand, if you would like to fill your life with excitement and passion while getting paid, you are a prime candidate for a great career.

How can you get that? Start planning now to get what you want. Define your goals and then start working toward them.

Not everyone starts off with a dream job. If you just sit and wait for your dream job to come to you, you could be sitting forever. What you can do, however, is take what you have and make it work for you until you get what you want.

What does that mean? It means that you can make whatever you do better, at least for the time being. The trick in this process is finding ways to give the job you have some meaning. Find a way to get some passion from what you're doing. If you get that mind set you'll never have a bad job. Focus on your ultimate career goal and then look at each job as a benchmark along the way to what you want.

How to Use This Book to Help You in the Music Industry

Ideally, I would love for you to read this book from beginning to end, but I know from experience that that's probably not the way it's going to happen. You might browse the contents and look for something that can help you *now,* you might see a subject that catches your eye, or you might be looking for an area of the book that solves a particular problem.

For this reason, as you read the book, you might see what appears to be some duplication of information. In this manner, I can be assured that when I suggest something that may be helpful to you in a certain area that you will get all the information you need, even if you didn't read a prior section.

You should be aware that even if you're interested in working on the talent end of the industry, knowing about the business end will be helpful to succeeding in your career and vice versa.

If you're on the talent end of the industry, understanding how the business end works, for example, will help assure that you are treated fairly, don't get ripped off, and know where the monies come from and go. If you're on the business end of the industry, understanding as much as possible about the talent area can help you be more effective in your job.

There's a great mystique to the music business, as there is in the entire entertainment industry. Many would have you think that the music industry is impossible to break into, impossible to succeed in. Trust me—it is not. If you're willing to put some effort into the process, you can make it.

You might have heard the saying that knowledge is power. This is true. The more you know about the music industry and how it works, the better your chances are of succeeding. This book is full of information to help you learn everything you need to know about the industry and how it works. I'm betting that you will refer to information in this book long after you've attained success.

As you read through the various sections, you'll find a variety of suggestions and ideas to help you succeed. Keep in mind that every idea and suggestion might not work in every situation and for every person. The idea is to keep trying things until one of them works. Use the book as a springboard to get you started. Just because something is not written here doesn't mean that it's not a good idea. Brainstorm to find solutions to barriers you might encounter in your career.

My job is to lead you on your journey to success in the music industry. Along the way you'll find exercises, tasks, and assignments that will help get you where you want to be faster. No one is going to be standing over your shoulder to make you do these tasks. You alone can make the decision on the amount of time and work you want to put into your career. While no one can guarantee you success, what you should know is that the more you put into your career, the better your chances of having the success you probably are dreaming about.

Are you worth the time and effort? I think you are! Is a career in the music industry worth it? I believe it's one of the best industries in the world in which to work. Aside from the opportunity to make a great living and fulfill your dreams, you can leave an imprint on the entertainment others enjoy.

No matter what level you're currently at in your career in the music business and in whatever capacity, this book is for you. You might not need every section or every page, but I can guarantee that parts of this book can help you.

Whether you're just starting out as an intern or administrative assistant, you're an up-and-coming music executive, or even the CEO of a record label, music publishing company, agency management firm, or other music industry business; whether you're a struggling songwriter, singer, or musician, or on the top of the charts, this book can help you experience more success in your career and a happier, more satisfying, and stress-free life.

Music Industry Overview

Whether through turning on the radio, playing a CD, seeing a concert, or singing a song, there are very few people whose lives the music industry doesn't touch. Even when we're not consciously listening, we hear jingles on radio and television commercials, background music on television shows and movies, and even music while riding elevators.

The music industry is huge. It is a multibillion-dollar industry that encompasses the talent and creative end of the music as well as the business end and everything in between.

Over the years the music industry has grown and changed dramatically. There are now new ways to enjoy music as well as new ways to make it. Thanks to portable CD players, MP3s, iPods, and the like, music is now easy to take with us wherever we go. Music television, video, and the Internet have joined radio in methods of garnering exposure for albums. An appearance or music video on music television, for example, can create a hit record almost instantaneously.

"Indies," or independent labels, have joined the ranks of major record labels. The industry is now diverse and filled with people of all ages, all backgrounds, and with various educational levels. There is no one type of music.

The corner record store is not the only place to buy music. As a matter of fact, finding a corner record store is becoming harder, if not impossible. Eager buyers can now purchase downloads of tunes as well as buy from mass retailers, chains, or Internet music sites. While cassettes are still available, CDs get the mass shelf space.

Affordable electronic instruments and updated computer technology allow people to write, play, and record music with ease. Affordable electronic audio and video equipment makes it possible for young artists to create both demos and videos easily.

The one thing that hasn't changed about the music industry is the desire many people have to be part of it. For many people who want to work in the music industry, the idea remains just a dream. The good news is that the dream can now become a reality.

The music industry today is a desirable career option, and it has never been easier to get in or succeed if you're prepared. Whether it's the glitz or the glamour or the gold at the end of the rainbow, or it's the genuine desire to express musical creativity or to share a music talent with others, there are many reasons that thousands of people are drawn to careers in music and find ways to succeed. I'm betting one of them will be you.

The Music Business and How It Works

Here's how the music business works in a nutshell. Some people make music. Other people buy it either directly or indirectly. In between there's a business organization that makes that possible. On a broad level, that's how the music business works. Do you want to be part of it? Then read on.

Let's look at the whole process a little closer. At one end of the spectrum there's the talent of the music industry encompassing singers, musicians, writers, and producers, among others. At the other end of the spectrum are the business people, including personal managers, agents, business managers, publicists, press agents, attorneys, record company executives, tour people, promoters, and other personnel. The music industry, like most other industries, has positions in peripheral areas, and these peripheral positions are important. As an example, reporters, journalists, and reviewers, talented in their own right, are the ones who write or speak about the music and music business. The industry also couldn't come full circle without people working in radio, education, and retailing, among other areas.

What's important to realize is that every position in the music industry, no matter what it is, is important. Every position can have an impact on the end result.

A songwriter, for example, can write a great song, but without someone promoting it, the song might not get to a great singer. The singer can have a perfect voice, but without a way to get it recorded, the number of people who hear it will be limited. Almost anyone can make a CD, but once it's recorded, if not marketed, promoted, and sold correctly, it can sit in a warehouse.

By the time a song becomes a hit and gets into stores, hundreds of different people have had an impact on it, from someone in the mailroom to the songwriter and the singer to the store clerk who ultimately sells the CD. Similarly, by the time you attend a concert, probably hundreds of people have worked toward that event. What all this means is that every job or career path in the industry is ultimately important. The job you do can, in reality, affect those who reap the benefits and pleasure of the music industry. With this in mind, if you need to take some jobs along the way to your dream career that you feel are beneath you, use them as a stepping-stone to get to your ultimate destination.

A Sampling of What This Book Covers

This informative guide to success in the music industry is written in a friendly, easy-to-read style. Let it be your everyday guide to success. Want to focus on what your really want to do? Check out the book!

Want to learn how to plan and prepare for your dream career? Do you want to know the best places to be for music business careers? Do you want to focus on search strategies especially for the music industry? How about tips for making those important music industry contacts, how to network, or how to create the ideal music industry resume or cover letter? Check out the book!

Do you need to know how to develop your bio or put together your press kit? Do you want to get your portfolio together? Want to know what business cards can do for you and your career? Check out the book!

Want to learn how to get your foot in the door? How about checking out tried-and-true methods to get people to call you back? Do you want to learn the best way to market yourself and why it's so important? Do you want to learn how to succeed in the workplace, deal with workplace politics, keep an eye out for opportunities, and climb the career ladder? You know what you have to do: Check out the book!

Do you want to know how to move from the garage to the recording studio and find gigs? Do you want to know about contracts, dealing with managers, agents, lawyers, and more? Are you interested in learning how to deal with the media, get exposure, and protect yourself? You need to read the book!

Do you need important contact information so you can more your career forward? Check out this book's listings of important associations, unions, organizations and Web sites.

Although this book won't teach you how to write a hit tune, sing a popular song, or play an instrument better, it will help you find ways to garner success whether your passion is the talent or business area.

If you dream of working in the music industry and don't know how to make that dream a reality, this book is for you. Have fun reading it. Know that if your heart is in it, you can achieve anything.

Now let's get started.

2

FOCUSING ON A GREAT CAREER IN THE MUSIC INDUSTRY

Focusing on What You Really Want to Do

Unless you're independently wealthy or just won the megamillion-dollar lottery, you, like most people, have to work. Just in case you're wondering, life is not supposed to be miserable. Neither is your job.

Here are some questions you might ask yourself. Do you wake up every morning dreading going to work? Do you ask yourself, "What should I be?" How about, "What should I do for the rest of my life?" or "What should I be when I grow up?" Do you daydream about working in the music industry? Do you wonder how you're going to make it in the industry?

Your life is supposed to have a purpose. That purpose is not sleeping, getting up, going to a job that you don't particularly care about, coming home, cooking dinner, and watching TV only to do it all over again the next day.

To be happy and fulfilled, you need to enjoy life. You need to do things that give you pleasure. As a good part of your life is spent working, the trick is to find a career that you love and that you're passionate about—the career of your dreams.

This is not something everyone does. Many people just fall into a career without thinking ahead of time about what it will entail. Someone who needs a job hears of an opening or answers an ad and then goes for it without thinking about the consequences of working at something for which they really have no passion. Once hired, either it's difficult to give up the money or just too hard to start job hunting again, or they don't know what else to do, so they stay. They wind up with a career that is okay but one they're not really passionate about.

Then there are the other people. The ones who have jobs they love, the lucky people. You've seen them. They're the people who have the jobs and life you wish you had.

Have you noticed that people who love their jobs are usually successful not only in their ca-

> ### Tip from the Coach
> Okay is just that: It's okay. Just so you know, you don't want just okay; you don't want to settle; you want *great!* That's what you deserve and that's what you should go after.

18

reer but in other aspects of life as well? They almost seem to have an aura around them of success, happiness, and prosperity. Do you want to be one of them? You can!

Finding a career that you want and love is challenging but possible. You are in a better position than most people. If you're reading this book, you've decided that the music business is what you're passionate about. Now all you have to do is determine exactly what you want to do in the industry.

What's your dream career? What do you really want to do? This is an important question to ask yourself. Once you know the answer, you can work toward achieving your goal.

If someone asks you right now what you really want to do, can you answer the question? Okay, one, two, three: "What do you want to do with your life?"

If you're saying, "Uh, um, well . . . What I really want to do is . . . well, it's hard to explain," then it's time to focus in on the subject. Sometimes the easiest way to figure out what you want to do is to focus in on what you don't want.

Most people can easily answer what they don't want to do. "I don't want to be a teacher. I don't want to work in a factory. I don't to work in a store," and the list goes on. The problem is that just saying what you don't like or don't want to do doesn't necessarily get you what you want to do.

It may seem simple, but sometimes just looking at a list of what you don't like will help you see more clearly what you do like.

Sit down with a sheet of paper or fill in the "Things I Don't Want to Do" worksheet on page 20 and make a list of work-related things you don't like to do. Remember that this list is for you. While you can show it to someone if you want, no one else really has to see it, so try to be honest with yourself.

Here's an example to get you started. When you make your list, add your personal likes and dislikes.

- ◎ I hate the idea of being cooped up in an office all day.
- ◎ I hate the idea of having to sing in front of a live audience.
- ◎ I don't want to have to commute for an hour each way every day.
- ◎ I don't like to be in the limelight.
- ◎ I don't like making decisions.
- ◎ I don't like getting up early in the morning to go to work.
- ◎ I don't want to work in retail sales.
- ◎ I don't want to have to travel for work.
- ◎ I don't like working with numbers.
- ◎ I don't like doing the same thing day after day.
- ◎ I don't like being in charge.

We know what you don't like. Now use this list as a starting point to see what you do like. If you look closely, you'll find that the things you enjoy are the opposite of the things you don't want to do.

Below are some examples to get you started. You might make another list as well as using the "Things I Enjoy Doing" worksheet on page 22. Remember that the reason you're writing everything down is so you can look at it, remember it, and focus in on getting exactly what you want.

- ◎ I hate the idea of being cooped up in an office all day.
  - ▫ But I'd really like to work on the road.
- ◎ I hate the idea of having to sing in front of a live audience.

Things I Don't Want to Do

- ⊡ But I'm a really good singer. Maybe I'll look into working as a background singer in a studio.
- ◎ I don't want to have to commute for an hour each way every day.
  - ⊡ But if I find a job in the city, perhaps I can find an apartment close by.
- ◎ I don't like to be in the limelight.
  - ⊡ But I really like supporting others who are there.
- ◎ I don't like making decisions.
  - ⊡ I like working in a situation where I'm given direction.
- ◎ I don't like getting up early in the morning to go to work.
  - ⊡ Maybe I can find a job where I work later in the day or work at night.
- ◎ I don't want to work in retail sales.
  - ⊡ But I'm really good at sales. I think I might be interested in working in the marketing department at a record label.
- ◎ I don't want to travel for extended periods of time, but I want to play in a band.
  - ⊡ Perhaps I can start off working local gigs and then see how it goes.

As you can see, once you've determined what you don't like doing, it's much easier to get ideas on what you'd like to do. It's kind of like brainstorming with yourself.

Many people in this world don't like what they do or are dissatisfied with their career. The good news is you don't have to be one of them.

You and you alone are in charge of your career. Not your mother, father, sister, brother, girlfriend, boyfriend, spouse, or best friend. Others can care, others can help, and others can offer you advice, but in essence, you need to be in control. What this means is that the path you take for your career is largely determined by the choices you make.

The fastest way to get the career you want is by making the choice to take actions now and going after it! You can have a career you love and you can have it in the music business. And when you're doing something you love, you'll be on the road to a great career and a satisfied and fulfilled life.

The next chapter discusses how to develop your career plan. This plan is your road map to success. It is full of actions you can do not only to get the career in the music industry you want but succeed in it as well. Before you get too involved in the plan, however, you need to zero in on exactly what you want your career to be.

At this point you might be in a number of different employment situations. You might still be in school planning your career, just out of school beginning your career, or in a job that you don't really care for. You might be in your late teens, 20s, 30s 40s, 50s, or even older.

The Inside Scoop

If you think working in music industry is just for those in their 20s and 30s, think again. Clive Davis, one of the most talented record executives in the world, is in his mid-70s. Davis, responsible for guiding the careers of recording stars such as Carlos Santana, Bruce Springsteen, Whitney Houston, and Alicia Keys, is so good at what he does that he was recently named chairman and CEO of BMG, North America.

Need some other examples? Carlos Santana won a Grammy in his early 50s. Bruce Springsteen is still going strong in his 50s. Mick Jagger, lead singer for the Rolling Stones, is in his 60s. Chubby Checker, king of "The Twist," hit the charts again in his 60s.

Things I Enjoy Doing

"Older? Did you say older?" you ask.

Yes. If you have a dream, it is never too late to pursue it.

Okay, you've decided that the music business is the industry for you, but do you know what your dream career is? There are hundreds of exciting career choices whether you want to be on the business end, in the talent area, or somewhere in between. It's up to you to decide which one you want to pursue.

What's Your Dream?

I bet that you have an idea of what your dream job is and I bet that you have an idea of what it should be like. I'm also betting that you don't have that job yet or if you do, you're not at the level you want to be. So, what can we do to make that dream a reality?

One of the problems many people have in getting their dream job is that they just don't think they deserve it. Dream jobs are something many people talk about and wish they had but just don't. Many people think that dream jobs are for the lucky ones.

Well, I'm here to tell you that you are the lucky one. You can get your dream job, a job you'll love, and it can be in the music business!

If I had a magic wand and could get you any job you wanted, what would it be? Do you want to be a songwriter? A singer? Part of a hot rock-and-roll group? Do you want to book acts in a major venue? Do you want to manage the career of a hot artist? Would you rather handle the press and media for a record label? How about the career of a respected record label exec? Not sure what you want to do?

Determining what you really want to do is not always easy. Take some time to think about it. Throughout this process, try to be as honest with yourself as possible. Otherwise, you stand

the chance of not going after the career you really want.

Let's get started. We're going to do another writing exercise. While you might think these are a pain now, if you follow through, you will find it easier to attain your dream.

Get a pen and a pad and find a place where you can get comfortable. Maybe it's your living room chair. Perhaps it's your couch or even your bed. Now all you have to do is sit down and daydream for a bit about what you wish you could be and what you wish you were doing.

"Why daydream?" you ask.

When you daydream your thinking becomes freer. You stop thinking about what you can't do and start thinking about what you can do. What is your dream? What is your passion? What do you really want to do? Admit it now or forever hold your peace.

Many people are embarrassed to admit when they want something because they fear looking stupid if they don't get it. They worry people are going to talk badly about them or call them a failure. Is this what you worry about? Do you really want to be a singer but are afraid you'll fail? Is your dream to be a record exec, but you don't think you'll make it?

First of all, don't ever let fear of failure stop you from going after something you want. While no one can guarantee you success, what I can guarantee you is that if you don't go after what you want, it is going to be very difficult to get it.

One thing you never want to do is get to the end of your life and say with regret, "I wish I had done this," or "I wish I had done that." Will you get each and every thing you want? I'd like to say a definitive "yes," but that probably wouldn't be true. The truth of the matter is you might not succeed at everything. But even if you fail, when

> ### Tip from the Coach
>
> While you're working on your day-dreaming exercise, don't get caught up in thinking any of your ideas are foolish or stupid. Let your imagination run freely. If these negative ideas come into your head, consciously push them way.

you try to do something, it usually is a stepping-stone to something else. And that something else can be the turning point in your career.

Think about things that make you happy. Think about things that make you smile. Continue to indulge your passions as you daydream. As ideas come to you, jot them down on your pad. Remember, nothing is foolish, so write down all the ideas you have for what you want to do. You're going to fine-tune them later.

Here's an example to get you started.

◎ I want to write a hit song. As a matter of fact, I'd love to write a lot of songs that turn into megahits.

◎ I'd love to be on stage singing my hit records.

◎ I want to work on the business end of the music industry.

◎ I want to be a press agent. I want to make other people famous. I think that would be fun.

◎ I want to be famous myself.

◎ I want to go on the road and travel around the country.

◎ I wish I were an attorney. Then I could work in a record label legal department, or I could work directly for an artist.

◎ I want to be a tour manager. I want to go from city to city with a top music group and handle all the details.

◎ Maybe I should just be teacher. It's a good profession and you help people. No, I definitely don't want to be a teacher. I hated school. That would be like continuing something I hated. I think I'll leave teaching for people who have the calling.

◎ I want to be an on-the-road publicist.

Do you need some help focusing on what you really want to do in the music industry? To choose just the right career, pinpoint your interests and what you really love doing. What are your skills? What are your personality traits? You might want to fill in the worksheet on the next page to help you zero in even more.

What's Stopping You from Getting What You Want?

Now that you have some ideas written down about what you want to do, go down the list. What has stopped you from attaining your goal? Is it that you told people what you wanted to do and they told you that you couldn't? Did they tell you it was too difficult and your chances of making it were slim? Is it that you don't have the confidence in yourself to get what you want? Or is it that you need more education or training? Perhaps it's because you aren't in the location most conducive to your dream career? If you can identify the obstacle, you usually can find a way to overcome it, but you need to identify the problem first.

> ### The Inside Scoop
>
> When you write down your ideas, you're giving them power. You now have them on paper, making it easier to go over them, look at them rationally, and fine-tune them.

Focusing on the Job of Your Dreams Worksheet

Finish the following sentences to help pinpoint your interests and find the job of your dreams.

In my free time I enjoy

_____

In my free time I enjoy going

_____

My hobbies are

_____

When I volunteer the types of projects I do are

_____

My skills are

_____

My best personality traits include

_____

My current job is

_____

Prior types of jobs have been

_____

The subjects I liked best in school were

_____

If I didn't have to worry about any obstacles, the three jobs I would want would be

_____

What steps can I take to get one of those jobs?

_____

Do you know exactly what you want to do but can't find an opening? For example, do you know you want to work at a record label but can't find a job? If this is the case, don't only keep looking, but look outside the box. Try to find ways to get your foot in the door, and once it's in, don't let it out until you get what you want.

Have you found the perfect job and interviewed for it, but then the job wasn't offered to you? While at the time you probably felt awful about this, there is some good news. Generally, when one door closes, another one opens. Hard to believe? It may be, but if you think about it, you'll see that it's true. Things work out for the best. If you lost what you thought was the job of your dreams, a better one is out there waiting for you. You just have to find it.

Sometimes while you know exactly what type of job you want, you just can't find a job like that available. Don't give up. Keep looking. Sometimes you have to think outside of the box to get what you want.

Perhaps you are just missing the skills necessary for the type of job you're looking for. This is a relatively easy thing to fix. Once you know the skills necessary for a specific type of job, take steps to get them. Take classes, go to workshops, attend seminars, or become an apprentice or intern.

"But," you say, "I'm missing the education necessary for the job I want. The ad I read said I needed a bachelor's degree and I don't have one."

Here's the deal. While you can't get a job as an attorney in a record label unless you have completed law school and you can't get a job as an accountant without the required education, educational requirements may be negotiable in many cases.

Just because an ad states that a job has a specific educational requirement doesn't mean you should just pass it by if your education doesn't meet that requirement. First of all, advertisements for jobs generally contain the highest hopes of the people placing the ads, not necessarily the reality of what they will settle for. Secondly, many companies will accept experience in lieu of education. Lastly, if you're a good candidate in other respects, many companies will hire you while you're finishing the required education.

Is a lack of experience stopping you from entering your dream career? This is easily fixed. If you can't get experience in the workplace, then volunteer. For example, do you need experience doing publicity for a career in a label publicity department? See if you can find an internship. What if that doesn't pan out? Volunteer to do publicity for a local not-for-profit group. Experience is transferable. Do you need experience performing? Offer to provide the entertainment for a local not-for-profit event. Perhaps you can join your church or community choir or chorus. Take every opportunity that presents itself to get the experience you need. Don't ever let a chance to perform pass you by.

One of the biggest obstacles many people encounter when trying to enter the music business is that the jobs are just not in the geographic location in which they live. If, for example, you're looking for a career at a major label, you're probably going to have to live in one of the major music capitals like New York, Los Angeles, or Nashville. If you don't live in these areas and want to work at a label, you might try to find a similar job at an independent label closer to where you live.

Is what's holding you back that you don't know anyone in the music business? Is it that you don't have any contacts? Here's the deal. You have to find ways to make contacts. Take classes, seminars, and workshops in subject areas related to the music industry. Volunteer. Make cold calls. Attend concerts. Go to clubs and network, network, network. Put yourself in situations where you can meet people in the industry, and sooner or a later, you will meet them.

"The only thing between me and success," you say, "is a big break." Getting your big break may take time. Keep plugging away. Most of all, don't give up. Your break will come when you least expect it.

Are you scared? Are you not sure you have the talent? If you start doubting yourself, other people might do the same. Don't let fear stop you from dong what you want.

Whatever you do, don't let anyone burst your bubble. What does that mean? You know how it is when you get so excited about doing something that you just can't keep it to yourself. So you share your ideas of what you want to do with your family and friends. If they start trying to destroy your dream by pointing out all the problems you might encounter, don't let them undermine you. It's not that they're trying to be unsupportive, but for some people it seems to be their nature to try to pick other people's dreams

apart. Why? There are a number of reasons. Let's look at a few scenarios.

Scenario 1—Sometimes people are just negative. "Oh," they might say to you. "You'll never make it. Do you know how many people want to be in the music business?"

"Well," you tell them. "I have talent."

Their response? "There are a lot of talented people who have never made it. Why don't you just get involved with the music business on the side? Be smart. Get a real job."

Scenario 2—Sometimes people are jealous. They might hate their job and be jealous that you are working toward finding a great career. Others might be trying to make it in the music business themselves and be jealous that you have a plan. They might be jealous that you might make it before they do.

Scenario 3—Sometimes people are scared of change. In many cases, friends or family are concerned about your well-being and are just scared of change. "You have a job working in a bank," your girlfriend may say. "Why don't you just stay there so you know you have a solid income?"

Scenario 4—Sometimes people just think you're pipe dreaming. "You're a pipe dreamer," your family may say. "What you need is a dose of reality. Just because you got a couple of gigs does not mean that you're going to make it big. There are thousands of people who want to work in the music business. You're just one in a million. The odds are not good."

Scenario 5—Sometimes people are under the impression that you can't make it if you don't have any connections. "You don't know anyone in the business," your friend says. "Don't be an idiot. You can't make it if you don't know anyone. You need connections."

Whatever the scenario, there you sit starting to question yourself. Well, stop! Do not let

---

Tip from the Coach

If there is something that you want to do or something that you want to try in your career or your life, my advice is go for it. No matter what the risk, no matter how scared you are, no matter what. Your life and career will benefit more than you can imagine and you'll never look back with regrets. Even if it doesn't work out, you'll feel successful because you tried.

anyone burst your bubble. Just remember, no matter what anyone says, at least you are trying to get the career you want. At least you are following your dream. I can promise you if that if you don't go after your dream, it will be very difficult to achieve. So don't listen to anyone, and keep working toward what you want.

What Gives You Joy? What Makes You Happy?

Let's zero in further on what you want to do. Let's talk about what gives you joy. Let's talk about what makes you happy. Have you ever noticed that when you're doing something that you love, you smile? It's probably subconscious, but you're smiling. You're happy inside. And it's not only that you're happy; you make others around you happy.

So let's think about it. What makes you happy? What gives you joy? Is it singing? Is it playing an instrument? Is it writing a song? Is it being on the road?

Does the thought of seeing a review you wrote about a rock concert in the newspaper make you smile? When you close your eyes, can you see yourself planning a press conference for one of your new clients? Can you almost hear the song you wrote being played on the radio? Are you smiling as you think about seeing your name on the charts? Then maybe that's what would make you happy.

Keep dreaming. Keep asking yourself what makes you happy. What gives you joy? Are you

having a hard time figuring it out? Many of us do. Here's an idea to help get your juices flowing.

Take out your pad and a pen again. Make a list of any jobs or volunteer activities you've done, things you do in your "off time," and hobbies. If you're still in school, you might add extracurricular activities in which you've participated.

Note what aspects of each you like and what you don't like. This will help you see what type of job you're going to enjoy.

What are your special talents, skills, and personality traits? What gives you joy and makes you happy? Have you been part of your church choir? Is your special talent singing? Can you rehearse for hours on end, because you want to be perfect?

"That's not fair," you might say. "Singers have it easy. They know what they want to be." Well, yes and no. Singers have to determine what type of career they want to go after. Do they want to be a classical singer, pop singer, country singer? Do they want to be a solo artist? Part of a group? A background singer? There's always a decision to make when it comes to your career. Are you up for the challenge?

Are you always volunteering to do the publicity for a charity? Do you thrive on the excitement of putting together events? If you love doing publicity for a not-for-profit, you might really love doing publicity for a record label or artist. If you love putting events together, you might consider going after a job as a special events coordinator at a label or perhaps at a nightclub or venue.

A few years back, I gave a seminar where the participants were working on this particular assignment. A woman raised her hand and said, "I don't know what to write down. I've never had a job that I liked. I don't even know what

I like. I guess it's because I always wanted to be in the music business in some fashion, but I just can't figure out how or where I would fit in. I can't sing. I don't play an instrument. I don't really even know anything about the music business, but I really want to be in it."

"Let's see," I said. "What are your hobbies? What do you like to do in your spare time?"

"I don't have any hobbies," she answered. "I go to work, come home, and make dinner. Cooking relaxes me."

"Really," I said. "You like cooking?"

She continued, "My only good vacations are when I take gourmet cooking classes. I'm the one who always makes all the food for all my neighbor's parties. As a matter of fact, the only good time I ever had at my job was when I made the food for a large office party. Everyone loves my cooking."

"Did you ever consider trying to parlay your cooking skills into a job in the music industry," I asked?

"No," she responded. "I don't have a degree in cooking and I didn't even consider doing anything like that. What could I do anyway?"

"There are a lot of options," I told her. "A lot of the bands on the road bring along either a personal chef or a caterer. Do you think you'd like to try something like that?"

To make a long story short, the woman really liked that idea and decided to put all her efforts into getting a job like that. She took some extra cooking and baking classes, made up business cards, and went to every concert she could find with samples of cookies and brownies. Then, after she got her foot in the door meeting people, she offered to make them a meal. Within four months or so, she was offered jobs to go on the road and cook for a number of different touring acts. Not only is it

> ### Words from the Wise
> The first requisite for success is the ability to apply your physical and mental energies to one problem incessantly without growing weary.
>
> –Thomas Edison

just what she wanted to do, but she loves her job and every act that retains her loves what she does too.

If you dream big and reach high, you can have a life and career that are better than you can ever imagine. If, on the other hand, you just settle, you will never feel fulfilled.

What Are Your Talents?

It's important to define what your talents are. Sometimes we're so good at something that we just don't even think twice about it. The problem with this is that we don't see the value in our talent. What does this mean? It means that we may overlook the possibilities associated with our talents.

Just as the woman in the previous story didn't see her cooking as a talent, you may be overlooking a talent you have. It's also important to know that you can have more than one talent. Just because you can sing doesn't mean you aren't a talented writer. Just because you can play an instrument doesn't mean you can't be a talented publicist. Most of us have more than one talent. The trick is making sure you know what your talents are and using them to your advantage.

Do you know your talents? This is another time you're going to have to sit down and start writing. Write down everything that you're good at. Write down all your talents.

This is not the time to be modest. Remember, this list is for you, so be honest with yourself.

Can you finish this sentence? I am a talented (fill in the blank). You might be a talented singer, songwriter, musician, or writer. You might be talented in organizing, supervising, cooking, or baking. You might be talented at negotiating, persuasion, painting, drawing, decorating, or public speaking. Whatever your talents, you can use them to help your career.

How? Let's say you want to be a hot recording artist. Your talents are singing and songwriting. You also know that you are a great negotiator and very good at persuasion. While your singing and songwriting can certainly help you become a hot recording artist, having the talent to persuade people to listen to your act and the talent to negotiate deals can help catapult you to the top.

Getting What You Want

You hear opportunity knocking. How do you get what you want? How do you turn your dream into reality? One of the most important things you need to do is have faith in yourself. It is essential that you believe that you can make it happen in order for it to happen.

As we've discussed, you need to focus on exactly what you really want. Otherwise, you'll be going in a million different directions. Remember that things may not always come as quickly as you want. Most people in the music industry are not overnight successes. You will probably have to "pay your dues." What's that mean? On the most basic level in the music industry, it means you probably have to start small to get to the big time. Before you get to ride in the limo, you're going to have to drive a lot of Chevys. (There's nothing wrong with a Chevy; it's just not the same as having a chauffeured limo.)

Depending on your situation, it might mean singing the national anthem at a local sports event before you're invited to sing it at the Super Bowl. You might have to play a lot of little clubs before you play a stadium. You may have to pound on a lot of doors before you become a major recording artist.

On the business end of the industry, you may have to take jobs that are not your ideal choice to get experience so you can move up the career ladder and get the job of your dreams. You may have to do a lot of the grunt work and stay in the background while others get the credit. While all this is going on, you have to be patient with the knowledge that everything you do is getting you closer to your goal.

If you look at every experience as a stepping-stone to get you to the next level of your career, it's a lot easier to get through the trying things you may have to go through.

Want to hear another story? Let me share how I finally got into the music industry. Perhaps my experience will help you in your quest for success.

I wanted to be in the music business for as long as I can remember. I thought I knew what I wanted to do. My dream job was to be a road manager. "Yes," I said. "I want to be a road manager." It wasn't the most glamorous job, but that's what I thought I wanted to do. I mentioned earlier how at that time no one wanted a woman as a road manager with a male act. Did that stop me? Not at all.

After dealing with disappointment after disappointment, interview upon interview, letter upon letter, and countless unreturned phone calls, I decided my traditional job search just wasn't working quick enough. I was sure that I wasn't going to let the lack of a job offer stop me from working in the industry I wanted to be in. I decided to look "outside of the box."

I tried a number of things. I looked at my talents, I looked at my skills, and then I tried to find a way to use them. I knew I could write and I knew I could do it well. I had been a part-time reporter/photographer for my local bi-weekly newspaper during summer vacations and stayed on part time after I had graduated college. I knew how to do public relations and publicity. My parents had their own public relations and marketing firm. I had literally grown up with press releases.

I knew I wanted to be a road manager, maybe even a tour manager, because I wanted to be on the road with music acts. Yet, I had already experienced that management often didn't feel comfortable having a woman on the road with their male acts. I also knew that no matter how many record labels, agents, publishing companies, or management companies I talked to, right or wrong, I might have the same problem with all of them.

What could I do? I had landed interviews, yet no one had hired me. I had made contacts, yet I still couldn't get a job.

I had a lightbulb moment. I knew what I had to do. I don't know why I hadn't thought of this before. I actually did know one person who would hire me, a person who thought I would be great at whatever I did. And not only did I know this person; I knew her very well. Guess what? It was me!

I decided to start my own business, a music industry public relations and publicity firm, and hired myself. My specialty would be "on the road" publicity. For some reason, no one seemed to mind my presence on the road if I was getting the act television, radio, and print exposure. As a matter of fact, they were happy I was there to make sure everything went well.

"Well, anyone can do that," you say. Technically you're right. Anyone can start their own business. Sometimes it's the right move and sometimes it's not. For me it was right. For you it may or may not be the correct path. The idea wasn't without problems. The challenge once you start a business is getting clients to utilize your services. I wasn't sure exactly where I was going to get clients, but I knew I would find a way to get them.

One of the main things I had going for me was the faith I had in myself that I *would* do it. No matter what obstacle anyone put in my way, I knew I could find a way around it. I also knew I wasn't going to quit until I got what I wanted. Could I have failed? Absolutely not. Once I made a commitment to myself, there was no turning back.

To make another very long story short, I hustled to get my first clients and I was on my way to living out my dream career. I'll share my story of how that happened later in the book, so you can use similar techniques to help you in your career.

"Well," you might be saying, "that's you. You were lucky."

Yes, I was lucky. But it was luck put together with focus, a lot of hard work, a huge commitment, and knowing I wasn't giving up, no matter what. Just so you know, I am no different from you. That means if I can do it, you can do it too. Whether your dream is to work on the business end or the talent end of the industry, if you focus on just what you want, use your talents, and don't give up, the dream can be yours.

Setting Goals

Throughout this process, it's essential to set goals. Why? Because if you don't have goals, it's hard to know where you're going. If you don't know where you're going, it's very difficult to

> ⭐ **Tip from the Top**
>
> Successful people continue setting goals throughout their career. That ensures their career doesn't get stagnant and they always feel passion for what they do.

get there. You might want to look at goals as the place you arrive at the end of a trip. Actions are trips you take to get to your destinations.

What's the best way to set goals? To start with, be as specific as you can. Instead of your goal being, "I want to be in the music business," your goal might be, "I want to work at a major record label as the director of publicity." Instead of your goal being, "I want to be a singer," your goal might be, "I want to be a singer creating a steady stream of hot number one singles and CDs." Instead of "I want to make a million dollars in the music business," your goal might be, "I want to make a million dollars in the music business through publishing deals on songs I have written."

Notice that the specific goals have actions attached to them. For example, in the goal, "I want to work at a major record label as the director of publicity," the action would be working at a major label.

You should also try to make sure your goals are clear and concise. You'll find it easier to focus on your goals if you write them down. "I know what my goals are," you say. "Do I really have to write them down?" No, you don't, but you'll find that writing down your goals will give them power, and power is what can make it happen. Writing down your goals will also help you see them more clearly.

So take out your pad or notebook and get started. As you think of new ideas and goals, jot

them down. Some people find it easier to work toward one main goal. Others find it easier to develop a series of goals leading up to their main goal.

To help you do this exercise, you might want to first develop a number of long-term goals. Where do you think you want to be in your career in the next year? How about the next two years, three years, five years, and even ten years?

Need some help? Here are some examples of long-term goals someone interested in working in the talent end of the industry might write down.

First-year goals:
◎ I want to have a signed recording contract in my hands with a major label.
◎ I want to write at least half of my first CD.
◎ I want to record my first professional CD.
◎ I want to go on tour.

Second-year goals:
◎ I want my CD on the charts.
◎ I want at least one number-one single.
◎ I want to have my CD go gold.
◎ I want to be playing major arenas.

Third-year goals:
◎ I want to be recognized as a major recording artist.
◎ I want at least one of my tunes to cross over to other charts.

Those interested in working on the business end of the industry might write down things like this:

First-year goals:
◎ I want to obtain an internship at a record label.
◎ I want to finish college and get my bachelor's degree.

◎ I want to make as many contacts as possible in the music industry.

Second-year goals:

◎ I want to find a job in the music industry working in the publicity department of a major label.

◎ I want to make take extra class and workshops specifically designed for public relations and publicity in the music industry.

Third-year goals:

◎ I want to be promoted to a management position in the publicity department of the record label.

◎ I want to design and develop publicity campaigns for major artists.

◎ I want to be respected by my peers.

Long-term goals:

◎ I want to start my own music-oriented public relations company.

◎ I want to open offices on the East Coast and West Coast.

Once you've zeroed in on your main goals, you can develop short-term goals you might want or need to accomplish to reach your long-term goals. Feel free to add details. Don't concern yourself with situations changing. You can always adjust your goals.

When focusing on your goals, remember that there are general work-related goals and specific work-related goals. What's the difference? Specific goals are just that. See the following examples:

◎ General goal: I want to get a promotion.
  ▫ *Specific goal*: I want to be promoted to the director of A&R by the end of the year.

◎ General goal: I want to work in the music industry.

  ▫ *Specific goal*: I want to work in the A&R department of a major label.

◎ General goal: I want to be an entertainer.
  ▫ *Specific goal*: I want to be a major touring recording artist with songs on the charts.

◎ General goal: I want to be a songwriter.
  ▫ *Specific goal*: I want a career as a songwriter. I want my songs to be performed and recorded by major recording acts. I want great publishing deals.

Whether you're interested in a career on the business end or in the talent area of the music industry, you can use your goals as a road map to help you realize your dreams.

Visualization Can Help Make It Happen

Visualization is a powerful tool for success in all aspects of your career and your life. What is it? Visualization is "seeing" or "visualizing" a situation the way you want it. It's setting up a picture in your mind of the way you would like a situation to unfold.

How do you do it? Simple. Close your eyes and visualize what you want. Visualize the situation that you desire. Think about each step you need to take to get where you want to go in your

---

⭐ The Inside Scoop

Visualization works for more than your career. Use it to help make all your dreams come true in all facets of your life.

---

career, and then see the result in your mind. Want to see how it's done?

Want to be a rock star? How about a major country music singer? Perhaps a huge pop singer? Visualize driving up to the venue in a limo—a long, black, stretch limo. Fans are waiting outside the stage door trying to get a glimpse of you. Do you see your name in lights on the marquee? Wow!

Visualize yourself as you would like others to see you on stage. The spotlights are on you. Can you feel the energy in the air? Your heart is pounding in a good way. You're in front of a huge audience. Most of them are wearing T-shirts with your picture on them. Do you hear all your fans cheering? Can you hear the music? Can you hear the horn player's solo?

Look out into the audience. People are holding banners saying they love you. You start your set. What an amazing feeling. But wait—as you finish your set, everyone stands. You're getting a standing ovation. Now another one. What a great night. And it's only one of many. You're a star! Got the picture? That's visualization!

No matter what you want to do, you can visualize it to help make it happen. Visualize your career working at a record company. Visualize yourself going for the interview, getting the job, and then sitting at your desk. Visualize speaking to coworkers, going to meetings, and doing your work.

The more details you can put into your visualizations, the better. Add the colors of things

around you: the fragrance of the flowers on your desk, the aroma of the coffee in your mug, the color of the suit you are wearing, and even the bright blue sky outside. Details will help bring your visualization to life.

Whatever your dreams, concentrate on them, think about them, and then visualize them. Here's the great news. If you can visualize it, you can make it happen! No one really knows why, but it does seem to work and it works well. Perhaps it's positive energy. Perhaps you're just concentrating more on what you want.

One of the tricks in visualizing to get what you want is actually visualizing all the actions you need to take to achieve your goal. If you don't know what these actions are or should be, an easy exercise that might help you is called reverse visualization. In essence, you're going to play the scenes in reverse.

Start by visualizing at the point in your life where you want to be and then go back to the point where you are currently. If your dream is to be a major recording artist, that's where you're going to start. If you currently are trying to get your act and band together, that's where you're going to end up in this process. Similarly, if your dream is to be an important record label executive, begin this exercise there. If you are still in school, that's where you're going to end up.

Let's go back to your dream of being a major rock star, pop star, or country singer. As we just did a moment ago, start visualizing that you have what you want. The stage, your clothing, the fans—everything. Now take one step back. Right before you got to that point in your career, what did you do? There were probably a number of things. Let's make a list of how events might have unfolded in reverse.

◎ You packed to go on tour.

◎ You rehearsed with your band.

◎ You auditioned new band members.

◎ Your agent told you about your upcoming tour.

◎ Your CD went platinum.

◎ Your CD went gold.

◎ Your single is number one.

◎ Your single hit the charts with a bullet.

◎ You heard your song for the first time on the radio.

◎ Your song was released.

◎ You did your video for your upcoming new single.

◎ You recorded your new CD.

◎ You wrote songs for your new CD.

◎ You signed a major recording contract.

◎ You looked for a label to sign with.

◎ You signed with a major booking agency.

◎ You shopped around for a new booking agency.

◎ You signed a new management contract.

◎ You met with a number of different managers.

◎ You opened for a top recording act at a local country fair.

◎ You played in a variety of small clubs.

◎ You began polishing and fine-tuning your act when you decided you wanted a career as a major music star. (This is where you are now.)

Here's a different example of the reverse visualization exercise you might do if you were interested in a career on the business end of the industry. It's the same concept, just a slightly different way of doing it.

Let's say you want a career as a record executive. Think about where you'd like to work. Add your office environment, the office décor.

> ### Tip from the Coach
> Make a commitment to your dream and stick to it. Without this commitment, your dream will turn into a bubble that will fly away and burst in mid-air.

Now add your coworkers. Next, put yourself in the picture. Remember to visualize what you're wearing, your accessories, and even the color of your suit.

Visualize yourself speaking to coworkers, supervisors, and label clients. Feel the excitement of the day. Now go backwards. Visualize yourself driving to work the first day. Keep visualizing. Now you're thinking about getting dressed that morning. Keep going. Remember hearing the alarm buzzing and how you just couldn't wait to get up to go to work.

Keep visualizing in reverse. Hear your cell phone ringing and remember the feeling you had when the voice at the other end told you that you got the job. Go back and visualize the feeling that you had waiting for that call. Visualize the thank-you note you wrote to the director of human resources. See the letter in your mind. Now remember leaving the interview. Visualize in detail what you wore, what the experience was like, the questions that you were asked, and the feelings you had at that moment. Remember how much you hoped you would be hired.

Visualize filling out the application and developing and sending in your resume with your perfectly tailored cover letter. Now visualize seeing the job advertised in the newspaper and the excited feeling you had.

Recall all the preparation you did to find that job; the skills you updated; the people you

Words from the Wise

I have learned this at least by my experiment: that if one advances confidently in the direction of his dreams, and endeavors to live the life which he has imagined, he will meet with a success unexpected in common hours.

–Henry David Thoreau

spoke to; the networking. Visualize the internship you went through.

You are now back at the position in the visualization process, where you currently are in your career. You have an idea of the steps needed to get where you want to go. This might not be the exact way your situation goes down, but it can get you started in the visualization process.

Paint a picture in your mind of what you want to achieve detail by detail. Whether you're using a reverse visualization or a traditional visualization technique, this powerful tool can help you get what you want. Give it a try. You'll be glad you did.

3

PLAN FOR SUCCESS IN THE MUSIC INDUSTRY

Take Control and Be Your Own Career Manager

No one cares about your career as much as you do. Not your mother, your father, your sister, or your brother. Not your best friend, girlfriend, boyfriend, or spouse. Not even people associated with your business. It's not that these people don't care at all. They probably all want you to be successful, but no one cares as much as you do.

With this in mind, an important career strategy is to become your own career manager. What does this mean? It means that you won't be leaving your career to chance. You will be in the driver's seat! You will have control and you can make your dream career happen!

Will it take a lot of work? Yes, being your own career manager can be a job in itself. The payoff, however, will be worth it.

If you look at many successful people in the entertainment business, you will notice that most have a tremendous dedication to their career. Of course, they have managers, agents, attorneys, financial professionals, and others who advise them, but when it comes to the final decision making, they are the ones who take the ultimate responsibility for their career.

Now that you've decided to be your own career manager, you have some work to do. Next on the list is putting together an action plan. Let's get started!

What Is an Action Plan?

Let's look at success a little closer. What's the one thing successful people, successful businesses, and successful events all have in common? Is it money? Luck? Talent? While money, luck, and talent all are certainly part of the mix, generally the common thread most share is a well-developed plan for success. Whatever your goal, be it short range or long range, if you have a plan to achieve it, you have a better chance of succeeding. With that in mind, let's discuss how you can create your own plan for success.

What can you do with a plan? The possibilities are endless.

People utilize all types of plans to help ensure success. Everyone has his or her own version of what is best. To some, just going over what they're going to do and how they're going to do it in their mind is plan enough. Some, especially those working on a new business, create formal business plans. Some people develop action plans. That's what we're going to talk about now.

What exactly is an action plan? In a nutshell, an action plan is a written plan detailing all the actions you need to and want to take to successfully accomplish your ultimate goal: success in your chosen career.

How an Action Plan Can Help You Succeed

Success is never easy, but you can stack the deck in your favor by creating your own personal action plan. Why is this so critical? To begin with, there are many different things you might want to accomplish to succeed in your career. If you go about them in a haphazard manner, however, your efforts might not be as effective as they could be. An action plan helps define the direction to go and the steps needed to get the job done. It helps increase your efficiency in your quest for success.

Another reason to develop an action plan is that seeing a plan in writing sometimes helps you see a major shortcoming or simply makes you notice something minor that may be missing. At that point, you can add the actions you need to take and the situation will be easily rectified.

With an action plan, you know exactly what you're going to be doing to reach your goals. It helps you focus so that everything you need to do is more organized. Many of us have had the experience of looking in a closet where everything is just jumbled up. If you need a jacket or a pair of pants from the closet, you can probably find them, but it may be frustrating and take you a long time. On the other hand, if you organize your closet, when you need that jacket or pair of pants, you can reach for them and find them in a second with no problem.

One of the main reasons you develop a plan is to have something organized to follow, and when you have something to follow, things are easier to accomplish and far less frustrating. In essence, what you're creating with your action plan is a method of finding and succeeding in your dream career, whether it be in the talent area, business area, or somewhere in between. When you put that plan into writing, you're going to have something to follow and something to refer to, making it easier to track your progress.

"Okay," you say. "How do I know what goes into the plan? How do I do this?"

Well, that depends a lot on what you want to do and what type of action plan you're putting together. For the most part, your action plan is going to comprise a lot of the little, detailed steps you're going to have to accomplish to obtain your goal.

Some people make very specific and lengthy action plans. Others develop general ones. You might create a separate action plan for each job you pursue, a plan for your next goal, or even a plan that details everything you're going to need to do from the point where you find yourself now up to the career of your dreams. As long as you have some type of plan to follow, the choice is yours.

★ Words from the Wise

Always keep control of your career. Even at the height of your success when you have lawyers, accountants, managers, and agents working for you, make sure *you* oversee things. This doesn't mean you can't delegate tasks. It just means that you should be aware of what is going on, whom you are dealing with, how much money is coming in and going out, and where your money is going.

Your Personal Action Plan for Success in the Music Industry

So you've decided to be your own career manager. It's now up to you to develop your personal action plan or plans for success in the music industry. Are you ready to get started?

A great deal of your action plan will depend on what area of the music industry you're interested in and exactly what you want to do. We're going to cover specialized action plans later, but right now, let's try look at some basics.

Sit down, take a notebook and pen, and start thinking about your career and the direction you want it to go. Start by doing some research. What do you want to find out? Almost any information can be useful in your career. Let's look at some of the things that might help you.

Your Market

One of the first things to research is your market. What does that mean? It means that you need to determine what jobs or employment situations you are interested in and where they are located. Who and where will your potential employers or clients be?

For example, if you want to work at a record label, you might determine that the largest number of employers might be in New York City, Los Angeles, and Nashville. Through research, however, you may also discover that there are a large number of independent labels that might offer opportunities in other geographical areas.

If the business end of the industry is where your dream career lies, you might research potential employers, where they might be located, and what the possibilities of working on your own would be.

If you want to work in the talent area as a singer, you should explore the various places to perform, who your audiences might be, and

Tip from the Coach

When you break large projects up into smaller tasks, they seem more manageable. It's like spring-cleaning. If you look at cleaning the whole house at one time, it can seem impossible. But if you break the job up into cleaning one or two rooms at a time, it seems easier to accomplish. When you look at the ultimate task of finding the perfect career and then becoming successful, it, too can seem like a huge undertaking. Breaking up the tasks you need to accomplish will help you reach your goal.

how you could bring your act to the attention of the movers and shakers in the music industry.

If you want to be a songwriter, you might look into who and how to develop interest in your songs. What labels might need songs in the style you write? Which publishers or artists might be possibilities? How about television shows, films, or commercials? Would any of them be possibilities?

What Do You Need to Do to Get What You Want?

Next, research what you need to do to get the career you want. Do you need additional skills? Training? Education? Experience? Do you need to move to a different location? Make new contacts? Get an internship? Take a songwriting workshop? In other words, what's standing between you and your career in the music business? If you are already in the business, what's standing between you and success? How can you climb the ladder of success and perhaps even skips a few rungs?

Spend some time thinking about this. If you can determine exactly what skills, qualifications,

What Stands Between Me and What I Want?	Possible Solution

or experience you're missing or what you need to do, you're halfway there.

It often helps to look at exactly what is standing between you and what you want on paper. Use the form on the previous page to help you clarify each situation and the possible solution.

How Can You Differentiate Yourself?

If you're looking for a career in the music business, you are not alone. Thousands of other people want to make it as a record executive, tour manager, singer, songwriter, musician, or recording artist. Thousands of people are seeking stardom.

Here's the challenge. How can you stand out in a positive way? What attributes do you have or what can you do so people choose you over others?

"I don't like to draw attention to myself," you say. "I just kind of like to blend into the crowd."

Well, you're going to have to drop that attitude. Why? Because the people who get the jobs, the ones who succeed, the ones who make it in music are the ones who have found a way to set themselves apart from others.

How? Perhaps it's your personality or the energy you exude. Maybe it's your sense of humor or the way you organize things. Some people just have a presence about them. Could it be the way you sing or play an instrument? Maybe it's the type of songs you write. Do you have a special or unique stage show? A special fashion style? Do you appeal to a unique group of fans or followers?

Everyone is special in some way. Everyone has a special something they do or say that makes them stand out in some manner. Most people have more than one thing. Spend some time determining what makes you special in a positive way so that you can use it to your advantage in your career.

Tip from the Coach

If you don't know what makes you special, take a cue from what others tell you. Listen to those conversations where someone says something in passing like, "You're so funny, I love being around you," or "You always know just what to say to make me feel better," or "You have such a beautiful voice. I love listening to you sing," or "You always are so helpful." Listen to what people say and always take compliments graciously.

How to Get Noticed

Catching the eye of people important to your career is another challenge. Take some time to try to figure out how to make yourself and your accomplishments known to others. This is the time to brainstorm. For example, let's say you're an aspiring singer. How can you bring your talent to the attention of those people who can make a difference to your career? See what talent competitions are available, either locally or nationally. What about television opportunities? How about putting together a showcase? Maybe you want to find an agent. Perhaps you want to put together a demo tape and video. What about appearing in a talent show? Maybe you'll volunteer to be the talent for a fundraiser. What about finding a way to get on the news? How about sending a brochure with a CD and video to agents? Just keep coming up with ideas and writing them down as you go. You can fine-tune them later.

Think about these questions. Can you come up with more? Once you determine the answers, it's easier to move on to the next step of writing your plan.

What Should Your Basic Action Plan Include?

Now that you've done some research and brain-stormed some great ideas, you're on your way. Here's what your basic action plan should include.

Career Goals

One of the most important parts of your action plan will be defining your career goals. Are you just starting your career? Are you looking for a new job or career? Are you already in the business and want climb the career ladder? Are you interested in exploring a different music industry career from the one you're in now? Do you want to be a singer, songwriter, or musician? Do you want to be a major recording artist? Do you want to be an A&R executive? The head of a record company? Want to be the VP of publicity at a major label? The sky is the limit if you know what your goals are.

When defining your goals, to try to make them as specific as possible. For example, instead of writing in your action plan that your goal is to be a singer, refine your goal to be a major recording and performance artist. Instead of defining your goal to be a record label executive, you might define it as being the vice president of A&R or whatever *your* career goal or aspiration might be.

It's important to include your short-range goals as well as your long-range ones. You might

even want to include mid-range plans. That way you'll be able to track your progress, which gives you great inspiration to slowly but surely meet your goals. For example, if you're interested in pursing a career on the business end of the industry, you might set your long-range goal to be the director of publicity at a major label. Your short-range goal might be to get an internship at a label and then secure a position in the publicity department.

Keep in mind that goals are not written in stone and it's okay to be flexible and change them along the way. The idea is that no matter what you want, moving forward is the best way to get somewhere.

What You Need to Reach Your Goals

The next step is to put in writing exactly what you need to reach your goals. Do you need training or more education? Do you need to learn new skills or brush up on old ones? Do you need to move to a different geographic location? Do you need to network more? Do you need to make more contacts?

Your Actions

This is the crux of your action plan. What actions do you need to attain your goals?

◎ Do you need to take some classes or attend some industry-related workshops?
  ▫ Your actions would be to identify, locate, and take classes and workshops.
◎ Do you need to find seminars and attend them?
  ▫ Your actions would be to investigate potential seminars to see if they will assist in accomplishing your goals, and if so, attend them.

Voice of Experience

Once you get the knack of creating action plans, you can use them for everything in your life, not just your career. You'll find everything goes more smoothly with a plan in place.

- Do you need to go to college, get a bachelor's degree, or even a law degree?
  - Your actions would be to go to college, get a degree, and so on.
- Do you need to learn how to play the guitar or take voice lessons?
  - Your actions would be to take music or vocal lessons.
- Do you need to move to New York, Los Angeles, Nashville, or any other geographic location?
  - Your actions would be to find a way to relocate.
- Do you need to attend industry events, conferences, and conventions?
  - Your actions would be to locate and investigate events, conferences, and conventions, and then attend them.
- Do you need to find more ways to network or just network more?
  - Your actions would be to develop opportunities and activities to network and follow through with those activities and opportunities.
- Do you need more experience?
  - Your actions might include becoming an intern, volunteering, or finding other ways to get experience. Talk to people who might be able to help you find opportunities to volunteer.

Tip from the Coach

Try to be realistic when setting your timetable. Unrealistic time requirements often set the groundwork for making you feel as though you've failed.

The Inside Scoop

Don't start panicking when you think you are never going to reach your career goals. Just because you estimate that you want to reach your long-range goals within the next five or seven years or whatever you choose does not mean that you can't get there faster. Your timetable is really just an estimate of the time you need to reach a specific goal.

Your Timetable

Your timetable is essential to your action plan. In this section, you're going to include what you're going to do (your actions) and when you're going to do them. The idea is to make sure you have a deadline for getting things done so your actions don't fall through the cracks.

Designing Your Action Plan

Remember, there is no right or wrong way to assemble your action plan. It's what you are comfortable with. You might want yours to look different in some manner from the examples that follow, have different items, or even have things in a different order. That's okay. The whole purpose of action plans is to help you achieve your career goals. Choose the one that works for you.

Let's look first at an example of a basic action plan, and then look at the same plan partly filled in by someone whose career goal is to be a country music artist. After that are examples of alternative action plans for an aspiring songwriter or composer and one for someone interested in the business of music.

After reviewing these samples, use the blank plan provided to help you create your own personal action plan.

Example 1

My Basic Action Plan

Career Goals

Long-range goals:
Mid-range goals:
Short-range goals:

My market:

What do I need to reach my goals?

How can I differentiate myself from others?

How can I catch the eye of people important to my career?

What actions can I take to reach my goals?

What actions do I absolutely need to take now?

What's my timetable?
   Short-range goals:
   Mid-range goals:
   Long-range goals:

Actions I've taken: Date completed:

Example 2

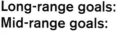

My Basic Action Plan

Career Goals

Long-range goals: To be a major recognized force in the music industry as a top country recording and performing artist.

Mid-range goals: To become a recognized force in the music industry; to record and tour earning enough to be financially stable.

Example 2, continued

Short-range goals: To put together an act and become a successful performer on a local and regional basis.

My market: Fans of country and country-rock music.

Possible people to book my act short-range: Local lounges and clubs; hotels; schools; colleges; local wedding planners and coordinators; booking agents.

Possible people to book my act mid-range: Booking agents; colleges; managers; promoters; wedding planners and coordinators; booking agents.

Possible people to book my act long-range: Major booking agents and promoters in United States and abroad for large venues, fairs, casinos, and hotels.

What do I need to reach my goals? Put together band and develop my act.
Find manager and agents.
Perfect my skills, talent, and craft.
Find venues to play.
Write songs to record.
Find label to record with.
Sing with record label.
Get exposure.
Tour.

How can I differentiate myself from others? Write songs people can relate to; come up with interesting stage act.

How can I catch the eye of people important to my career? Get media exposure; send out press releases; develop and send out brochures and press kits; donate my services to not-for-profit organizations I support; become spokesperson for some cause or product I believe in.

What actions can I take to reach my goals? Take vocal and/or instrument lessons; attend songwriting workshops; attend industry events and conventions; become member of local chamber of commerce for networking opportunities; network more.

What actions do I absolutely need to take now? Develop act and band; rehearse on regular basis; develop press kit and bio; get professional photos done; send out mailing to get bookings; follow up on mailings; find and attend industry events.

(continues)

Example 2, continued

What's my timetable?
Short-range goals: Within the next six months
Mid-range goals: Within the next year and a half to two years
Long-range goals: Within the next seven years

Actions I've taken: **Date completed:**
Attended songwriting workshop.   October
Put together new band.   October
Rehearse twice a week.
Spoke to local country radio station   December
     and arranged to be their station
     band, playing at all their events.
Continue with actions.

Example 3

My Personal Action Plan

CAREER GOALS (Long-range):   Become successful Grammy award–winning songwriter with many songs published and recorded by top artists.

CAREER GOALS (Short-range):   Write songs and get them published.

Action To Be Taken	Comments	Timetable/ Deadline	Date Accomplished
Short Range			
Look for songwriter's workshops.	Check with local community colleges, trade associations, local music store.	ASAP	
Attend songwriter's workshops.	Try to take a number of different ones to get input from different people.		

Example 3, continued

ACTION TO BE TAKEN	COMMENTS	TIMETABLE/ DEADLINE	DATE ACCOMPLISHED
SHORT RANGE			
Join trade associations.	Check on Internet for trade associations; look in directories.	ASAP	
Look for seminars, workshops, etc. in business end of the industry to learn more about it.	Check directories, music stores, Internet, and so on.	Within six months; By June	
Find listing of names and addresses and Web sites of music publishers.	Check directories and Internet.	Within six months; By June	
Read *Billboard* to get familiar with music industry news and trends. Check out classified section.	See if library subscribes to *Billboard;* check with local radio stations to see if they will let me borrow magazines.	ASAP	
Look into industry conferences and conventions to network.	Try to attend one or two. Call up in advance to see if they have special fee structure for students or nonprofessionals.	Within six or eight months; By August	
Read books about music industry, songwriting, songwriters, etc.	Do search on Amazon, then go to library to borrow books.	Browse through at least one a week. Start now.	
Look for a mentor or teacher.	Talk to people at songwriting workshops.	Start looking now.	
Learn about copyright.	Do research online; call government copyright office; talk to people.	Immediately	
Copyright songs.		As I write them	
Write songs.	Regularly write new material.	Start now!	

(continues)

Example 3, continued

Action To Be Taken	Comments	Timetable/ Deadline	Date Accomplished
Short Range			
Make up business cards.		Within two months	
Find ways to meet and network with artists.	Attend concerts, clubs, and so on. Go to industry events.	Continually, beginning now	
Develop my bio.			
Develop my press kit.	Get professional photos done.		
Find ways to exploit my talent.			
Find ways to get publicity.			
Write a song for a not-for-profit or charity event to get exposure.	Talk to organization I believe in and see if they would be interested.	Within the year	
Consider collaborating with other songwriters.	Think about pros and cons.		
Find ways to meet and network with publishers and producers.	Visit recording studios, publishing houses, and so on.		
Find industry networking events.	Contact radio stations, club owners, concert promoters, singers, musicians, music teachers.	Start now and keep going.	
Long Range			
Make demo of songs.		Within eight months but sooner if possible	
Publish songs.		Within a year	
Pitch songs to artists, publishers, record companies, television shows, film producers, and so on.		Within a year to eighteen months	
Continue recording demos.			

Example 3, continued

Action To Be Taken	Comments	Timetable/ Deadline	Date Accomplished
Long Range			
Get three or four songs recorded.		Within two years	
Record a top ten hit.	Sooner would be really nice	Within six years	
Collaborate with top artists.		Within six years	
Have film producers and directors call you to write music for their top films.	Sooner if possible	Within eight years	
Win a Grammy!	I really want one within two years, but I'm going to try to be more realistic.	Within eight years	

Example 4

My Personal Action Plan

CAREER GOALS (Long-range):   VP of Publicity at Major Record Label

CAREER GOALS (Short-range):   Obtain position at major record label in publicity department.

Action To Be Taken	Comments	Timetable/ Deadline	Date Accomplished
Short Range			
Look into internship possibilities at record labels or music-oriented publicity firms.	Contact college advisor to see if school has internship programs with labels; write to record labels and music industry publicity and PR firms.	ASAP so I possibly find an internship my last semester	October

(continues)

Example 4, continued

Action To Be Taken	Comments	Timetable/ Deadline	Date Accomplished
Short Range			
Fill in internship application.	Get references from former employers and college advisor.	ASAP	November
Go through internship at record label.	Get letters of recommendation and visit human resources (HR) department.	This semester	May
Look for seminars and workshops in entertainment and music publicity and public relations.	Contact the Public Relations Society of America (PRSA), colleges, industry associations; look on Internet.	Find by January	
Find listing of names and addresses and Web sites of record labels and music industry publicity and PR firms.	Check directories and Internet.	This month	
Read *Billboard* to get familiar with music industry news and trends; check out classified section.	See if library subscribes to *Billboard;* check with local radio stations to see if they will let me borrow magazines.	This week and continually	
Get letters of recommendation from internship coordinator and directors of departments in which I interned.		Before internship ends	
Make appointment with HR director.	Check into possibility of getting job at label after graduation.		
Look into industry conferences and conventions to network.	Try to attend one or two; call up in advance to see if they have career fairs.		

Example 4, continued

Action To Be Taken	Comments	Timetable/ Deadline	Date Accomplished
Short Range			
Read books about music industry.	Do search on Amazon, then go to library to borrow books.	Browse through at least one a week.	
Take classes in publicity.		This semester	
Volunteer to do publicity for a not-for-profit entertainment event.	Call my contact at General Hospital Foundation to see if I can help with the publicity for their fund-raising concert.	Call this week.	
Work on school paper or look into part time job at local newspaper.	Contact *Daily Record* to see if they would be interested in reviews of entertainment events.		
Start working on resume.		Finish first draft by end of next week.	
Start building career portfolio.		Start now and keep going.	
Find industry networking events.	Contact radio stations, club owners, concert promoters, singers, musicians, music teachers, and so on.	Start now and continue.	
Make up business cards.	Find printer; check out other people's business cards for ideas.		
Long Range			
Develop marketing package and brochure.		Finish by mid-March.	

(continues)

Example 4, continued

Action To Be Taken	Comments	Timetable/ Deadline	Date Accomplished
Long Range			
Send out marketing package and brochures to record labels, music industry P.R. and publicity firms, radio stations, etc.		ASAP after marketing package and brochures are completed.	
Contact record label HR departments.	Send letters and resumes asking about openings.	Start in March.	
Contact Public Relations Society of America.	See if they know of any openings.	Start in April.	
Contact entertainment industry associations.	Check to see if there are any networking events or career fairs.	Start in April.	
Check out *Billboard* and other music industry trades for job openings.			
Continue with actions.			

Specialized Action Plans

What things might be in your specialized action plan? That depends on the area in which you're interested in working. Let's look at some of the specific actions you might take if the career to which you aspire is on the business end of the industry. Remember, these are just to get you started. When you sit down and think about it, you'll find tons of actions you're going to need to take.

The Business Side of the Industry

◎ Identify your skills.
◎ Identify your talents.
◎ Identify your passions.
◎ Look for internships.
◎ Develop different forms of your resume.
◎ Develop cover letters.
◎ Network.
◎ Go to industry events.
◎ Make contacts.
◎ Volunteer to get experience.
◎ Obtain reference letters.
◎ Get permission to use people's names as references.
◎ Develop your career portfolio.
◎ Attend career fairs.

My Personal Action Plan

CAREER GOALS (Long-range):

CAREER GOALS (Short-range):

ACTION TO BE TAKEN	COMMENTS	TIMETABLE/ DEADLINE	DATE ACCOMPLISHED
SHORT RANGE			
LONG RANGE			

- Look for industry events in your area of interest.
- Take seminars, workshops, and classes.
- Get a college degree.
- Make business cards.
- Perform research online.
- Learn about industry trends.
- Make cold calls to obtain job interviews.
- Read books about the industry.

If your career aspirations are in the creative talent area, you'll need to take a different set of specific actions to achieve your goals. Let's go over a few of them. Remember, this list is just to get you started thinking. It is by no means complete.

The Talent Side of the Industry

- Find vocal teacher.
- Take vocal lessons.
- Take music lessons.
- Subscribe to trade journals.
- Find songwriting courses and workshops.
- Join trade associations.

- Become affiliated with a performance rights society such as the American Society of Composers, Authors, and Publishers (ASCAP) or Broadcast Music, Inc. (BMI).
- Rehearse on regular basis.
- Develop press kits.
- Develop bio.
- Look for agents.
- Look for and sign with personal manager.
- Develop booking brochures and pieces.
- Make up business cards.
- Perform in showcases.
- Perform in competitions.

Using Action Plans for Specific Jobs

Action plans can be useful in a number of ways. In addition to developing a plan for your career, you might utilize action plans to look for specific jobs. Let's look at an example for someone hoping to succeed as a booking agent.

Action Plan Looking for Specific Job

Job title: Booking Agent Trainee

Job description: Make phone calls, learn how to negotiate fees; learn how to write contracts; make sure contracts are signed; look for new business; take phone calls from potential clients.

Company name: Best Talent USA

Contact name: Jeff Post

Secondary contact name: Anita Dobson

Company address: 1214 West 111 St., Some City, NY 11111

Company phone number: (212) 111-1111

Company fax number: (212) 222-2222

Company Web site address: No Web site

Company e-mail: besttalentusa@besttalent.com

Secondary e-mail:

Where I heard about job: Read ad in *Billboard* 3/3

Actions taken: Tailored resume and cover letter to job; spoke to references to tell them I was applying for job and make sure I could still use them as references; faxed resume and cover letter.

Actions needed to follow up: Make sure suit and other clothing needed for interview is clean and pressed; review portfolio; make extra copies of my resume; read *Billboard* and other trade information to keep up-to-date on trends; do research on company to see who their clients are and find out extra information; call if I don't hear back within a week.

Interview time, date, and location: Received call on 3/10; they want me to come in for interview; interview set for 2:00 P.M. on 3/12 with Jeff Post at agency office.

More actions to follow up on: Get directions to building; pick out clothes for interview; try everything on to make sure it looks good; rehearse giving answers to questions most likely to be asked during interview; noticed that company didn't have a Web site; develop a simple sample Web site to show initiative.

Comments: Went to interview; nice office and very nice people working there; I would like the job; Mr. Post seemed impressed that I had put together a sample Web site; he said most people wouldn't take the time to do something like that before they got a job; he also seemed interested in my portfolio; the only thing that bothered me was that I didn't know the specific computer program they used; he said he was conducting interviews for the next week and would get back to me one way or another in a couple of weeks.

Extra actions: Write note thanking Mr. Post for interview.

Results: 3/19 Mr. Post called; I didn't get that job; they gave it to someone who had been an intern at the company. He offered me a different job; he said that they had been talking

(continues)

(continued)

about a Web site for a while and my sample site motivated them to move on the idea. While they are retaining a company to put together a professional Web site, my job would be to coordinate the information included on the site. I would also be the liaison between the agency and their clients, getting information, working on bios, and so on; he still would want me to learn about booking and if I am interested, could start to do a little of that as well. I'm going to meet with him tomorrow to discuss salary and benefits.

Use the blank plan provided on page 57 to keep track of your actions when you find specific jobs you're interested in.

How to Use Your Action Plan

Creating your dream career takes time, patience, and a lot of work. In order for your action plan to be useful, you're going to have to use it. It's important to set aside some time every day to work on your career. During this time, you're going to be *taking actions*. The number of actions you take, of course, will depend on your situation. If you are currently employed, you may not be able to tackle as many actions as someone who is unemployed and has more time available every day. Keep in mind that some actions may take longer than others. Putting together your career portfolio will take longer than making a phone call, so if you're working on your portfolio, you might not accomplish more than one action in a day.

Try to make a commitment to yourself to take at least one positive action each day toward getting your dream career or becoming more successful in the one you currently have. Do more if you can. Whatever your situation, just make sure you take *some* action every single day.

Keeping a Daily Action Journal

In addition to creating an action plan, you might find it helpful to keep an action journal recording all the career-related activities and actions you take on a daily basis. What you're going to do is write down all the things that you do on a daily basis to help you attain your career goals. You then have a record of all the actions you have taken in one place. Like your action plan, your action journal can help you track your progress.

How do you do this? The sample on page 58 will get you started. Names and phone numbers are fabricated.

With your daily action journal, you can look back and see exactly what you've done, who you've called, who you've written to, and what the result was. Additionally you have the names, phone numbers, times,

(continues on page 59)

⭐ The Inside Scoop
Once you start writing in your daily action journal, you'll be even more motivated to fulfill your career goals.

Action Plan for Specific Job

Job title:

Job description:

Company name:

Contact name:

Secondary contact name:

Company address:

Company phone number:

Company fax number:

Company Web site address:

Company e-mail:

Secondary e-mail:

Where I heard about job:

Actions taken:

Actions needed to follow up:

Interview time, date, and location:

Comments:

Results:

Daily Action Journal

Monday, January 8

Read daily papers.

Called John Lopez, H.R. Director, CBE Records (212) 222-3333. Cold call, not in. His secretary Donna said he would be in on Wednesday and to call back.

Read *Billboard*. Noticed an advertisement for entertainment attorney at Big L Records. Took name of H.R. director and sent my resume and cover letter asking about opening in promotion or marketing department.

Tuesday, January 9

Read daily paper and scanned classifieds.

Called Gina Young, station director at WPDA-FM 999-1111; asked if I could come in for informational interview. Tentative appointment for next week, Monday, January 15 at 5 P.M. Check on Friday.

Worked on career portfolio.

Did research on Internet about CBE records.

Wednesday, January 10

Called John Lopez, H.R. Director, CBE Records (212) 222-3333. I got Donna on phone, she said he was in and he got on the phone. I told him I had just graduated college with a major in communications and was looking for an entry-level job in the music industry in the promotion or publicity departments. He told me there were no positions open at the time in those departments but if I was interested, I could come in and fill out an application. I asked what departments usually had openings and he told me the only opening currently available was for an administrative assistant in artist development. Yay!!! I asked if I could come in and fill in an application and he said yes. I'm going in on Monday at 1:00.

Worked on career portfolio.

Reviewed my resume.

Thursday, January 11

Called Bill Jones 999-2222 to tell him about going in to fill in job application and make sure it was still alright to use him as a reference.

Called Vanessa Hampton 999-1111 to tell her about going in to fill in job application and make sure it is still okay to use her as reference.

Called Jen Brown 111-1112 to check about using her as reference. Left message.

Printed out clean copies of my resume.

Checked on suit to wear on Monday.

(continued from page 56)
dates, and other information at your fingertips. As an added bonus, as you review your daily action journal, instead of feeling like you're not doing enough, you are often motivated to do more.

The next step is to discuss your personal career success book.

My Daily Action Journal

Date:
_____

Date:
_____

Date:
_____

Date:
_____

Date:
_____

Your Personal Career Success Book

What's your personal career success book? It's a folder, scrapbook, notebook, binder, or group of notebooks where you keep all your career information. Eventually, you might have so much that you'll need to put everything in a file drawer or cabinet, and that's okay. That means your career is progressing.

What can go in your personal success career book? You can keep your action plans, your daily action journals, and all of the information you need to get your career to the level you want to reach.

What else can go into your personal success career book? Whether you're pursuing a career on the talent or business end of the industry or anywhere in between, you will probably be sending and receiving a lot of correspondence. It's a good idea to keep copies of all the letters you send out as well as the ones you receive from people in the industry. Don't forget copies of e-mail.

Why do you want to keep correspondence? First of all, it gives you a record of people you wrote to and people who wrote to you. You might also find ways to make use of letters people send you. For example, instead of getting a rejection letter, reading it, crumpling it up, and throwing it in the trash, take the name of the person who signed it, wait a period of time, and see if you can pitch another idea, another song, another job possibility, or anything that might further your career or get you closer to where you want to be.

What else can go in your book? Keep copies of advertisements for jobs that you might want or be interested in now and in the future. If you hope to be a performer, keep copies of information on locations you might perform, clubs, lounges, arenas, concert halls, and so on. Keep lists in this book of your potential support staff: agents, managers, attorneys, accountants, publicists, and press agents. Have you seen someone's professional photos that you think are great? Find out who did them and note it in your book. Then you have the information when you need it.

What else? Lists of media possibilities, names, addresses, phone and fax numbers, and e-mail addresses. Let's say you're watching television and see an interesting interview about the music industry. At the time, you think you're going to remember exactly what you saw, when you saw it, and who the reporter or producer was. Unfortunately, you will probably forget some of the details. You now have a place to jot down the information in a section of your book. When you need it, you know where to look!

Don't forget to clip out interesting interviews, articles, and feature stories. Instead of having them floating all over your house, file them in this book. Want to network a bit? Write the reporter a note saying you enjoyed his or her piece and mentioning why you found it so interesting. Everyone likes to be recognized, even people in the media. You can never tell when you might make a contact or even a friend.

It goes without saying that you should also clip and make copies of all articles, stories, and features that appear in the print media about you. Having all this information together will make it easier later to put together your career portfolio.

What else is going into your personal career success book? Copies of letters of recommendation, notes that club owners have sent you, and even fan mail.

As your career progresses, you will have various resumes, background sheets, and bios. Keep copies of them in your book as well. What about your networking and contact worksheets? They now have a place too.

We've discussed the importance of determining your *markets*. This is where you can keep these lists as well. Then, when you find new possibilities, just jot them down in your book. With your personal career success book, everything will be at your fingertips.

You know how you sometimes go to seminars or workshops and get handouts or take notes? You now know where to keep them so you can refer to them when needed. The same goes for conference and convention material. Keep it in your personal career success book.

You'll find success is easier to come by if you're more organized and have everything you need in one place.

If you're now asking yourself, "Isn't there a lot of work involved in obtaining a career you want?" the answer is a definite yes.

"Can't I just leave everything to chance and hope I get what I want?" you ask.

You can, but if your ultimate goal is to succeed in the music industry, you need to do everything possible to give yourself the best opportunity for success.

4

GET READY, GET SET, GO:
PREPARATION

Opportunity Is Knocking. Are You Ready?

Imagine you have a fairy godmother, who comes to you one day and says, "I can get you a one-on-one meeting with the head of the number-one record label in the world. The only catch is you have to be ready to walk in their office door in half an hour." Would you be ready? Would you miss your big break because you weren't prepared? If your answer is, "Hmm, I might be ready . . . well, not really," then read on.

Here's the deal on opportunity: It may knock. As a matter of fact, it probably will knock, but if you don't open the door, opportunity won't stand there forever. If you don't answer the door, opportunity, even if it's *your* opportunity, will go visit someone else's door.

While you might not believe in fairy godmothers, you should believe this: In life and in your career, you will run into situations where you need to be ready "now" or miss your chance. When opportunity knocks, you need to be ready to open the door and let it in.

How can you do that? Make a commitment to get ready now. It's time to prepare. Ready, set, let's go!

Look Out for Opportunities

Being aware of available opportunities is essential to taking advantage of them. While it's always nice when unexpected opportunities present themselves, you sometimes have to go out looking for them as well.

How many times have you turned on the television or radio or opened the newspaper and seen an opportunity you wished you had known about so *you* could have taken advantage of it? For example, would you rather open the newspaper and read a feature story profiling up-and-coming entertainers or be the entertainer they are profiling? Would you rather see an advertisement for an evening of entertainment showcasing new acts or be the act being showcased? Would you rather meet the record label exec who is visiting your campus to work on an internship program or hear from your friend that he or she got the job?

Of course, if your goal is a hot career in the music industry, you want to be the one taking advantage of the available opportunities. Here's the deal: If you don't know about opportunities, you might miss them. It's important to take some time to look for opportunities that might be of value to you.

Where can you find opportunities? You can find them all over the place. Read through the papers, listen to the radio, look through the trade journals, and watch television. Check out music stores, Web sites, and college campuses. Even if you're not a student, schools, universities, and colleges often offer seminars or have programs that might be of interest and are open to the public for a small fee. Contact associations and ask about opportunities. Network, network, and network, continuously looking for further opportunities.

What kind of opportunities do you have? What types of opportunities are facing you? Is there a talent competition coming up? Is *American Idol* coming to your part of the country? Is a record label executive coming to your school in search of campus representatives? Have you heard that a booking agency is seeking out new clients? Will internship opportunities at a label or agency be announced soon? Will a trade association conference be hosting a career fair? Is there an opening at the label you're working at, in the department you want to work? These are all potential opportunities. Be on the lookout for them. They can be your key to success.

Keep track of the opportunities you find and hear about in a notebook. If you prefer, use the Opportunities Worksheet provided. There is a sample at the top of page 64 to get you started.

The Inside Scoop

For some reason we never understood, my grandmother always kept a suitcase packed. "Why?" we always asked her. "You can never tell when you'll have an opportunity to go someplace," she replied. "If you're ready, you can go. If you're not prepared, you might miss an opportunity."

Evidently she was right. Here's her story.

My grandfather was a physician. After he died, my grandmother worked at a number of different jobs, both to keep herself busy and to earn a living. At one point she worked as a sales associate in a women's clothing store in a well-known resort hotel. The hotel always had the top stars of the day in theater, music, film and television performing nightclub shows on holiday weekends. One weekend, Judy Garland was doing a show at the hotel. According to the story we were told as children, Judy Garland evidently wanted a few things from the clothing store and called the store to see if someone could bring up a few pieces for her to choose from.

The store was busy and the manager assigned my grandmother the job. She quickly chose some items and brought them up to the star's room. Judy was pleased with my grandmother's choices and after talking to her for a short time was evidently impressed with her demeanor and attitude.

While signing for the purchases, she said to my grandmother, "I need a nanny for my children. I think you would be the right one for the job. I'm leaving tomorrow morning. If you're interested, I need to know now." Without missing a beat, my grandmother took the job and by the next afternoon was on the road with Judy Garland serving as nanny to her children.

While clearly she didn't give two weeks notice to her sales job, being in the right place at the right time certainly landed her an interesting job she seemed to love. I don't really remember how long she kept the position. What I do know, however, is that when an opportunity presented itself, my grandmother was ready. Had she not been ready or hesitated, someone else would have gotten the job.

The moral of the story is when opportunity knocks, you have to be ready to open the door.

Opportunities Worksheet

Local radio/television stations hosting talent competition. Winner gets appearance on nationwide TV and meeting with major record company executive. Must fill in application and submit tape by 5/10. Competition is during Memorial Day Celebration. Judges will be established record company execs, booking agents, DJ, and TV station personalities.

Local portion of national telethon seeking entertainment—will be televised 6/9.

Music television stations holding contest for unsigned talent ends 9/3.

New booking agency, Dome Booking, opening in city.

Daily News is looking for up-and-coming entertainment acts to profile for feature in newspaper.

Chamber of Commerce is holding large networking event.

Self-Assessment and Taking Inventory

Now let's make sure you're ready for every opportunity. One of the best ways to prepare for anything is by first determining what you want and then seeing what you need to get it. Remembering that you are your own career manager, this might be the time to do a self-assessment.

Your self-assessment involves taking an inventory of what you have and what you have to offer and then seeing how you can relate it to what you want to do. Self-assessment involves thinking about yourself and your career goals.

Self-assessment helps you define your strengths and weaknesses. It helps you define your skills, interests, goals, and passions, giving you the ability to see them at a glance. Your self-assessment can help you develop and write your resume and make it easier to prepare for interviews.

Do you know what you want? Do you know what your strengths and weaknesses are? Can you identify the areas in which you are interested? Can you identify what's important to you in your career?

"But I already *know* what I want to do," you say. "This is a waste of my time."

Well, that's up to you, but answering these questions now can help your career dreams come to fruition quicker. It will help give you the edge others might not have.

Doing a self-assessment is a good idea no matter whether your career goal is on the business end of the industry or in the talent area. If you're thinking that since your career goal is to become a singer or musician or even a recording artist, so you don't need to do this, think again. Even in the talent area, before someone

Opportunities Worksheet

_____

_____

_____

_____

_____

_____

_____

takes a chance on you, they are going to want to know about you. If you have this done, you'll be prepared.

Strengths and Weaknesses

We all have certain strengths and weaknesses. Strengths are things you do well. They are advantages that most others don't have. You can exploit them to help your career. Weaknesses are things that you can improve. They are things you don't do as well as you could.

What are your strengths and weaknesses? Can you identify them? Why are these questions important? Once you know the answers, you know what you have to work on.

For example, if one of your weaknesses is shyness and you don't like speaking in front of groups of people, you might take some public

speaking classes, or you might force yourself to network and go into situations that could help make you more comfortable around people. If you need better written communication skills, you might take a couple of writing classes to make you a better writer.

Are you a good singer who needs to be great? Consider taking some vocal lessons. Do your songwriting skills need some help? A songwriting workshop might help get you on track.

Take some time now to define your strengths and weaknesses. Then jot them down in a notebook or use the Strengths and Weaknesses Worksheet on page 67. Be honest and realistic. The next page contains two sample worksheets to help you get started. One was filled in by someone interested in the business end of the industry and the other by someone pursing a career in the talent area.

Strengths and Weaknesses Worksheet—Business Career

My strengths:
I have a lot of energy.
I can get along with almost everyone.
I can follow instructions.
I'm a team player yet can work on my own.
I'm organized.
I am good at teaching others.
I know how to do Web design and am an accomplished Web designer.

My weaknesses:
I'm a perfectionist.
I don't like speaking in front of groups of people.
I'm shy.
I need better written communication skills.

What's important in my career?
Working as a record company exec at a major record label in the artist development area. I want to work in one of the music capitals. I want a top job. I want to work directly with artists. I want to be the top person in my field.

Strengths and Weaknesses Worksheet—Talent Career

My strengths:
I have a great voice.
I get along with others.
I can write my own music.
I'm organized.
I have good business relationships with bankers and people interested in investing in good projects.

My weaknesses:
I'm a perfectionist.
I don't like traveling.
I'm shy.

What's important in my career?
Singing, performing, and entertaining are all important to me and that's what I want in a career. While I would love to be a top recording artist, I would be happy finding a way to earn a good living singing and performing until I get there.

Strengths and Weaknesses Worksheet

My strengths:

_____

_____

_____

_____

My weaknesses:

_____

_____

_____

_____

What's important in my career?

_____

_____

_____

_____

Tip from the Coach

If a human resource director, headhunter, or interviewer asks what your weaknesses are, you might say you are a perfectionist but probably don't want to give him or her any information on any of your *real* weaknesses. Remember that as friendly as these people might seem during interviews, their job is screening candidates. You don't want to give anyone a reason not to hire you.

The Inside Scoop

A good way to deal with an interviewer asking you how you will deal with a specific weakness that they identify is by saying you are actively trying to change it into strength. For example, if one of your weaknesses is that you don't like speaking in public, you might say you are working on turning that into a strength by taking a public speaking class. Telling an interviewer you are working on your shortcomings helps him or her form a much better picture of you.

Once you know some of your strengths and weaknesses, it's time to focus on your personal inventory. Your combination of skills, talents, and personality traits are what help to determine your marketability.

What Are Your Skills?

Skills are acquired things that you have learned to do well. They are part of your selling tools. Keep in mind that there are a variety of relevant skills. There are job-related skills that you use at your present job. Transferable skills are ones that you used on one job and that you can transfer to another. Life skills are ones you use in everyday living such as problem solving, time management, decision making, and interpersonal skills. Hobby or leisure time skills are related to activities you do during your spare time for enjoyment. These might or might not be pertinent to your career. There are also technical skills connected to the use of machinery. Many of these types of skills overlap.

Most people don't realize just how many skills they have. They aren't aware of the specialized knowledge they possess. Are you one of them?

While it's sometimes difficult to put your skills down on paper, it's essential so you can see what they are and where you can use them in your career. Your skills, along with your talents and personality traits, make you unique. They can set you apart from other job applicants, singers, musicians, and songwriters and help you land the career of your dreams.

Once you've given some thought to your skills, it's time to start putting them down on paper. You can either use the worksheet or a page in a notebook. Begin with the skills you know you have. What are you good at? What can you do? What have you done? Include everything you can think of from basic skills on up, and then think of the things people have told you you're good at.

Don't get caught up thinking that "everyone can do that" and so a particular skill of yours is not special. *All* your skills are special. Include them all in your list.

Tip from the Coach

Don't limit the skills you list just to those that relate to the music industry. Include all your skills. Even when a skill seems irrelevant, you can never tell when it might come in handy.

Skills Worksheet

_____

_____

_____

_____

_____

_____

_____

_____

_____

_____

_____

_____

_____

_____

_____

Review these skill examples to help get you started. Remember, this is just a beginning.

◎ computer proficiency
◎ public speaking
◎ time management
◎ analytical skills
◎ organizational skills
◎ writing skills
◎ listening skills
◎ verbal communications
◎ management
◎ selling
◎ problem solving
◎ language skills
◎ leadership
◎ math skills
◎ decision-making skills
◎ negotiating skills
◎ money management
◎ word processing skills
◎ computer repair
◎ teaching
◎ customer service
◎ cooking
◎ Web design
◎ singing
◎ songwriting
◎ playing an instrument
◎ interior decorating
◎ instrument repair
◎ engineering skills

Your Talents

You are born with your talents. They aren't acquired like skills, but they may be refined and perfected. Many people are reluctant to admit what their talents are, but if you don't identify and use them, you'll be wasting them.

What are your talents? You probably already know what some of them are. What are you not only good at but better at than most people? What can you do with ease? What has been your passion for as long as you can remember? These will be your talents. Are you a great singer? A talented musician? A prolific songwriter? Are you a talented writer? A talented artist? Does your talent fall in the science area? How about math? Do you have an "ear" for being able to choose just the right song? Can you *see* raw talent?

Think about it for a bit and then jot your talents in your notebook or in the Talent Worksheet. Here are a couple of examples to get you started, the first for an individual interested in becoming an entertainer and recording artist and the second for someone hoping to become a record label executive.

Fill in your talents.

Your Personality Traits

We all have different personality traits. The combination of these traits is what sets us apart from others. Certain personality traits can help you move ahead whether you're interested in a career on the talent end or the business end of the music industry. Let's look at what some of them are.

◎ ability to get along well with others
◎ adaptable
◎ ambitious
◎ analytical
◎ assertive
◎ charismatic
◎ clever
◎ compassionate
◎ competitive
◎ conscientious
◎ creative
◎ dependable
◎ efficient
◎ energetic

My Talents Worksheet—Entertainer

I have a unique vocal style. I am a talented singer.

I am a talented musician. I can play five instruments well: guitar, keyboards, sax, bass, and violin.

I am a good songwriter.

I am a charismatic entertainer.

My Talents Worksheet—Record Label Executive

I have the ability to hear a hit song ahead of time and the ability to see raw talent.

I am a talented writer.

I have a great sense of humor. I can make almost everyone I'm around feel better by making them laugh.

◎ enterprising
◎ enthusiastic
◎ flexible
◎ friendly
◎ hard worker
◎ helpful
◎ honest
◎ imaginative
◎ innovative
◎ inquisitive
◎ insightful
◎ observant
◎ optimistic
◎ outgoing
◎ passionate
◎ personable

◎ persuasive
◎ positive
◎ practical
◎ problem solver
◎ reliable
◎ resourceful
◎ self-confident
◎ self-starter
◎ sociable
◎ successful
◎ team player
◎ understanding

What are your special personality traits? What helps make you unique? Think about it, and then jot them down in your notebook or in the Personality Traits Worksheet on page 73.

Talents Worksheet

Personality Traits Worksheet

Special Accomplishments

What special accomplishments have you achieved? Special accomplishments help distinguish you. They make you unique and often will give you an edge over others.

Have you won any awards? Were you awarded a scholarship? Did you write a song that won an award, even on a local level? Were you asked to sing the national anthem at a special event? Have you or your act won talent competitions? Were you the president of your class? Were you the chairperson of a special event? Have you won a community service award? Were you nominated for an award even if you didn't win? Has an article about you appeared in a regional or national magazine or newspaper? Have you been a special guest on a radio or television show? Are you sought out as an expert on some subject, music-related or otherwise?

All these things are examples of some of the special accomplishments you may have experienced. Think about it for a while and you'll be able to come up with your own list. Once you identify your accomplishments, jot them down in your notebook or on your Special Accomplishments Worksheet.

Special Accomplishments Worksheet

_____

_____

_____

_____

_____

_____

_____

_____

Education and Training

A college background can't guarantee you a job in the music industry, but it often helps prepare you for life in the workplace. If your goal is a career as a top record executive at a major label, you probably want to pursue a college education. College is also helpful if your goal is a career on the talent end.

Keep in mind that in addition to college, education may encompass other training opportunities. This may include classes, courses, seminars, programs, and learning from your peers. What type of education and training do you already possess? What type of education and training do you need to get to the career of your dreams? What type of education will help you get where you want to go? Would private vocal lessons help you reach your career goal?

How about private music lessons? Is a college degree what you're missing to give you an edge over other applicants seeking jobs at a record label or booking agency? How about some workshops or seminars? What about attending some conferences?

Now is the time to determine what education or training you have and what you need so that you can go after it. Below is a sample to get you started.

> ### Tip from the Coach
> Courses, seminars, and workshops are great ways to meet and network with industry insiders. Actively seek them out and attend them.

Education and Training Worksheet

What education and training do I have? Associate's degree with a major in business
Two semesters away from bachelor's degree
Private vocal lessons

What education or training do I need to reach my goals?
Go on to get my bachelor's degree
Seminars in music business

What classes, seminars, and workshops have I taken that are useful to my career aspirations? Music theory
Music business overview
Vocal lessons
Songwriting workshops

What classes, seminars, workshops, courses, and other steps can I take to help my career? Take electives in music business
Attend more music industry business workshops
Look for internship at record label

Education and Training Worksheet

What education and training do I have?

_____

_____

_____

What education or training do I need to reach my goals?

_____

_____

_____

What classes, seminars, and workshops have I taken that are useful to my career aspirations?

_____

_____

_____

What classes, seminars, workshops, courses, and other steps can I take to help my career?

_____

_____

_____

Fill in the Education and Training Worksheet on page 76 with your information so you know what you need to further your career and meet your goals.

Location, Location, Location. Where Do You Want to Be?

It's possible to make it in other regions, but New York City, Los Angeles, and Nashville are the best places to be for a top career in the music or recording industry. Why? Because these are the music capitals. These are the cities where the headquarters for most of the major recording labels in the United States are located. This is where it's happening.

If you have the opportunity to work in one of the major music cities, seriously consider it. One of the reasons it's helpful to be where it's happening is that you will have more opportunities to meet the people you need to meet to help you get to the top level of your career quicker. You will also have more opportunities to make contacts necessary to your career success.

There's also something to be said about being at the right place at the right time. What does that mean? Let's say you happen to hear about an opening at Highlight Records in New York City. If you live locally, you can put on a suit, grab your resume, and stop by the human resources department. They might or might not interview you that day, but at least you've gotten your resume to them and they are aware of your interest in the position. If they want to set up an interview later in the week, no one has to worry about flying you in, because you're already there.

Let's look at another example. Say you're a songwriter or composer. An advertising agency is working on a campaign. They're on deadline. They need a jingle or a tune to go with one of their new advertisements. If you're in town

Words from the Wise

Before you pack up and move to one of the music capitals, be aware that living in New York, Los Angeles, or Nashville can be quite expensive. If you come from a smaller or less populated area, city living can also bring a radically different lifestyle. Try to secure employment and a place to live *before* you make a big move. That way you can concentrate on your career.

when the advertising agency calls, you might be the one to get the job. Are they going to wait until you fly in? They might, but they might not.

As we'll discuss throughout this book, success in the music industry comes from a number of things such as talent, luck, perseverance, and being in the right place at the right time.

"Well, what am I going to do?" you ask. "I want to be in the music industry and I *don't* live in one of those cities. Now what?"

Before you panic, remember that the key words here are *best places.* They are not the only places. If you don't live in one of the music capitals, you might consider other options. Depending on the career you want to pursue, other metropolitan areas such as Philadelphia, Chicago, Seattle, Atlanta, Boston, Las Vegas, and Atlanta may offer possibilities. You might, for example, start your career in one area and, as it progresses, move closer to one of the music capitals.

Do you have your heart set on a job at a record label but don't live in New York, Los Angeles, or Nashville? What about looking for a job at an indie label? These independent labels are scattered throughout the country. While many of the major booking agencies, entertainment publicity firms, entertainment attorneys, and

Location Worksheet

Type of area I reside in now:

_____

_____

_____

_____

Location of job I want:

_____

_____

_____

_____

Other possible locations:

_____

_____

_____

_____

other important industry players are located in New York, Los Angeles, and Nashville, these types of businesses exist in other areas of the country, too.

One advantage of *not* going directly into one of the major music markets is that it is usually easier to break into the regional industry. Whether you're hoping to work at a record label, publicity firm, booking agency, promotion company, venue, or other branch of the industry, you will have a better chance of getting a job without a lot of experience in a smaller market. Once you're in, you will have the opportunity to learn the ropes, gain experience, and move onward and upward, if that's your dream.

If you're hoping to succeed in the talent area, it's also easier to get your foot in the door by starting off in a small area rather than in one of the very competitive major music capitals. Once you're in the door, you can build a following and move up the ladder to the top.

People working as singers, musicians, and recording artists and the people who support them might also travel extensively. Once you're established, you might need or want to tour on a regular basis. Is this what you want? Are you physically and emotionally prepared to leave family and friends for extended periods of time?

The Inside Scoop

One of the great things about being a touring artist is that it really doesn't matter where you're headquartered. As long as you can get to an airport or get a car or tour bus on the road, you can usually get where you're going.

Reviewing Your Past

Let's look at your past. What have you done that can help you succeed in your career in the music business?

"I haven't done anything that can help," you might say.

I'm betting you have.

Make a list of all the jobs you have had and the general functions you were responsible for when you held them. Look at this information and see what functions or skills you can transfer to your career in the music business. Have you worked in a local radio station? How about the record department of a major retailer? Are you a music teacher? Have you worked at a local music club in any capacity? What about your job at the concession stand at the local movie theater? Have you worked in the ticket booth at a local entertainment venue?

"None of my jobs have had anything to do with the music business," you say. That's okay. Many skills are transferable.

"Give me examples," you say.

Have you held a job as a reporter for a local newspaper? That shows that you know how to develop and write an article or news story and can do it in a timely fashion. These skills can easily be transferred if you are interested in a career as an entertainment journalist or publicist.

Have you worked as a bookkeeper? What about a job in an agency's or label's bookkeeping department? With education and certification, you might be able to fulfill your goals of working as an accountant for entertainment clients.

Are you a schoolteacher and wish you could be on tour with a major recording act? Your talents, skills, and education might get you into a position teaching the children of the recording stars when they're on the road.

Remember that the idea is to use your existing talents, skills, and accomplishments to get your foot in the door. Once in, you can find ways to move up the ladder so you can achieve the career of your dreams. When going over your list of positions, include both part-time jobs you had as well as full-time ones. Look at the entire picture, including not only your jobs but your accomplishments and see what they might tell about you.

"Like what?" you ask.

Did you graduate from high school in three years instead of four? That illustrates that you're driven and can accomplish your goals. Were you the chairperson for a not-for-profit charity event? That illustrates that you take initiative, work well with people, and can delegate and organize well. Do you sing in your church choir? Have you volunteered to handle the choir's music? This shows you can sing and that you have the dedication to attend rehearsals. Handling the music illustrates your organizational skills.

Now that you have some ideas, think about what you've done and see how you can relate it to your dream career. Everything you have done, including your past jobs, volunteer and civic activities, and other endeavors, can help create your future dream career in the music industry.

Using Your Past to Create Your Future

Review your past jobs and volunteer activities to see how they can be used to help you get what you want in the music industry. Answer the following questions:

◎ What parts of each job accomplishment or volunteer activity did you love?
◎ What parts made you happy?

> ### Tip from the Top
> If you're just out of school, your accomplishments will probably be more focused on what you did while in school. As you get more established in your career, your accomplishments will be more focused on what you've done during your career.

◎ What parts gave you joy?
◎ What parts of your previous jobs excited you?
◎ What skills did you learn while on those jobs?
◎ What skills can be transferred to your career in the music industry?
◎ What accomplishments can help your career in the music industry?

Jot down your answers in your notebook or use the Using Your Past to Create Your Future worksheet provided.

The more ways you can find to use past accomplishments and experience to move closer to success in your career in the music business, the better you will be. Look outside the box to find ways to transfer your skills and use jobs and activities as stepping-stones to get where you're going.

Passions and Goals

Once you know what you have, it's easier to determine what you need to get what you want. You've made a lot of progress by working on your self-assessment, but you have a few more things to do. At this point, you need to focus on exactly what job you want to do. In what types of music industry functions do you want to be involved? What are you interested in? Do you

Using Your Past to Create Your Future		
Past Job/ Volunteer Activity/ Accomplishment	Parts of Job/ Volunteer Activity/ Accomplishment that I Enjoyed	Skills I Learned and Can Transfer to Career in Music Industry

want to be a singer, songwriter, or musician? Do you like working with numbers, public speaking, or organizing things? Is selling your passion? What about teaching? Do you want to help musicians create a unique sound by producing, engineering, or arranging it? Do you want to travel? Do you want to entertain or work behind the scenes in the industry?

You began working on this task with the worksheets in Chapter 2. Continue to refine your list of things that you enjoy and want to do. Previously you defined your career goals. Now that you've assessed the situation, are they still the same?

What are your passions? You can be the most talented singer in the world, but if you don't have a passion for singing, it's a bad career choice. You owe it to yourself to have a career that you love, that you're passionate about, and that you deserve. Take the time now to make sure that you get it by going after your passions. Believe it or not, passion in many cases can override talent. What does that mean? It means that while talent is important, the desire to do something you're passionate about can make it happen.

There are thousands of people in all aspects of the music industry who are less talented than others, yet they've made it big. They've succeeded where their more talented counterparts have not. What's the difference? They have more passion for what they want, and they never give up on their goals. If *you* have that passion, you can reach your goals too.

The Talent Support Team

If you're working toward a successful career as a singer, musician, recording artist, songwriter or any of the other areas on the talent end of the industry, take some time to think about your support team. In the beginning of your career, you might be managing yourself, booking yourself, and advising yourself. Sooner or later, however, if you're on the talent end of the industry, you probably are going to have a support team.

What exactly is a support team? It's the team of people who help guide your career. They might include managers, booking agents, business managers, attorneys, publicists, press agents, and record producers, among others.

While we're going to discuss more about your support team later, take some time to assess your situation now. Who is handling your career? Is it you? A friend or family member? Do you currently have a manager? How about an agent? What about an attorney?

When do you need these members of your team? To help you decide, ask yourself a few questions.

Personal Manager

◎ Are you committed enough to your career that you're ready for a manager?
◎ Do you think if you had a manager he or she could help you further your career?
◎ Are you ready to go professional or have you gone pro already?

If the answer to these questions is yes, it might be time to start looking for potential managers. Don't rush into signing with a manager until you're sure that he or she is right for you. While a good manager can push your career to the next level, one who is not right for you can hold your career back.

Booking Agent

◎ Is your act tight enough to take it to an agent or agents?

- Are you getting gigs on your own?
- Do you think that an agent could land you more gigs and higher fees?

If your stage act is rehearsed and tight, even if you are getting gigs on your own, you might start looking for agents to represent you. An agent can help your act become more established by booking gigs you might not be able to book yourself. Remember that unless you are signed to a booking agency exclusively, you can work with more than one agent or agency.

Lawyer

- Are you in a position where you are being asked to sign contracts and agreements?

If your answer is yes, it's time to find an attorney. Your best bet is an attorney who specializes in the music industry. A music industry attorney will be up on lingo and have more knowledge

Tip from the Top

While anyone can be a manager, it doesn't mean any manager will be good for your career. In addition to believing in you and your act, there are other considerations. Does the potential manager have the contacts to get you where you need to get? Does he or she have the knowledge and ability to get to those people? Check out qualifications before you sign a contract.

Words from the Wise

Contracts are legally binding agreements. Before you sign any agreement, read and fully understand the contracts and documents you are asked to sign. It's a good idea to have an attorney review your contracts before you sign them as well.

about the music industry and its contracts. Additionally, he or she may have contacts within the industry that could be helpful to you.

"What about press agents and publicists?" you ask. "When do I need them?"

That depends to a great extent on where you are in your career. If you're just starting out and you can put together professional-looking bios and press kits, you might be able to do it yourself. You might also have some creative friends or family members put together your bios and press kits.

If your career is becoming more established or you want to create some buzz, consider retaining a publicist or press agent. In addition to music industry publicists and press agents, many publicists freelance and will work on a per-project basis. It's okay to ask to see a portfolio of *their* work and ask for references.

Whether your career choice is on the business end of the music industry, in the talent area, or anywhere in between, you've taken another step toward preparing for success.

5

JOB SEARCH STRATEGIES

Using a Job to Create a Career

No one goes out and gets a career; you usually have to create one. This can be especially true in the music business. How can you create your dream career? You have to take each job you get along the way and make it work for you. Developing the ultimate career requires a lot of things, including sweat, stamina, and creativity. Think of every job as a rung on the career ladder, every assignment within that job as a stepping-stone. Completing the puzzle takes lots of pieces and lots of work, but it will be worth it.

Except for a lucky few or those with specialized skills, breaking into the music business often requires starting at low-level, low-paying, or even volunteer positions. But every job helps to sharpen your skills and adds another line to your resume. Every job is an opportunity to network, learn, and most of all get noticed.

Of course, if you know that your ultimate goal is a career in the music industry, it's much easier to see how each job you do can get you a little closer. And this doesn't just apply to the business end of the industry. For performing artists, every engagement or gig, no matter how small, gives you experience, hones your skills, helps you gain confidence in front of an audience, and gives you the opportunity to be dis-

covered. Every job can lead you to the career you've been dreaming about.

While almost anyone can get a job, not everyone ends up with a career. As discussed in a previous section, the difference between a job and a career is that a job is just a means to an end. It's something you do to get things done and to earn a living. Your career, on the other hand, is a series of related jobs you build using your skills, talents, and passions. It's a progressive path of achievement.

When you were a child, perhaps your parents dangled the proverbial carrot on a stick in front of you, tempting you to eat your dinner so that you could have chocolate ice cream and cake for dessert. Whether dinner was food you liked, didn't particularly care for, or a combination, you probably ate it most of the time to get to what you wanted—dessert. In this case, your dessert will be ultimate success in your career in the music industry.

Use every experience, every job, and every opportunity for the ultimate goal of filling your life with excitement and passion while getting paid. Will there be things you don't enjoy doing and jobs you wish you didn't have along the way? Perhaps, but there will also be things you love doing and jobs you look back on and remember with joy.

The Inside Scoop

When many of the people who have succeeded on the talent end of the music industry get together and start talking, they refer to the days when they were up-and-coming, struggling acts as the "good old days." That's not to say they aren't thrilled to be where they are now—just that, looking back, they went though some great experiences and had a lot of good times.

Moving into the Music Biz— Changing Careers

Are you currently working in another industry and want to be in the music business? If so, you're not alone. Many people have dreamed about a career in the music business and for a variety of reasons have ended up in other industries. Is this you?

Perhaps at the time you needed a job or it looked too difficult to get into the music industry. Maybe you just didn't know how to go about it. Maybe you weren't ready. Maybe people around you told you that you were pipe dreaming. Maybe you were scared. Or maybe someone offered you a job in a different industry and you took it for security. There might be hundreds of reasons why you didn't get into the music industry. The question is, do you want to be there now?

"Well," you say. "I do, but . . ."

Before you go through your list of *buts,* ask yourself these questions: Do you want to give up your dream? Do you want to live your life saying, "I wish I had," but never trying? Wouldn't you rather find a way to do what you want than never really be happy with what you're doing? Wouldn't it be great to look at others who are

doing what they want and know that you are one of them? You just have to make the decision to do it!

How can you move into the music business from a different industry? How can you change your career path? Let's begin with the business end of the industry, and then we'll discuss moving into the talent and creative area.

First, take stock of what you have and what you don't have. One of the easiest ways to move into the music industry is by transferring skills. That means going over your skills and finding ways you can use them in the career of your choice.

Do you have strong writing skills? Consider seeking a position at a record label in the publicity or marketing department. What about a job in a music industry public relations or publicity firm. How about starting your own music industry publicity firm? What about looking for a job as an entertainment reporter for a newspaper, magazine, or music trade?

Are your skills in the number-crunching area? What about seeking a position at a record label in the accounting department? What about working with a CPA who handles clients in the music industry? What about going on the road

Tip from the Coach

Are you living someone else's dream? You can't change your past, but you can change your future. If your dream is to work in the music business, go for it. Things might not change overnight, but the first step you take toward your new career will get you closer to your dream. Every day you put it off is one more day you're wasting doing something you don't love. You deserve more. You deserve the best.

with a major recording artist to handle their finances on tour?

Do you have office skills? Are you a good manager? Do you have good organizational skills? Consider a job as an administrative assistant at a record label, booking agent, or other music industry business. One of the good things about this type of job is that you get to learn the ropes and often have a great chance of moving up the career ladder.

Do you have information technology (IT) skills? Are you a webmaster? Do you have other computer skills? Most every agency and record label has a Web site even if they have no IT department. What about doing Web sites for individual artists?

Are your skills in marketing? Are you working in marketing in another industry? Consider a position in the marketing department at a record label. What about a position in a management firm helping to market its artists? What about the marketing department of a radio station? How about a marketing position at a club, arena, or other venue?

Are your skills in sales? Lucky you. The possibilities are endless. Every record label needs salespeople. What about a position in a booking agency? A great deal of the work involved in booking artists is selling. What about selling advertising for a radio station? What about selling your own songs or those of another artist?

Are your skills in education? What about teaching music? What about becoming a private music teacher? What about giving vocal lessons?

"Wait a minute," you say. "What if I don't want to work in the area where my skills are? What if I want to be a record label exec? What then?"

Here's the deal. Use your skills and your talents to get your foot in the door. Once in, you

> **Voice of Experience**
> Start saving up your vacation and personal days now to use when you need to take a trip to a city where a potential job is located, go on interviews, make important phone calls, or finish up a project.

have a better opportunity to move into the area you want.

Should you quit your present job to go after your dream? And if so, when should you do it? Good questions. Generally, you are much more employable if you are employed. You don't have that desperate "I need a job" look. You don't have the worries about financially supporting yourself. You don't have to take the wrong job because you've been out of work so long that *anything* looks good. It's best to work on starting your dream career while you have a job to support yourself. Ideally, you'll be able to leave on job directly for another much more to your liking.

You must focus on exactly what you want to do, set your goals, prepare your action plan, and start taking actions now. You're going to have to begin moving toward your goals every day: not just a job, but a job that can lead to the career of your dreams.

Now let's talk about the talent end of the industry. To survive financially, many aspiring singers, musicians, and songwriters hold down a "day job" to make a living. Is this what you're doing? Whether you're working as a waiter, waitress, secretary, administrative assistant, sales associate, administrator, or manager (no matter whether you work full time, part time, or temp), your goal should be to make enough money to support yourself until you make it in the music business.

The question many ask is, "When do I quit my day job?" No one can answer this for you, but try to be realistic. You don't want to be in the position where you *can't* do what you want because you don't have any funds. To have the best shot at what you want to do, you need to be as financially stable as possible.

Before you quit your day job, ask yourself a few questions.

- Are you getting gigs on a consistent basis?
- Are your fees for engagements increasing?
- Are you earning more money from gigs in the music business than you are in your job?
- Are you turning down paying engagements because of your job?
- Do you have a nest egg put away in case of emergencies?
- Can you support yourself on the monies you're earning from your music career?

Once you answer these questions, you'll know what you have to do. If you can't support yourself on what you're earning from your music career, keep your day job until things change.

This doesn't mean you shouldn't work toward your goals. Continue searching out ways to make your music career more lucrative. Later chapters discuss some ways to do this.

"But I don't have time to do everything," you say.

You're going to have to make time. It's amazing how you can expand your time when you need to. Remember your action plan? It's imperative that you carve time out of your day to perform some of those actions.

If you think you don't have the time, look at your day a little closer. What can you eliminate

---

Words from the Wise

As excited as you might be about your new career, keep your job search to yourself at work. Don't talk about it during work to your friends, your coworkers, and certainly not to your boss.

---

doing? Will getting up a half an hour early give you more time to work on your career? How about cutting out an hour of TV during the day or staying off the computer for an hour? Even if you can only afford to take time in 15-minute increments, you usually can find an hour to put into your career.

Finding the Job You Want

Perseverance is essential to your success in the music industry no matter what you want to do, what area of the industry you want to enter, and what career level you want to achieve. Do you want to know why most people don't find their perfect job in the music industry? It's because they gave up looking *before* they found it.

Difficult as it might be to realize at this point, remember that your job is out there waiting for you. You just have to locate it. How do you find that all-elusive position you want in the music industry?

For the most part, jobs are located in two areas: the open job market and the hidden job market. What's the difference? The open job market is composed of jobs advertised and announced to the public. The hidden job market is composed of jobs not advertised or announced to the public.

Where can you find the largest number of jobs: the hidden job market or the open job market? A lot depends exactly on what you want to do in the industry, but be aware that there are a great many jobs in the music business that just aren't advertised. Why? There are a few reasons, but basically because positions in the music industry are often so coveted, putting an ad in the classified section of the newspaper might mean that there could be hundreds of responses, if not more.

"But isn't that what employers want?" you ask. "Someone to *fill* their job openings?"

Of course they want their job openings filled, but they don't want to have to go through hundreds of resumes and cover letters to get to that point. It is much easier to try to find qualified applicants in other ways, and that is where the hidden job market comes in.

This doesn't mean, however, that you shouldn't look into the open market. The smart thing to do to boost your job hunt is utilize every avenue to find your job. With that being said, let's discuss the open job market a bit and then we'll go on to talk about the hidden job market in more detail.

The Open Job Market

When you think of looking for a job, where do you start? Most people head straight for the classifieds. While, as I just noted, this strategy may not always be the best bet, it's at least worth checking out. Let's go over some ways to increase your chances of success in locating job openings this way.

The Sunday newspapers usually have the largest collection of help wanted ads. Start by focusing on those. You can never tell when a company will advertise job openings, though, so you might also want to browse through the classified section on a daily basis if possible. Will you find a music industry job advertised in your local hometown newspaper? That depends

on what type of job you're seeking and where you live. If you live in a small town and you're looking for a position at a major record label, probably not. If you're looking for a position at a local radio station or in a local club, your chances are better.

If you're seeking a position at a major record label or agency, check out the classified sections of newspapers from the music capitals of New York, Los Angeles, and Nashville. You might also find jobs advertised in newspapers in other large metropolitan cities including Chicago, Atlanta, Detroit, Philadelphia, Boston, and Seattle.

"But I don't live in those areas," you say. "How can I get the papers? What am I going to do?"

There are a number of solutions. Larger bookstores and libraries often carry Sunday newspapers from many metropolitan cities in the country. If you're interested in getting newspapers from most areas, you can also usually order short-term subscriptions. One of the easiest ways to view the classified sections of newspapers from around the country is by going online to the newspapers' Web sites. The home page will direct you to the classified or employment section. Start your search from there.

What do you look for? That depends on the specific job you're after, but generally look for keywords. If you want a job at a label, for example, you might look for keywords such as record label, music business, music industry, music, record label executive, and entertainment. You might also look under the names of specific job titles or departments such as "A&R Executive," "Publicity-Music Business," "Record Producer," "Administrative Assistant-Record Label," "Artist Development Coordinator," and so on. Don't forget to look for specific company names as well.

Sometimes major companies such as large record labels, booking agencies, and music publishers also use boxed or display classified ads. These are large ads that may advertise more than one job and usually have a company name and/or logo. There are also employment agencies specializing in the music industry that may advertise openings in the employment agency area of the classifieds. These will usually be located in newspapers in the music capitals.

The Trades, Industry Publications, Newsletters, and Web Sites

Where else are jobs advertised? Trade journals are often a good source. Trades are periodicals geared toward a specific industry. Every industry has trade magazines and newspapers, and the music business is no exception.

The most recognized trade in the music industry is *Billboard*. This weekly publication is chock full of information on the music business, trends, the music charts, and people in the news and offers a classified advertisement section where music industry businesses often advertise job openings.

How can you use the trades to your advantage? Read them faithfully. If you don't want to invest in a subscription, go to your local or college library to see if they subscribe. If all else fails, visit your local radio station and ask if it

would be possible for you to look at their copy of the magazine. Browse through the Help Wanted ads in the classified section every week to see if your dream job is there.

Don't forget to check out some of the other trades too. *Pollstar,* for example, is the trade for the touring industry. *Cashbox* and *Radio and Records* are the trades for radio. Refer to the bibliography at the back of this book for information about more music trades.

Newsletters related to the music industry might offer other possibilities for job openings. What about Web sites such as Monster.com, Hotjobs.com, and others? Don't forget company Web sites. Record labels; booking agencies; music industry publicity and public relations firms; music publishers; venues; clubs; and other music industry businesses now usually host Web sites. Many of these sites have specific sections listing career opportunities at their company. They are worth checking out. Some companies in the music business also host job hotlines that let you call a phone number and hear about openings at the company.

Are you already working at a label, agency, or other music industry company and seeking to move up the career ladder? Many companies post their employment listings in the human resources department or in employee newsletters. What if you don't have a job there already and are interested in finding out about internal postings? This is where networking comes into play. A contact at the company can keep you informed.

If you're still in college or graduated from a school that had a music business program, check with the career placement office. In some cases, record labels searching to fill specific positions may go to colleges and universities where they had internship programs.

As noted previously, a number of employment agencies specialize in jobs in the music industry or have clients in the music industry for which they fill jobs. Check out the newspapers in the music capitals to see which agencies are advertising music industry jobs. While these are often entry or mid-level jobs, remember that the idea is to get your foot in the door. Even if the agency is not advertising for a job in which you're interested, you might call or stop by to talk to someone just to make contact.

The Hidden Job Market

Let's talk about the hidden job market. Many people think that their job search begins and ends with the classified ads. If they get the Sunday paper and their dream job isn't in there, they give up and wait until the next Sunday. I am betting that once you have made the decision to have a career in the music industry, you're not going to let something small like not finding a job opening in the classifieds stop you. So what are you going to do?

While there may be job openings in your field that are in the classifieds, it's essential to realize that many jobs are not advertised at all. Why? In addition to not wanting to be bombarded and inundated by tons of resumes and phone calls, for example, some employers may not want someone in another company to know that they are looking for a new director of A&R or a new director of publicity until they

hire one. As a matter of fact, they may not want the person who currently holds the job to know that he or she is about to be let go. Whatever the reason, once you're aware that all jobs aren't advertised you can go about finding them in a different manner.

Why do you want to find jobs in the hidden job market? The main reason is that you will have a better shot at getting the job. Why? To begin with, there is a lot less competition. Because positions aren't being actively advertised, there aren't hundreds of people sending in their resumes trying to get the jobs. Not everyone knows how to find the hidden job market, nor do they want to take the extra time to find it, so you also have an edge over other job applicants. Many applicants in the hidden job market also often come recommended by someone who knew about the opening. This means that you are starting off with one foot in the door.

While there are entry-level jobs to be found in the hidden job market, there are also a good number of high-level jobs. This can be valuable when you're trying to move up the career ladder.

How does the hidden job market work? When a company needs to fill a position, instead of placing an ad, they quietly look for the perfect candidate. How do they find candidates without advertising? Let's look at some ways this is accomplished and how you can take advantage of each situation.

◎ Employees may be promoted from within the company.

  ⊡ That is why it is so important once you get your foot in the door and get a job to keep yourself visible in a positive manner. You want supervisors to think about you when an opening occurs. For example, if you're working in publicity and your goal is a career in artist development, drop subtle hints during conversations with supervisors of your department and artist development. You might, for example, say something like, "I love working in publicity. Learning how to publicize acts was one of my goals when I decided to work in this industry. I've also always wanted to learn about artist development." You're not saying you don't like your job. You're not saying you want to leave your job. What you're doing is planting a seed. If you have been doing an amazing job in your current position and anything opens up in artist development, you just might be suggested.

◎ An employee working in the company may recommend a candidate for the position.

  ▫ This is another time when networking helps. Don't keep your dreams to yourself. Tell others what type of job you're looking for and what your qualifications are. You can never tell when a position at a label, agency, publishing house, or other music industry business becomes available. Employers often ask their staff if they know anyone who would be good for this job. If you've shared your qualifications and dreams, someone just might recommend you.

◎ Someone who knows about an opening may tell their friends, relatives, or coworkers, who then apply for the job.

  ▫ In some cases, it's not another employee who knows about an opening, but it might be someone who has contact with the company. For example, a performing act's accountant might hear that the act's record label is looking for a marketing manager and an administrative assistant. He or she might tell his or her daughter to call up and apply for the job. Sometimes it may be someone outside the company who hears about the job. The UPS delivery person, for example, may be delivering packages at a booking agency when he or she overhears a conversation about the company needing an agent in training. If you have networked with the UPS delivery person and mentioned you are looking for a job in the music business, he or she might stop by and tell you about the opportunity. All you have to do is contact the agency.

◎ People may have filled in applications or sent resumes and cover letters to the company, asking that they be kept on file. When an opening exists, the human resources department might review the resumes and call one of the applicants.

  ▫ Even if jobs are advertised, it is often worth your while to send a letter and your resume to the human resources department to ask about openings. Be sure to ask that your resume be kept on file.

◎ Suitable candidates may place cold calls at just the right time.

  ▫ Difficult as it can be to place cold calls, it might pay off. Consider committing yourself to make a couple of cold calls every day. Do some research, choose the labels, agencies, publishing houses, publicity firms, and venues in which you are interested and call the director of human resources or the director of one of the departments in an attempt to set up an interview. Make sure you get the person's name ahead of time so you can ask for someone by name.

◎ People may have networked and caught the eye of those who need to fill the jobs.

  ▫ Finding positions in the hidden job market is a skill in itself. One of the best ways to do this is by networking. Through networking you can make contacts, and your contacts are the people who will know about the jobs in the hidden market.

Networking in the Music Business

Often, it's not just what you know but who you know. In the music business, as we've discussed, contacts are key. Networking is an important part of succeeding. It's so important that it can often make or break you.

How so, you ask?

You may be the most talented singer in the world, but if you can't get the right people to hear you, it's going to be difficult to find an agent and a record label. You might be a great singer, but you might just end up just singing in the shower.

The importance of networking is not limited to the talent area of the industry. Networking is just as important on the business end. The fact of the matter is that without the power of networking, it is often difficult to get your foot in the door.

Earlier chapters have touched on networking because of its importance to your success, and it will be discussed further throughout the book. What is essential to understand is that networking isn't just something you do at the beginning of your career. It's something you're going to have to continue doing for as long as you work.

How do you network? Basically, you put yourself into situations where you can meet people and introduce yourself. Chapter 7 discusses more about networking basics and offers some networking exercises. However, right now, you're going to have to learn to get comfortable walking up to people, extending your hand, and introducing yourself.

"Hi, I'm Lisa Cable. Isn't this an interesting event? What a great opportunity this was to learn more about record promotion," you might say at a seminar.

The person you meet will then tell you their name and perhaps something about themselves. You can then keep talking or say, "It was nice meeting you. Do you have a card?"

Make sure you have your business cards handy, and when you are given a card, give yours as well.

Voice of Experience

You never want to be in a position where someone remembers that they met you and remembers that you would be perfect for a job, yet they have no idea how to get in touch with you. Don't be stingy with your business cards. Give them out freely.

Every business situation can ultimately be an opportunity to network, but some are more effective than others. Look for seminars, workshops, and classes that music industry professionals might attend. Why would an industry professional be at a workshop or seminar? There are many reasons. They might want to network just like you, or they might want to learn something new, or they might be teaching or facilitating the workshop.

Where else can you meet music industry professionals to network with? It probably will be difficult (if not impossible) to go to a record company, music distributor, or booking agency, knock on doors, and introduce yourself to the president of the company. So what can you do? You're next best bet is trying to network with employees of those companies. How? Here's a strategy to try if you live near an area where there are music industry companies.

Find one or two of the companies in which you are interested and locate the street address. Choose a day when you have some time to spare, but it must be a weekday. Get dressed in some appropriate clothing, and go to the office of the company you've chosen. Now stand outside the building and look around. Are there restaurants, coffee shops, diners, or bars nearby? There probably are. Why does that matter? Because people from the offices have to eat lunch somewhere, get their coffee somewhere, and after work on Friday might stop into the bar on the corner for happy hour. What does that mean to you? If you can determine where the company employees hang out, you can put yourself in situations in which to network with them.

Can you find out which restaurants and coffee shops the employees frequent? Sometimes you can if you stand outside around lunchtime and watch to see who goes where. Some office buildings have thousands of employees in different businesses, so how do you know which are the employees from the company you have targeted? You might have to eavesdrop a little and listen for clues in things people say as they walk out the door. You might stop in the building and ask someone. Get on the elevator for the floor the company is located and ask the elevator operator. Ask the security guard standing in the lobby. You might even stop into a couple of the coffee shops or restaurants and ask the hostess.

"Hi, I was supposed to have a lunch meeting with someone from ABC records, the record company next door and I'm embarrassed to say, I'm not sure which coffee shop the meeting was set for," you might say. "Do a lot of the employees from the record company come in here?"

At this point, the hostess will either give you a blank look that means you probably are in the wrong place or tell you that you are indeed in the right location. Once you've found the correct location, wait until it's nice and busy and there is a slight line. People will usually talk to other people even if they don't know them when they are standing in lines. Start up conversations

---

Tip from the Top

When networking at an event, don't just zero in on the people you think are the important industry insiders and ignore the rest. Try to meet as many people as you can, and always be pleasant and polite to everyone. You never can tell who knows who and who might be a great contact later.

and hope that you're standing near the people from the company you're looking for. What about sitting at the counter? It you get lucky, you might end up sitting next to someone from the company.

The tricky part in all of this is being able to network in this type of situation. Some people are really good at it, and some people find it very difficult. What you're dealing with when doing this is first finding the correct people and then starting a conversation that may let you turn the person into a networking contact. If you do it right, it can pay off significantly. You might meet someone who works at the company and strike up a conversation about how you want to work at the company or in the music business. You never can tell what might happen from there. Your new contact might tell you they are looking for someone in the marketing department or the A&R department. You might get a referral, set up an interview, or even get a job.

I have often discussed this technique at seminars and workshops and once described it on a radio show about getting into the music business. I knew the area where the show aired, so I mentioned the name of a gourmet coffee shop near a music industry company where I knew all the employees congregated before and after work and at various times during the day. A few months later, I started getting calls and e-mails from people who had tried the technique and found that it worked. Did they all get a job? Some of them did. Some of them didn't. The important thing to know is that many of them got their foot in the door where they otherwise might not have.

If you find networking in this manner difficult, it might be easier for you to do at a bar during a happy hour because people tend to talk more in these situations. Remember, though, that while it's okay to drink socially, your main goal is to network and make contacts. You won't do yourself any favors becoming intoxicated and then acting outrageously or saying something inappropriate.

Where else might music industry professionals congregate? What about clubs, concert halls, or other venues? How do you get to the right people? Call the venue manager or assistant manager. Tell him or her about your career aspirations and ask if he or she would be willing to give you the names of a couple of industry people that you might call.

"Why would anyone want to help me?" you ask. Most people like to help others. It makes them feel good. Don't expect everyone to be courteous or to go out of their way for you, but if you find one or two helpful people, you may wind up with some useful contacts.

To get you started thinking, here's a sample script of how such a conversation might go.

Venue Manager: Hello, Jim Robertson.

You: Hi, this is Jill Wilson. I'm not sure if you're the right person to speak to about this, but is it okay if I tell you what I'm looking for and you can point me in the right direction?

⭐ The Inside Scoop

It's great to network with those at the top, but a good and often more practical strategy is to try networking with their assistants and support team. The people at the top might not always remember you; those a step or two down the line usually will. Not only that, but a recommendation from these people about you to their boss can do wonders for your career.

Venue Manager: Sure, go ahead.

You: Thanks. First of all, I'm not selling anything. I live in the area and work at the hospital in the public relations department. It's my goal to get a job in the music industry, but I don't really know any of the right people. I was wondering if you might have some ideas about who I could talk to or how I can meet some people in the industry. I know a lot of the big concerts in the area are at your venue and I thought you might be able to give me some suggestions.

Venue Manager: I mainly deal with the agents and the managers. You probably want a job at a record label. I don't deal with those people too often. Sorry.

You: Well, at this point, I'm just trying to get my foot in the door. Would it be a big imposition for me to come in one day when you're not busy to get a couple of names and numbers?

Venue Manager: I'm pretty busy this week. We have a couple of big concerts going off next week. You know, you might want to come over and meet some of those folks. Are you free next Thursday afternoon? The publicist for one of the groups is coming by with the act to do a couple of interviews and I think one of the agents will be there.

You: That would be great. Just tell me exactly when to be there and where to meet you.

Venue Manager: Why don't you come up to my office around 3:00 on Thursday? Bring your resume. I don't know if you're interested in any freelance work, but we're looking for someone. We can talk Thursday.

You: Thanks. I look forward to meeting you.

See how easy it is? You just have to ask.

"But what if they say no?" you ask.

That might happen. The conversation may not go in the direction you want it to. Some people will say no. So what? If you don't ask, you'll never know.

"But what do I say if someone says no?"

Simply thank them nicely for their time and hang up. Don't belabor the point. Just say, "Thanks anyway. I appreciate your time."

It will be difficult the first couple of times you make a call like that, but as you begin to reach out to others, it will get easier. Pretty soon, you won't even think about it.

Where else can you network with music industry professionals? What about concerts? Concerts are full of people involved in the music business.

"But how do I get through to them?" you ask.

You're going to have to be creative.

Radio stations often sponsor or co-sponsor concerts and other entertainment events, and when they do so, they sometimes hold contests to win concert tickets and, more important, "meet and greets" with the performers. Look for these and enter them.

"But I'm not lucky," you might say. "I never win anything."

Even so, it's worth entering your name and taking a chance. But it's true that only a limited number of people win, so here's your next plan of attack. Call up the radio station owner, manager, or promotion director and tell him or her your plight. Explain that you are trying to network with some people in the music industry with the ultimate goal of not only getting a job but having a career. Ask if they have any ideas about who you could speak to within the support team with the act appearing at the event. If they say they don't have any ideas, ask if they would consider letting you go along to the meet and greet.

"I know I wasn't a winner in the promotion, but I would really appreciate the opportunity to attend the meet and greet. I'll be glad to buy my own tickets to the show, so that's not a consideration," you might say. "I promise to give your station first dibs when I become head of A&R at the biggest record label in the world. If it would help you to know, I'm serious about my career and would be glad to fax over my resume."

If someone has taken the time to speak with you on the phone, there's a good chance they will invite you and tell you when to be there. In that case, thank the person you're speaking to, get the spelling of his or her name, and confirm the time and place of the meeting. If there is time, drop a thank-you note to the person you spoke to confirming the conversation.

When you arrive at the meet and greet, remember that you are a guest at a business function. Behave professionally and make sure to watch for any opportunities to network, the main reason that you're there. Here are some tips on what to do and what not to do:

- Do not bring anyone with you. Go alone. If your girlfriend, boyfriend, spouse, or significant other wants to go, meet them afterwards. No exceptions.
- Do not drink alcoholic beverages while you're there, even if someone asks you if you want a drink or a beer. A soft drink is fine.
- Do not smoke even if other people are. You can never tell what makes someone remember you. You don't want it to be that you smell of tobacco.

- Don't wear strong perfume, cologne, or aftershave. Aside from the possibility of some people being allergic to it, you don't want this to be the reason people remember you.
- Do not use any drugs, even if other people are.
- Don't get in people's way. The support staff may be getting ready for the show.
- Don't overstay your welcome. When everyone is instructed to leave the area or most people start to go, thank the radio station personnel and go.
- Do bring business cards to give out to everyone.
- Do bring a pen and a pad to take down names and phone numbers of people who don't have cards.
- Do meet as many people as possible. Briefly tell them what your goal is and ask if they have any suggestion about who you can contact. Don't forget to talk to roadies, sound engineers, and light technicians. They often have the pulse of what's happening and may be more approachable than the performing stars and their high-level support staff.
- Do send a thank-you note to the contact at the radio station the day after the event.

Here's a sample letter thanking your radio station contact:

Mr. John Stevens
WAAA
PO Box
Anytown, NY 11111

Dear Mr. Stevens,
　　Thanks for helping an aspiring record label artist development director get his start. I can't

tell you how much I appreciate the opportunity you gave me to attend the meet and greet your station sponsored. While I haven't gotten a job yet (it's only been three days), I did network and met a number of people who gave me some great contact information. I will be calling them this week to see if I can set up interviews.

I'll let you know how it works out. If there is anything I can ever do for you, please let me know. Thanks again.

Sincerely yours,
Bobby Carmendy

The next step is to follow up on the contacts and information you gathered at the meet and greet. Here is a sample letter you might send to someone you were referred to by a contact you met at the meet and greet.

Ms. Charma Harmon
DND Records
1111 Broadway
New York, NY

Dear Ms. Harmon:

I met John Henricks, the road manager for the Book Bank Band, at a radio station–sponsored event, and he suggested I write to you. I've recently completed my bachelor's degree with a major in music business management and am interested in a career in artist development. While in college I was on the concert committee for our school, and I interned for Bada Records in both the artist development and A&R departments.

I was wondering if it would be possible to set up an appointment with you to discuss opportunities at DND Records. I have enclosed a copy of my resume for your review.

Thanks for your consideration.

Sincerely,
Bobby Carmendy

Words from the Wise

Never, ever come off as a groupie when meeting either the support team or the musical artists you are trying to get a job with. Networking in this way will not get you a job.

What other networking opportunities can you find? Whether or not a station sponsors or cosponsors a concert, it is worth your while to network with radio station personnel. Record label representatives often visit radio station personnel in an attempt to get their artists on the station's playlist. Recording artists may visit to do interviews or to promote their CDs. Station personnel may also know other music industry professionals.

Almost every station sponsors events and special broadcasts from remote locations. Get into your networking mode, go to these events, and introduce yourself to the on-air personality or the engineer or anyone who is there. Tell them you enjoy their station, briefly mention your career aspirations, and give out your cards. If you go to enough events, pretty soon, the station employees will know you and likely call you over and ask you how it's going when they see you. Once you develop a networking relationship, when an artist or label representative comes into town, you can either call your contact and ask for an invitation, or they might just call you.

Trade Shows, Conferences, and Conventions

Trade shows, conferences, and conventions geared toward the music industry are a treasure trove for making contacts. Those who attend

> ## ⭐ Tip from the Coach
>
> Remember that networking is a two-way street. If you want people to help you, it's important to reciprocate. When you see something you can do for someone else's career, do it and do it graciously.

are going for a specific reason. Most are industry professionals. By attending a good trade show, you probably will find businesses within the music industry that you might not even have known existed, and you'll meet more people as well.

A trade show and conference can dramatically increase the contacts in your network very quickly. You will have the opportunity to meet literally hundreds of people in the industry, and you're meeting them in an atmosphere where you're on a more level playing field than if you make cold calls trying to meet them.

Most trade shows and conferences also have an educational track chock full of seminars, workshops, and keynote presentations. Some even have certification programs in various areas. More important, many shows now incorporate career fairs where you have the opportunity to meet people from actual companies with job openings to fill.

Chapter 7 discusses trade shows and conferences and how to get the most out of attending them in more detail. What you should remember now is that when you go to any of these events, it's essential to introduce yourself, spend time talking to people, and let them know you are in the market for a job.

The Right Place at the Right Time

Have you ever looked down while you were walking and seen some money sitting on the ground? It could have been there for a while, but no one else happened to look down at that time. You just happened to be in the right place at the right time.

It can happen any time. Sometimes you hear about an interesting job opening from an unlikely source. You might, for example, be visiting your neighbor at the hospital and her roommate turns out to be a record label executive who had come into town to see one of her acts perform. While there, she had a severe allergic reaction and was hospitalized. Over the course of the day, she had mentioned to your neighbor that she hoped she was going to be released the following morning because her assistant had recently quit and she needed to fill the position. Your neighbor remembered that you were trying to get a job in the music industry, mentioned it to her roommate, and told her all about you. You walked into the hospital room and practically were interviewed on the spot. Before the week was up, you got a call from the label's human resources department asking you if it would be possible for you to come in for a formal interview. By the next week, you were offered a job. Think it can't happen? It can and it does. It's just a matter of being in the right place at the right time.

Many people in the music industry tell stories of their success, saying something to the effect of, "We were just in the right place at the right time." Perhaps the "right" person may have been sitting in the audience when your act filled in for another one that unexpectedly dropped out of a show. Perhaps you sat next to an A&R exec on the airplane. There is no question that being in the right place at the right time can help. The question is, however, what is the right place and the right time, and how do you recognize it?

The simple answer is, it's almost impossible to know what the right place and right time is. You can, however, stack the deck in your favor. How? While you never know what the right place or the right time to be someplace is, you can put yourself in situations where you can network. Networking with people outside of the industry can be just as effective and just as important as networking with industry professionals.

The larger your network, the more opportunities you will have to find the job you want. The more people who know what you have to offer and what you want to do, the better. Who do you deal with every day? Who do these people know and deal with? Any of these people in your network and your extended network may know about your dream career in the music industry.

If you aren't employed and don't have to worry about a current boss or supervisor hearing about your aspirations, spread the news about your job search. Don't keep it a secret. The more people who know you're looking to be in the music industry, the more people who potentially can let you know when and where there is a job possibility.

Cold Calls

What exactly is a cold call? In relation to your career, a cold call is an unsolicited contact in person or by phone, letter, or e-mail with someone you don't know in hopes of obtaining some information, an interview, or a job. It is a proactive strategy.

Let's focus on the cold calls you make by phone. Many find this form of contact too intimidating to try. Why? Because not only are you calling and trying to sell yourself to someone who may be busy and doesn't want to be bothered, but you are also afraid of rejection. None of us like rejection. We fear that we will

> **Voice of Experience**
> You will find it easier to make cold calls if you not only create a script but practice it as well. To be successful in cold calling, you need to sound professional, friendly, and confident.

get on the phone, try to talk to someone, and they will not take our call, hang up on us, or say no to our requests.

The majority of telemarketing calls made to homes every day are cold calls. In those cases, the people on the other end of the phone aren't trying to get a job or an interview. Instead, they are attempting to sell something such as a product or a service. When you get those calls, the first thing on your mind is usually how to get off the phone. The last thing you want to do is buy anything from someone on the other end. But the fact of the matter is that people do buy things from telemarketers if they want what they're selling.

With that in mind, your job in making cold calls is to make your call compelling enough that the person on the other end responds positively. Why would you even bother making a cold call to someone? It's simply another job search strategy, and it's one that not everyone attempts, which gives you an edge over others.

How do you make a cold call? The phone call to the radio station and the venue manager we just discussed above give you a basic idea. If you wanted to make a cold call to a potential employer, do it in the same way. Identify who you want to call, put together a script to make it easier for you, and then make your call. Keep track of the calls you make. You may think you'll remember who said what and who

Cold Call Tracking Worksheet

Company	Phone Number	Name of Contact	Date Called	Follow-Up Activities	Results
ABDA Records	212-111-6666	John Carter	4/9	Send resume	Asked for resume, will get back to me after reviewing my qualifications.
Dell Publicity Services	212-222-3355	Missy Faitch	4/9		Couldn't get through. Does not take unsolicited employment calls.
QRZ Records	212-233-4444	Joan Diamond	4/9	Come in to fill in application/ interview	They are looking for marketing department coordinator.

you didn't reach, but after a couple of calls, it gets confusing. Use the Cold Call Tracking Worksheet provided on page 101 and see the sample above for the type of information you should record.

Who do you call? That depends on who you're trying to reach. If you want to pursue a career as a booking agent, you might call a booking agency owner directly.

You: Hi, Ms. Jacks. This is Tom Gere. I'm not sure you're the right person to speak to, but I was hoping I could tell you what I was looking for and perhaps you could point me in the right direction. Are you in the middle of something now or would it be better if I call back later?

Ms. Jacks: Are you trying to book a show?

You: No, I'm actually looking for a job. I was wondering if you knew of any opportunities for agent trainees. I don't have a lot of experience in the music industry, but I'm great at sales. I'm working in sales now and I have a 75 percent conversion rate.

Ms. Jacks: Seventy-five percent conversion. That's pretty good. What are you selling?

You: Web site advertising. I would really like to come in to talk to you. Would it be possible for me to make an appointment when you have some time for me to come in? I understand that you might not have a position, but you might know

Cold Call Tracking Worksheet

Company	Phone Number	Name of Contact	Date Called	Follow-Up Activities	Results

someone or might be able to give me some advice.

Ms. Jacks: I'm pretty busy for the next couple of weeks.

You: When would be good for you then? I'm flexible.

Ms. Jacks: Why don't you come in next Thursday. I'll probably have some time then. I'm going to put you on with Darla, my secretary, and she'll set up an appointment.

You: Thanks for your time. I look forward to meeting you.

Ms. Jacks: See you then. Hold for Darla.

It's not that difficult once you get someone on the phone.

"But what if they say no?" you ask.

So they say no. Don't take it personally. Just go on to your next call and use your previous call as practice.

Where do you find people to call? Browse company Web sites for names. Read the trade journals. Watch television and listen to the radio. Go through the yellow pages. You can get names from almost anyplace. Is there a record label you're interested in? What about a record distributor? How about a music industry publicity firm? What about an entertainment magazine or a newspaper's entertainment editor? Call up. Take a chance. It may pay off.

In many cases, when you start your conversation during a cold call, the person you're speaking to will direct you to the human resources (HR) department. If this is the case, ask who you should speak to in HR. Try to get a name. Then thank the person who gave you the information and call the HR department, asking for the name of the person you were given. Being referred by someone else in the company will often get you through. Try something like this:

You: Good afternoon, would Rick Robbins be in please.

Secretary: Who's calling?

You: This is Tony Williams. Mr. Adams suggested I call him.

Believe it or not, the more calls you make, the more you will increase your chances of success in getting potential interviews.

If you're really uncomfortable making calls or you can't get through to the people you're trying to reach by phone, consider writing letters. It takes more time than a phone call, but it is another proactive method for you to get through to someone.

Any of these techniques can be used even if you have a job and are trying to move up the career ladder. What you'll find is that once you're working in the business, it will usually be a lot easier to get through to people in the industry.

Creating Your Career

Do you want one more really good reason to find the hidden job market in the music business? If you're creative and savvy enough, you might even be able to *create* a position for yourself even if you are only on the first or second rung of the career ladder. What does that mean?

⭐ Tip from the Coach

Expect rejection when making cold calls. Some people may not want to talk to you. Rejection is a lot easier to deal with when you decide ahead of time it isn't personally directed toward you.

Let's say you're working as an administrative assistant at a label in the artist development department. In the course of your job, you get an idea. Wouldn't it be great to have a newsletter about new artists that goes out a couple of times a week via e-mail to fans? That way, fans can request that the artist's music videos be played on music television and CDs be played on radio. You do a prototype and bring it to your supervisor. He or she may speak to the publicity department. While there was no position planned for this job, they ask you if you would be interested in taking over this project. Voila! You've created your own position and you've moved up the ladder.

"What if I don't yet have a job. Is it still possible to create a position?"

If you are creative, have some initiative, and are assertive enough to push your idea, you can. Come up with something that you could do for the company that you want to work for that isn't being done now or that you could do better. Do you have any ideas? What about being a concierge for one of the label's major acts? What about being a media trainer, someone who coaches a label's performers on dealing with the press so that the act can be effective when doing interviews?

Get creative. Come up with an idea, develop it fully, and put it on paper so you can see any problems and then fine-tune it. Then call up the company that you want to work with, lay out the idea, and sell them on it. You've just created your own job!

6

TOOLS FOR SUCCESS

Your Resume as a Selling Tool

Every successful company markets and advertises their products or services. Some use ads in newspapers or magazines. Others use television or radio commercials. Some utilize billboards, banners, or a variety of other marketing vehicles. The main reason companies advertise and market themselves is to make sure others are aware of their product or service and to find ways to entice potential customers to buy or use that product or service.

When trying to succeed in your career, it is sometimes easier to look at yourself as a *product*. With that concept in mind, how can you market yourself so people know you exist? How can you entice potential employers to hire you?

The answer is simple. Start by making your resume a selling tool! Make it your own personal printed marketing piece. Everyone sends out resumes. The trick is making yours so powerful that it will grab the attention of potential employers.

Does your resume do a great job of selling your credentials? Does it showcase your skills, personality traits, and special talents? Is your resume the one that is going to impress the employers or human resources directors who can call you in for that all-important interview and ultimately land you the music business job you're after?

If an employer doesn't know you, their first impression of you might very well be your resume. This makes your resume a crucial part of getting an interview that might ultimately lead to your dream job.

A strong resume illustrates that you have the experience and qualifications to fill a potential employer's needs. How can you do this? To begin with, learn to tailor your resume to the job you're pursuing. One of the biggest mistakes people make is to create one resume and then use the same one every single time they apply for a position, regardless of the type of job.

How can you break this habit? Start by crafting your main resume. Then, don't be afraid to edit it to fit the needs of each specific job opening or opportunity.

"But," you say, "I want to work in the music industry. Can't all my resumes be the same?"

They can be *only if* you are going for the exact same type of job in each instance. For example, let's say you apply for a position as an administrative assistant at one record label. You then apply for a similar position as an administrative assistant at a different record label. In this instance, you can probably use the same resume.

On the other hand, let's say you're pursuing a job in the marketing department of a label. Another opening you're interested in is in the A&R department of a different label. In a case like this, while your resume might generally be the same, you should change it slightly by highlighting your skills and experiences most relevant to each post.

Before computers became commonplace, preparing a different resume for every job was far more difficult. In many cases, people would prepare a resume and then have it professionally printed by a resume service or printer. That was it. If you wanted to change your resume, you had to go back to the printer and have it done again and incur a major expense.

Today, however, most of us have access to computers, making it far easier to change resumes at will. Do you want to change your career objective? What about the order of components on your resume? Do you want to add something? You can create the perfect resume every time with the click of a mouse.

Always keep a copy of your resume on your computer and make sure you note the date it was done and its main focus. For example, you might save your resumes as "marketing resume," "PR resume," "record label resume," "booking agency resume," and so on. If you don't have your own computer, keep your resume on a CD or disk so you always have access to it without having to type it all over again.

Words from the Wise

If you're using different resumes, make sure you know which one you send to which company. Keep a copy of the resume you use for a specific job with a copy of the cover letter you send.

Tip from the Top

Keep updated copies of your resume on CDs or disks. You can never tell when your computer hard drive will die just when you see an advertisement in *Billboard* for the perfect job. If your resume is on a CD, you simply need to just put it in another computer, tailor your resume for that particular job, and send it off. You can also toss a CD in your briefcase or bag to keep with you if you are away from home and want to add something to your resume quickly. Adding a handwritten line when you change your phone number or address or even whiting out the wrong information is just not acceptable.

How can you make your resume a better marketing tool? Present it in a clear, concise manner, highlighting your best assets. Organize things in an order that makes it easy for someone just glancing at your resume to see the points that sell you the best and then want to take a second look.

The decision about the sequence of items in your resume should be based on what is most impressive in relation to the position you are pursuing. Do you have a lot of experience in the music industry? Put that first. Are your accomplishments extraordinary? If so, highlight those first. Do you have little experience, but you just graduated cum laude with a degree in music business management? Then perhaps your education should be where your resume should start.

Imagine if you received your resume. What would make you glance at it and say, "Wow," and keep on reading? One of the most important things to remember is that there really is no right or wrong type of resume. The right one for you will end up being the one that

> ### ⭐ Tip from the Top
>
> When replying to a job advertisement, use words from the advertisement in both your resume and your cover letter. It makes you look like more of a fit with the company's expectations.

ultimately gets you the position you want. There are so many ways to prepare your resume that it is often difficult to choose one. My advice is to craft several different ones, put them away overnight, and then look at them the next day. Which one looks best to you? That probably will be the style you want to use.

Here are some tips that might help:

◎ Tailor every resume for every position.
◎ Make sure you check for incorrect word usage. No matter what position you're pursuing, most employers prefer to have someone who has a command of the English language. Check to make sure you haven't inadvertently used the word *their* for *there, to* for *too* or *two, effect* for *affect, you're* for *your, it's* for *its,* and so on.
  ▫ Don't rely solely on your computer's spell and grammar checker. Carefully go over your work yourself as well.
◎ Every time you edit your resume or make a change, check carefully for errors.
  ▫ It is very easy to miss a double word, a misspelled word, or a wrong tense. Have a friend or family member look over your resume. It is often difficult to see mistakes in your own work.
◎ Tempting as it is to use different colored inks when preparing your resume, don't. Use only black ink.

◎ Use a high-quality paper of at least 40-pound weight for printing your resumes. Paper with texture often *feels* different, so it stands out. While you can use white, beige, or cream colored papers, soft light colors such as light blue, salmon pink, gray, or light green will help your resume stand out from the hundreds of white and beige ones.
◎ Make sure your resume layout looks attractive. You can have the greatest content in the world, but if your resume just doesn't look right, people may not actually read it.
  ▫ You know the saying, "You can't judge a book by its cover?" Well, you really can't, but if you don't know anything about the book or its contents you just might not pick it up unless the cover looks interesting.
◎ When sending your resume and cover letter, instead of using a standard number 10 business envelope and folding your resume, use a large manila envelope. That way you won't have to fold your resume and your information gets there looking clean, crisp, and flat.
◎ Don't use odd fonts or typefaces. Why? In many large companies, resumes are scanned by machine. Certain fonts don't scan well. What should you use? Helvetica, Times, Arial, and Courier work well.

> ### ⭐ Words from the Wise
>
> Whatever color paper you use for your resume and cover letters, make sure it photocopies well. Some colored papers photocopy dark or look messy.

◎ When preparing your resume, make your name larger and bolder than the rest of your resume. For example, if your resume is done in 12-point type, use 14-, 16-, or 18-point type for your name. Your name will stand out from those on other resumes.

Redefining Your Resume

You probably already have a resume in some form. How has it been working? Is it getting you the interviews you want? If it is, great. If not, you might want to consider redefining it.

You want your resume to stand out. You want it to illustrate that you have been successful in your accomplishments. You want potential employers to look at your resume and say to themselves, "That's who I want working here!"

How do you do that? Make your resume compelling. Demonstrate through your resume that you believe in yourself, because if you don't believe in you, no one else will. Show that you have the ability to solve problems and bring fresh ideas to the table.

First decide how you want to present yourself. What type of resume is best for you? There are a couple of basic types of resumes. The chronological resume lists your jobs and accomplishments beginning with the most current and going backwards. Functional resumes, which may also be referred to as skills-based resumes, emphasize your accomplishments and abilities. One of the good things about this type of resume is that it allows you to lay it out in a manner that spotlights your key areas whether they be your qualifications, skills, or employment history.

What's the best type of resume for you? That depends on a number of factors, including where you are in your career. If you are just entering the job market and you haven't held down

Voice of Experience

Your resume is your place to toot your own horn. If you don't, no one will know what you have accomplished.

a lot of jobs, but you have relevant experience through internships and/or volunteer activities, you might want to use the functional type. If, on the other hand, you have held a number of jobs in the field and climbed the ladder each time you moved, you might want to use the chronological variety. You can also sometimes combine elements from both types. This is called a combination resume. There is no one right way. You have to look at the whole picture and make a decision.

Use common sense. Make your best assets prominent on your resume. Do you have a lot of experience? Are your accomplishments above the bar? Did you graduate cum laude with a degree in music business management? Determine what would grab your eye and find a way to focus on that first.

What Should Your Resume Contain?

What should you have in your resume? Some components are required and some are optional. Let's look at some of them.

What do you definitely need? Your name, address, phone number, and e-mail address. What else? Your education, professional or work experience, accomplishments, and professional memberships. What else might you want to put in your resume? Your career objective, a summary of skills, and a career summary.

What shouldn't you put in your resume? Your age, marital status, any health problems, current or past salaries, and whether or not you have children.

Career Summary

Let's discuss your career summary. While a career summary isn't a required component, it often is helpful when an employer gets a huge number of resumes and gives each a short glance. A career summary is a short professional biography—no longer than 12 sentences—that tells your professional story. You can do it in a number of ways. Here's an example:

> Bachelor's degree with a major in music business and a minor in communications. Proven ability to deal with media on the local, regional, and national level. Fully knowledgeable in all aspects of public relations, publicity, advertising, and marketing. Accomplished entrepreneur in a variety of areas including artist merchandising. Increased merchandising revenues for three acts by 40 percent. Fluent in English, Spanish, and French. Assisted in the development and coordination of major marketing events for five new CD releases. Energetic, passionate, and articulate team player with a good sense of humor and the goal of making a success out of every opportunity.

A potential employer looking at this might think, "This Jody Walker has a degree in the music business, so she probably at least knows something about the industry. She also has managed her own business in music industry merchandising and increased revenues so she has a business sense. The ability to speak more than one language is always a plus. It looks like she has an understanding of marketing, publicity, promotion, and the like, and on top of that she looks successful. Why don't I give her a chance

to tell me more? I think I want to bring her in for an interview."

"What if I'm just out of college and have no experience?" you ask. "What would my career summary look like?"

In situations like this, you have to look toward experience and jobs you held prior to graduating. How about this:

> Recent graduate of State University with a major in music business management and a minor in merchandising with a GPA of 4.0. Intern in rotating departments at ABEL Records, an independent label. Proven ability to handle various tasks quickly, effectively, and efficiently. Ability to successfully bring a project to fruition on time and under budget. Handled the booking, tour coordination, travel arrangements, and publicity for a popular campus solo artist while still in college. Member of college campus activities board, assisting in the booking of all college entertainment events as well as handling artist rider fulfillment on days of events. Entertainment reviewer for *Hot Shots,* a local entertainment newspaper.

If you prefer, you can use a bulleted list to do your career summary.

- Recent graduate of State University with a major in music business management and a minor in merchandising; GPA of 4.0
- Intern at ABEL Records, an independent label
- Member of college campus activities board, assisting in the booking of all college entertainment events
- Entertainment reviewer for *Hot Shots,* a local entertainment newspaper

Career Objective

Do you need a career objective in your resume? It isn't always necessary, but in certain cases it helps. For example, if you are just starting out in your career, having a career objective illustrates that you have some direction. Because there are so many people who aspire to be in the music industry, showing that you have a direction or a specific goal is often positive.

When replying to a job opening, make sure the career objective on your resume is as close to the job you are applying for as possible. For example, if you are applying for a job as a marketing coordinator at a record label, you might make your career objective, "To work in the marketing department of a record label in a position where I can fully utilize my marketing, promotion, and sales skills."

If, on the other hand, you are sending your resume to a company "cold" or not for a specific job opening, don't limit yourself unnecessarily by stating a specific career objective. If you use a career objective in this type of situation, make sure it is general.

In many instances, you might send copies of your resume with a cover letter to companies you want to work for who aren't actively looking to fill a job. Your hope is to garner an interview. If your resume indicates that your sole goal is to work in the label artist development department, you might be overlooked for a position in the marketing department. Your career goal in this situation instead might be, "To work at a record label in a position where my people skills can be combined with my love and understanding of the music business and my degree in marketing." Remember, you want the person reviewing your resume to think of all the possible places you might fit in the organization.

Education

Where should you put education on your resume? That depends. If you recently have graduated from college and especially if you have a degree in something related to the music industry, put it toward the top. If you graduated a number of years ago, put your education toward the end of your resume. Do you need to put the year you graduated? Recent graduates might want to. If not, just indicate the college or university you graduated from and your major.

If you went to college but didn't graduate, simply write that you attended or attended taking coursework toward a degree. Will anyone question you on it? That's hard to say. Someone might. If questioned, simply say something like, "I attended college and then unfortunately found it necessary to go to work full time. I plan on getting my degree as soon as possible. I only have nine credits left to go, so it will be an easy goal to complete."

In addition to your college education, don't forget to include any relevant noncredit courses, seminars, and workshops you have attended. While you probably wouldn't want to add in classes like flower arranging (unless this had to do with your job in some way), you might include educational courses which are not music industry oriented but might help you in your career such as public speaking, writing, communications, or team work.

Professional and Work Experience

List your work experience in this section of your resume. What jobs have you had? Where did you work? What did you do? How far back do you go? That, once again, depends where you are in your career. Don't go back to your job as a babysitter when you were 15, but you need to show your work history.

In addition to your full-time jobs in or out of the music industry, include any part-time work that relates to the music industry or illustrates transferable job skills, accomplishments, or achievements.

Skills and Personality Traits

There is an advertising saying to the effect of "Don't sell the steak, sell the sizzle." When selling yourself through your resume, do the same. Don't only state your skills and personality traits; make them sizzle! Do this by using descriptive language and key phrases.

Need some help? Here are a few words and phrases to get you started:

◎ creative
◎ dedicated
◎ hard working
◎ highly motivated
◎ energetic
◎ self-starter
◎ knowledgeable
◎ strong work ethic

Accomplishments and Achievements

What have you accomplished in your career in or out of the music industry? Have you increased sales? Coordinated a major music event? Written a weekly entertainment column? Won an industry award? Your achievements inform potential employers not only about what you have done but also about what you might do for them.

Sit down and think about it for a while. What are you most proud of in your career? What have you done that has made a difference or had a positive impact on the company for which you worked? If you are new to the work force, what did you do in school? What about in a volunteer capacity?

Just as you made your skills and personality traits sizzle with words, you want to do the same

thing with your accomplishments and achievements. Put yourself in the position of a human resources director for a moment. You get two resumes. Under the accomplishments section, one says, "Planned and executed concert for charity." The other says, "Planned, coordinated, and successfully executed charity concert from inception through fruition generating $35,000 profit for Community Hospital." Which resume would catch your eye?

Do this by adding action verbs to your accomplishments. Use words such as *achieved, administered, applied, accomplished, assisted, strengthened,* and others.

When drafting your resume, include any honors you have received, whether or not they have anything to do with the music industry. These honors help set you apart from other candidates. Were you honored with the "Volunteer of the Year" award at a local hospital? While this has absolutely nothing to do with the music industry, it does show that you are a hard worker and good at what you do.

Community Service and Volunteer Activities

If you perform community service or volunteer activities on a regular basis, include it on your resume. Community service and volunteer activities you perform illustrate to potential employers that you "do a little extra." Additionally, you can never predict when the person reviewing your resume might be a member of the organization with which you volunteer. An unexpected connection like that can help you stand out.

Hobbies and Interests

What are your hobbies and interests? Do you collect old 45s? Do you go to concerts? Do you collect cookbooks? Are you a hiker? Do you volunteer with a literacy program? Many career counselors feel that hobbies or personal interests have no place on a professional resume, but I disagree. Why?

Here's a secret. You can never tell what will cause the person or persons reviewing the resumes to make a connection. Perhaps he or she has the same hobby as you. Perhaps he or she is a volunteer with a literacy program in which you participate. Anything that causes you to stand out in a positive manner or that causes a connection with your potential interviewer will help your resume garner attention, helping you to land an interview.

References

If you list your references on your resume, someone may check them to help them decide if they should interview you. The goal for your resume is to have it help you *obtain* an interview. You don't really want people giving their opinions about you until you have the chance to sell yourself. With this in mind, it usually isn't a good idea to list your references on your resume.

If you are uncomfortable with this, include a line on your resume stating that "references are available upon request."

Your Resume Writing Style

How important is writing style in your resume? Very important. Aside from conveying your message, your writing style helps to illustrate that you have written communication skills.

When preparing your resume, write clearly and concisely and do not use the pronoun "I" to describe your accomplishments. Instead of

writing "I developed key PR campaigns for entertainment industry clients. I got clients over 1,000 appearances and mentions in major media," try "Developed key PR campaigns for entertainment industry clients resulting in over 1,000 major media appearances, interviews, and mentions in a two-month period." Note the inclusion of a time period. It's good to be specific about your achievements.

Creating Music Industry–Specific Resumes

How can you create music industry–specific resumes? Tailor each resume for the specific position or area you are pursuing, and find ways to relate your existing skills to the music industry. If you can sell one product or service, with a little training, you can usually sell another. If you can publicize one product or service, you can publicize another. Similarly, if you can market one product, you can do so for another. Use all your experiences, talents, and skills to get the career you want.

The music business is known as a glamorous industry. Make sure your resume sparkles with enthusiasm and passion.

One thing you should *never* do is lie on your resume. Don't lie about your education. Don't lie about experience. Don't lie about places you've worked. If you haven't picked up on it yet, *do not lie*. As large as the music industry is, it is a very close-knit community. Once someone knows you have lied, that is what they will remember about you.

"Oh, no one is going to find out," you might say.

Don't bet on it. Someone might find out by chance, deduce the truth based on their industry knowledge, or hear the facts from a coworker or industry colleague. When the truth comes out, it tends to blow up in your face.

"By that time, I'll be doing such a good job, no one will fire me," you say.

That's the best-case scenario and there's a chance that could happen, but think about this. Once someone lies to you, do you ever trust them again? Probably not, and no one will trust you or anything you say. That will hurt your chances of climbing the career ladder. The worst-case scenario is that you will be fired, left without references, lose some of your contacts, and make it much more difficult to find your next job.

Believe it or not, whether you're interested in working at a record label, an agency, a recording studio, a music business publicity firm, a music-oriented law firm, or any other music business company, the people who are doing the hiring know everyone has to start someplace. If you don't have the experience, impress them with other parts of your resume and your cover letter. If, on the other hand, you have the experience and you are trying to advance your career, this is the time to redefine your resume. Add action verbs. Add your accomplishments. Make your new resume shine. Create a marketing piece that will make an employer say, "We need to interview this person. Look at everything he's done."

What About References?

References are another of your selling tools. References are the individuals who will vouch for your skills, ethics, and work history when a potential employer calls. A good reference can set you apart from the crowd and give you the edge over other applicants. A bad one can seriously hinder your career goals.

It's always a good idea to bring the names, addresses, and phone numbers of the people you are using for references with you when you apply for a job or when you are going on an interview. If you're asked to list them on an employment application, you'll be prepared.

Who should you use for references? To begin with, you'll need professional references. These are people you've worked with or who know you on a professional level. They might be current or former supervisors or bosses, the director of a not-for-profit organization you've worked with, internship program coordinators, a former professor, and so on.

Do your references have to be in the music industry? If you have references in the industry, it can't hurt. What you are looking for, however, are people who you can count on to help sell you to potential employers. Those will be your best references.

Always ask people if they are willing to be a reference before you use them. Only use people you are absolutely positive will say good things about you. Additionally, try to find people who are articulate and professional.

Who would be a bad reference? A boss who fired you, a supervisor you didn't get along with, or anyone you had any kind of problem with whatsoever. Do not use these people for references even if they tell you that they'll give you a good one. They might keep their word, but they might not, and you won't know until it's too late.

Consider this scenario. A potential employer named Mr. Elvins is calling your former supervisor Ms. Clifton, who never gave you a good review even though you did your best to get along with her. The conversation might go something like this:

Mr. Elvins: Hi, this is Chuck Elvins. I just interviewed one of your former employees, John Hillman. We're thinking of hiring him for a position at our publishing company. What can you tell me about him?

Ms. Clifton: He worked here for two years and we let him go.

Mr. Elvins: What else can you tell me about him? Was he responsible? Did he come in on time? What was his work ethic?

Ms. Clifton: Um, he was always on time I guess. I don't know what to tell you.

Mr. Elvins: Was he responsible?

Ms. Clifton: Yes, I guess so.

Mr. Elvins: You don't sound very excited about him.

Ms. Clifton: Well, I'm sure he'll work out nicely for your company.

Mr. Elvins: Thanks for your time. I appreciate it.

As you can see, Ms. Clifton didn't really say anything bad about John Hillman; she just didn't say anything good. You definitely don't want a reference like this.

"But," you say, "she was my supervisor. Isn't he going to call her anyway?"

The Inside Scoop

If you give your references an idea of what type of job you're pursuing, what skills are important in that position, or even what you want them to say, you stand a better chance of them leading the conversation in the direction you want it to go. You might tell a reference, for example that you're applying for a position as an assistant facility manager, and that the job description calls for someone very organized with an ability to multitask. In most cases, when your reference gets a call, he or she will remember what you said and stress your important selling points.

Maybe, but the trick here is getting a list of three to five good references, so no matter what anyone else says, you still look good.

You might be asked to list references on an employment application, but it's a good idea to prepare a printed sheet of your professional references that you can leave with the interviewer. This sheet will contain your list of three to five references, including their names, positions, and contact information. As with your resume, make sure it is printed on a high-quality paper.

Here's an example to get you started:

PROFESSIONAL REFERENCE SHEET FOR TONY BLAST

Mr. Jim Conners
President
Conners Booking Agency
121 Broadway
Anytown, NY 11111
(212) 222-3333, ext. 232
jconners@conners.com

Mr. Daniel Evans
Intern Coordinator
IBF Records
303 West End Avenue
Anytown, NY 11111
(212) 333-4444
danielevans@ibf.com

Ms. Rosanne Blouson
Editor
Music Pro Magazine
491 Fifth Avenue South
Cityville, NY 12222
(444) 4444-4444
editor@musicpro.com

Personal References

In addition to professional references, you might also be asked to provide personal references. These are friends, family members, or others who know you. You probably won't need to print out a reference sheet for your personal references, but make sure you have all their contact information in case you need it quickly.

As with professional references, make sure the people you are using know you are listing them as references. Give them a call when you're going on an interview to let them know someone might be contacting them. Ask them to let you know if they get a call.

Letters of Recommendation

As you go through your career, it's a good idea to get letters of recommendation from people who have been impressed with your work. Along with references, these help give potential employers a better sense of your worth. How do you get a letter of recommendation? You usually simply have to ask. For example, let's say you are close to completing an internship at a label. While the label is in a hiring freeze, things have gone well and everyone has been pleased with your work.

Say to your supervisor, "Would it be possible to get a letter of recommendation from you for my files?"

Most people will be glad to provide this. In some cases, people might even ask you to write it yourself for them to sign. Don't forego these opportunities even if you feel embarrassed about blowing your own horn. The easiest way to do it is by trying to imagine you aren't writing about yourself. In that way you can be honest and write a great letter. Give it to the person and say, "Here's the letter we discussed. Let me know if you want anything changed or you aren't comfortable with any piece of it." Nine times out of 10, the person will sign the letter as is.

Who should you ask for letters of recommendation? If you are still in school or close to graduating, ask professors with whom you have developed a good relationship. Don't forget internship coordinators or supervisors, former and current employers, executive directors of not-for-profit, civic, or charity organizations you have volunteered with, and so on.

In some situations the people you ask may just write generic letters of recommendation stating that you were a pleasure to work with or were good at your job. If the person writing the letter knows the type of position you're pursuing, he or she might gear the letter toward specific skills, traits, and talents needed.

Your letters of recommendation will become another powerful marketing tool in your quest to career success in the music industry. What do you do with them? Begin by photocopying each letter you get on high-quality white paper, making sure you get clean copies. Once that's done, you can make them part of your career portfolio, send them with your resume when applying for position, or bring them with you to interviews.

Creating Captivating Cover Letters

Unless instructed otherwise by a potential employer or in an advertisement, always send your resume with a cover letter. Why? Mainly because if your resume grabs the eye of someone in the position to interview you, he or she often looks at the cover letter to evaluate your written communications skills, as well as to get a sense of your personal side. If your letter is good, it might just get you the phone call you've been waiting for. On the other hand, a poorly written letter might just keep you from getting that call.

What can make your letter stand out? Try to make sure your letter is directed to the person to whom you are sending it instead of "Hiring Manager," "To Whom It May Concern," or "Sir or Madam."

"But the name of the person isn't in the ad," you say. "How do I know what it is?"

You might not always be able to get the correct name, but at least do some research. You might, for example, call the company and ask the name of the person to which responses are directed.

If you are sending your resume to a company cold, it's even more important to send it to a specific person. It gives you a better shot at someone not only reviewing it but taking action on it.

It's okay to call the company and say to the receptionist or secretary, "Hi, I was wondering if you could give me some information? I'm trying to send my resume to someone at your company, and I'm not sure who to send it to. Could you please give me the name of the human resources director?"

If he or she won't give it to you for some reason, say thank you and hang up. Because so many people try to get through to executives in A&R, artist development, and other popular departments, receptionists often don't give out names easily.

How do you get around this? Wait until lunch time or around 5:15 P.M. when the person you spoke to might be at lunch or done with work, call back, and say something to the effect of, "Hi, I was wondering if you could please give me the spelling of your director of artist development's name?"

If the person on the other end of the line asks you to be more specific about the name, simply say, "Let's see, I think it was Brownson or something like that. It sounded like Brown something."

Don't worry about sounding stupid on the phone. The person at the other end doesn't know you. This system usually works. Believe it not, most companies have someone working there whose name sounds like Brown or Smith.

The person on the phone may say to you, "No, it's not Brownson. Our director of artist development is Ryan Lawson. Is that who you're looking for?"

Then all you have to say is, "You know what, you're right, sorry, I was looking at the wrong notes. So that's R-Y-A-N L-A-W-S-O-N?"

Voila. You have the name. Is it a lot of effort? Well, it's a little effort, but if it gets you the name of someone you need and ultimately helps get you an interview, isn't it worth it?

You sometimes can get names from the Internet. Perhaps the company Web site lists the names of their key people. Key names for large companies may also often be located on Hoovers.com, an online database of information about businesses, but this is a paid service. Do what you must to get the names you need. It can make a big difference when you direct your letters to someone specific within the company.

People in the position to hire you in the music business receive a large number of resumes, letters, and phone calls. What else can help your letters stand out? Make them grab the attention of the reader. How? Develop some creative cover letters.

Take some time and think about it. What would make you keep reading? Of course, there will be situations where you might be better off sending the traditional, "In response to your ad letter." But what about trying out a couple of other ideas?

Take a look at the following sample cover letter. Would this letter grab your attention? Would it make you keep reading? Chances are it would. After grabbing the reader's attention, it quickly offers some of the applicant's skills,

talents, and achievements. Would you bring in Doug Fedder for an interview? I think most employers would.

DOUGLAS FEDDERS
322 Avenue J
Different Town, NY 22222
Phone: 111-222-3333
dfedders@moreinernet.com

Ms. Ginny Cunningham
Human Resources Manager
Rescue Records
P.O. Box 1222
Anytown, NY 11111

Dear Ms. Cunningham:

Congratulations!

I'm pleased to inform you that you have just received the resume that can end your search for Rescue Records' new marketing manager. In order to claim your "prize," please review my resume and call as soon as possible to arrange an interview. I can guarantee you'll be pleased you did!

As the marketing manager for a 3,000-seat facility for the past two years, I have developed a number of creative, innovative events to bring people in during "off" times as well as for major concert and entertainment events. Through these extra events, the bottom line revenue has increased dramatically and attendance has jumped 200 percent. In this position I have also worked with other large corporate businesses developing sponsorship opportunities for facility events, saving monies for the facility while generating large amounts of media attention for both entities.

While I love what I do now, my dream and passion since graduation has been a career in marketing at a major label. When I saw this opportunity, I was even more excited because not only am I a fan of your label's artists, but I have successfully marketed their concerts at our facility.

I believe my experience, skills, talents and passion would be an asset to Rescue Records. I would welcome the challenge and opportunity to work with your label to make it even more successful than it is now.

I look forward to hearing from you.

Sincerely yours,
Douglas Fedders

Now check out some other creative cover letters.

CARNIE PHILLIPS
322 Bayles Avenue
Different Town, NY 33333
Phone: 999-999-9999
cphillips@moreinternet.com

Mr. Phil Wilson
Promotion Manager
BLZ Records
912 Broadway
Anytown, NY 11111

Dear Mr. Wilson:

ARE YOU LOOKING FOR YOUR LABEL'S NEXT NUMBER-ONE RECORD?

While I can't guarantee a number-one record, I can promise you I'll be your label's number-one promotion staffer . . . if you give me a chance.

I'm an enthusiastic, pleasantly aggressive individual with a bachelor's degree in marketing. While still in school, I worked at Tower Records, moving up from a sales associate to a third key management position in two years.

In college I began working as a part-time receptionist at WMAX radio. Within two months I was promoted to the position of administrative assistant in the traffic department. Six months after that, I moved into the promotion department working as an assistant. Upon college graduation, I was offered my current position of assistant station promotion director.

While I enjoy my job and have been getting excellent employment reviews, my career goal is to work at a major record label. I believe with my love for music, ability to sell, and knowledge of both music and radio industries, I have the skills and talents to be an asset to your label in the promotion department.

I have enclosed my resume for your review and would very much appreciate the opportunity to meet with you to discuss opportunities at your label. In the event that you have no current openings, I was hoping you could still take a few minutes to speak to me to give me some ideas.

Thanks for your consideration. If I don't hear from you within a couple of weeks, I'll give you a call.

I look forward to hearing from you.

Sincerely yours,
Carnie Phillips

ART DAYTON
Different Town, NY 33333
Phone: 222-222-9999
artdayton@moreinternet.com

Mr. Bernard Katz
Amadaz Recording Studios
3121 Broadway
Anytown, NY 11111

Dear Mr. Katz:

I met your studio manager, Sharon Glover, at a recent music conference I was attending and she suggested I contact you regarding possible employment at your company.

I'm an enthusiastic, hard-working recording assistant searching for a job as a recording engineer at a larger studio.

In addition to earning a bachelor's degree from State University, where I took courses in sound engineering and recording technology, I have attended numerous workshops and seminars.

While in college I apprenticed at Fortune Studios.

I have a good musical ear and appreciation of music and have always been electronically and mechanically inclined.

I have enclosed my resume as well as a CD of several projects I have worked on in the past. I would very much appreciate an opportunity to speak with you regarding employment.

Thanks for your consideration. If I don't hear from you within a couple of weeks, I'll give you a call.

Sincerely yours,
Art Dayton

More Selling Tools—Business and Networking Cards

The best way to succeed at things is to do everything possible to stack the deck in your favor. Most people use a resume to sell themselves. As we just discussed, done right, your resume can be a great selling tool. It can get you in the door for an interview. But putting all your eggs in one basket is never a good idea. What else can you do to help sell yourself? What other tools can you use?

Business cards are small but powerful tools that can positively affect your career if used correctly. We've discussed the importance of business cards throughout the book. Let's look at them more closely.

Whatever level you're at in your career, whatever area of the industry you're interested

Tip from the Coach

Business cards are networking cards. You give them to people you meet so they not only remember you and what you do but how to contact you if necessary.

in pursuing, business cards can help you progress. If you don't have a job yet, business cards are essential. At this point, they may also be known as networking cards because that is what they are going to help you do. If you already have a job, business cards can help you climb the ladder to success. Get your business cards made up, and get them made up now!

Why are cards so important? For a lot of reasons but mainly because they help people not only remember you but find you. Networking is so essential to your success in the industry that once you go through all the trouble of doing it, if someone doesn't remember who you are or how they can contact you, it's almost useless.

How many times have you met someone during the day or at a party and then gone your separate ways? A couple days later, something will come up where you wish you could remember the person's name or you remember their name but have no idea how to get a hold of them. How bad would you feel if you found out that you met someone, told him or her that you were looking for a job in the industry, they ran into someone else who was looking for someone with your skills and talents, and they didn't know how to get a hold of you? Business cards could have helped solve that problem.

When was the last time you ran into someone successful who didn't have business cards? They boost your prestige and make you feel more successful. If you feel more successful, you'll be more successful. And cards are not just for those interested in the business end of the industry. If you are a singer, musician, in a group, a songwriter, or other performer, business cards are even more important to your career.

So, what's your next step? Start by determining what you want your business cards to look like. There are a variety of styles to choose from. You might want to go to a print shop or an office supply store such as Staples or Office Max to look at samples or you can create your own style.

Order at least 1,000 cards. What are you going to do with 1,000 cards? You're going to give them to everyone. While everyone might not keep your resume, most people in all aspects of business keep cards, and those in the music industry are no exception.

Simple cards are the least expensive. They probably will cost approximately $18 to $25 to print an order of 1,000. The more features you add, the more the cost goes up.

What should your cards say? At minimum, include your name, address, e-mail, and phone

Samples of Business and Networking Cards

Jim Gilman

Career Goal: Position in music industry utilizing degree in music business management

PO Box 1400   Phone: 111-111-1111
Anytown, NY 11111   Cell: 888-999-0000
E-mail: jim@moreinternet.com

420 Edwards Avenue
Anytown, NY 11111

Ivy Betula

Excellent verbal and written communication skills
Accomplish entertainment publicist
Marketing skills

Phone: 111-111-1111
Cell: 888-999-0000
Ivy@moreinternet.com

---

420 Edwards Avenue   Phone: 111-111-1111
Anytown, NY 11111   Cell: 888-999-0000
E-mail: jodi@moreinternet.com

Jodi Frand

Graduate of State University—Communications Major
Summer Intern - ABC Music Publishing
Excellent verbal and written communications skills
Sales skills
Detail oriented

Topper

Country/Pop

You won't be able to stay in your seats

Mark Toomy-Lead Singer

321 L Boulevard   Phone: 444-444-4444
Anytown, NY 11111   Cell: 999-999-9999
mark@topperband.com   www.topperband.com

---

number (both home and cell if you have one). It's a good idea to add your job or your career goal or objective. You might even briefly describe your talents, skills, or traits. Your business card is your selling piece, so think about what you want to sell. Check out some of the samples to get ideas.

At every seminar I give, someone raises their hand and says something to the effect of "I don't have a job yet. What kind of cards do I make up? What would they say? 'Unemployed but wants to be in the music industry'?"

So before you think it or say it, the answer is no; you definitely don't put "unemployed" on your card. You will put your name, contact information, and career goals on your business card, and you work on becoming employed in the industry.

Remember that cards are small, and that limits the number of words that can fit, so the card looks attractive and can be read easily. If you want more room, you might use a double-sided card (front and back) or a double-sized card that is folded over, in effect giving you four times as much space. I've seen both used successfully. The double-sized card can be very effective for a mini-resume.

You have a lot of decisions on how you want your business cards to look. What kind of card stock do you want? Do you want your card smooth or textured; flat or shiny? What about color? Do you want white, beige, or a colored card? Do you want flat print or raised print? What fonts or type faces do you want to use? Do you want graphics? How do you want information laid out? Do you want it straight or on an angle? The decisions are yours. It just depends what you like and what you think will sell you the best.

Brochures Can Tell Your Story

While you're always going to need a resume, consider developing your own brochure, too. A brochure can tell your story and help you sell yourself. The music business is a creative industry and sometimes something out of the ordinary can help grab the attention of someone important.

What's a brochure? Basically, it is a selling piece that gives information about a product, place, event, or person, among other things. In this situation, the brochure is going to be about you. While your resume tells your full story, your brochure is going to illustrate your key points.

Why do you need one? A brochure can make you stand out from other job seekers, songwriters, singers, musicians, or groups.

What should a brochure contain? Definitely your name and contact information. Then add your selling points. Maybe those are your skills. Perhaps they are your talents or accomplishments. What about something unique or special that you do? Definitely try to illustrate what *you*

can do for a company and what benefits they will obtain by hiring you. A brief bio is often helpful to illustrate your credentials and credibility. What about three or four quotes from some of your letters of recommendation? For example:

- ◎ "One of the best interns we ever had participate in our internship program." Marie Sanders, Internship Coordinator, Greatest Hits Records, NY
- ◎ "A real team player who motivates the team." Edward Jennings, New Tunes Publishing

Keep your wording simple. Make it clear, concise, and interesting.

What should your brochure look like? The possibilities are endless. Brochures can be simple or elaborate. Your brochure can be designed in different sizes, papers, folds, inks, and colors. You can use photographs, drawings, illustrations, or other graphics.

If you have graphic design ability and talent, lay out your brochure yourself. If you don't, ask a friend or family member who is talented in that area. There are also software programs that help you design brochures. With these programs you simply type your information in and print it out. If you have access to a color copier or printer, you can often create a very professional-looking piece. The beauty of doing it yourself is that after you've sent out a number of brochures, you can improve and redesign them if they aren't doing anything for you and send out another batch. Even with the expense of good paper, it is usually more cost effective to do it yourself.

If you want to design your brochure but want it printed professionally, consider bringing your camera-ready brochure to a professional print shop. Camera-ready means your document is ready to be printed, and any consumer print shop should be able to help guide you through the steps needed to prepare your work for them. In addition to print shops, you might consider office supply stores like Staples and Office Max that do printing.

If you don't feel comfortable designing your own brochure, you can ask a printer in your area if there is an artist on staff. Professional design and printing of a brochure can get expensive. Is it worth it? Only you can decide, but if it helps get your career started or makes the one you have more successful, probably the answer is yes.

Can brochures be effective? I certainly think so. Not only do I know a great number of people who have used them successfully; I personally

> ### Tip from the Coach
> You don't need 1,000 brochures. Start off with 100 or so and see how they work for you. Remember that in order for brochures to be effective, you have to send them out, so be sure you start working on a list of companies you want to target.

> ### Words from the Wise
> It is very easy to miss errors. Before you have your brochure printed, proofread it and then proofread it again. Then ask a friend or family member to proofread it as well.

used one when I was breaking into the music business and have continued using them ever since. Here's my story.

At the time, I was sending out a lot of resumes and making a lot of calls in an attempt to obtain interviews. I had learned a lot about marketing and noticed that many companies used brochures. My father, who was a marketing professional, suggested that a brochure might just be what I needed. By that time I had realized that if I wanted to *sell* myself, I might need to market myself a little more aggressively than I was doing, so I decided to try the brochure idea.

We designed a brochure that was printed on an 11-by-17-inch piece of paper folded in half, giving me four pages to tell my story. We artistically mounted a head shot on the front page and printed it in hot-pink ink. The inside was crafted with carefully selected words indicating my accomplishments, skills, talents, and the areas in which I could help a company who hired me. The brochures were professionally printed, and I sent them to various record labels, music instrument manufacturers, music publishers, music industry publicity companies, artist managers, and so on. I started getting calls from some of the people who received the brochure, obtained a number of interviews, and even landed a couple of job offers. None of them, however, interested me.

Five years after I sent out my first brochure, I received a call from a major record company

Tip from the Coach

You are going to use your brochure in addition to your resume, not in place of it.

who told me that at the time they first received my brochure, they didn't need anyone with my skills or talents, but they thought the brochure was so original that they kept it on file. Voila. Five years passed, and they needed an individual with my skills, so someone remembered my brochure, pulled it out, and called me. By that time I was already on the road with another group and couldn't take the job, but it was nice to be called.

What is really interesting, however, is that companies and people I originally sent that first brochure years ago still remember it. They can describe it perfectly and many of them still have it in their files.

When creating your brochure, make sure it represents the image you want to portray. Try to make it as unique and eye catching as possible. You can never tell how long someone in the industry is going to keep it.

Your Career Portfolio: Have Experience, Will Travel

People in creative careers have always used portfolios to illustrate what they have done and can accomplish. You can do the same.

What exactly is a career portfolio? Basically, it's a portfolio or book that contains your career information and illustrates your best work. Your portfolio is a visual representation of your potential. Why do you need one? Because your career portfolio can help you get the positions you want in the music business.

What would you believe more—something someone told you or something you saw with your own eyes? If you're like most people, you would believe something you saw. And that's what a good career portfolio can do for you. It can provide actual illustrations of what you've done and what you can do.

For example, you might tell a potential employer that you can write press releases. Can you really? If you have samples in your portfolio, you can pull out a couple and show your work.

What would be more impressive to you? Reading over someone's resume and reading that they won the salesperson of the month award or actually seeing a copy of the award certificate?

Have you written press releases about your accomplishments that led to articles in the paper? Have others done articles or feature stories about you that appeared in the media?

Copies of all these documents can be part of your career portfolio. Often, in a potential employer's mind, if you have buzz around you, you will be a commodity to the company.

Don't think that your portfolio is only going to be useful when you're first obtaining a job in the music industry. If you continue adding in your accomplishments, new skills, and samples of projects you've worked on, your portfolio can especially be useful in advancement throughout your career. Of course, as time goes on, omit some of your earlier documents and replace them with more current ones. Having an organized system to present your achievements and successes is also helpful when going through employment reviews, or asking for a promotion or a raise. It also is very effective in illustrating what you've done if you're trying to move up the ladder at a different company.

After attending one of my *Making It in Music* seminars, a woman who was in a lower-level job in the artist relations and development department at a record label decided to document projects she worked on at the label where she worked. She took pictures at the label's artist events, made copies of things she had worked on as well as copies of media stories which resulted from projects in which she was involved. When she heard about a mid-level position in artist relations and development at another label, she called up, managed to obtain an interview, brought her career portfolio, and got the job. Within a year she was promoted to the assistant director of the department. When I last heard from her, she was being courted by a number of other labels. She still uses her career portfolio.

Your portfolio is portable. You can bring it with you when you go on interviews so you can show it to potential employers. You can make copies of things in your portfolio to give to potential employers or have everything at hand when you want to answer an ad or send out cold letters.

How do you build a detailed portfolio illustrating your skills, talents, experiences, and accomplishments? What goes into it? You want your portfolio to document your work-related talents and accomplishments. These are the assets that you will be *selling* to your potential employers. Let's look at some of the things you might want to include.

- your profile
- resume
- bio
- reference sheets
- skill and abilities
- degrees, licenses, and certifications
- experience sheet
- summary of accomplishments
- professional associations
- professional development activities (conferences, seminars, and workshops attended as well as any other professional development activities)
- awards and honors
- volunteer activities and community service
- supporting documents
- samples of work
- newspaper, magazine, and other articles and/or feature stories about you
- articles you have written and published
- reports you've done
- letters or notes people have written to tell you what a good job you've done
- photos of you accepting an award or at an event you worked on
- photos of events you were involved in
- news stories or feature articles generated by your execution of a project (For example, if you did the publicity for concert and the paper did a feature story on the act or the concert.)

Remember that this list is just to get you started. You can use anything in your portfolio that will help illustrate your skills, talents, and accomplishments.

Here are some sample portfolio documents:

Tip from the Top

When compiling your portfolio be careful not to use any confidential work or documents from a company even if you were the one who wrote the report or the letter. A potential employer might be concerned about how you will deal with their confidential issues if you aren't keeping other confidences.

Sample of Profile for Portfolio

PROFILE

Sharon Williams

Education:
- State University—Bachelor's Degree
- Major: Music Business Management
- Minor: Communications

Additional Training:
- Seminar: Understanding Entertainment Contracts
- Seminar: Entertainment Law
- Workshop: The Music Business—An Overview
- Workshop: Music Industry Publicity

Goals:
- To work in the music industry in artist management

Qualifications:
- Hard working, motivated, energetic
- Knowledge of industry
- Understanding of entertainment law and contracts
- Computer skills—Microsoft Office and various other programs
- Ability to develop and build Web sites
- Verbal and written communication skills

Sample of Professional Development Sheet for Portfolio

CERTIFICATES OF PROFESSIONAL DEVELOPMENT

Sharon Williams

Communications:
- Certificate of Completion: Music Business Publicity and Promotion
- Toastmasters Certification

Music Industry:
- Certificate of Professional Development in Entertainment Law
- Certificate of Professional Development in Entertainment
- Workshop: The Music Business—An Overview
- Workshop: Music Industry Publicity

Goals:
- To work in the music industry in artist management

Qualifications:
- Hard working, motivated, energetic
- Knowledge of industry
- Understanding of entertainment law and contracts
- Computer skills—Microsoft Office and various other programs
- Ability to develop and build Web sites
- Verbal and written communication skills

Those on the talent end of the industry can effectively use a portfolio, too. In these situations, your target market might be agents or managers. It might be club owners or other people who could potentially need your services. If you're a songwriter, your portfolio audience might be record company executives, singers or groups, or music publishers looking for new material. You might include items like some of the following:

◎ reference sheets (from people you've performed for)
◎ skill sheet (singer, songwriter, ability to read and write music)
◎ experience sheet
◎ summary of accomplishments (sang national anthem at National Basketball Association [NBA] game, went on tour with three top recording acts, wrote song for local literacy fund-raising dinner dance)
◎ supporting documents
◎ samples of work
◎ newspaper, magazine, or other articles and/or feature stories done on you/your act
◎ audio or videos of radio interviews, television interviews, and so on
◎ audio recordings of songs you've written or your performances
◎ video of a performance
◎ photos of your act
◎ photos at events you played
◎ press releases

If you're on the talent end of the industry, your portfolio will be much like a press kit. That's okay. You can use the portfolio in conjunction with your press kit or in situations where a press kit isn't needed.

> ★ **Tip from the Top**
> Make good quality copies of key items in your portfolio to leave with interviewers or potential employers. Visit an office supply store to find some professional-looking presentation folders to hold all the support documents you bring to an interview.

While you can compile your portfolio in a variety of booklets, binders, or other formats, make sure whatever you choose is clean, neat, and professional looking. Depending on your contents, a large three-ring binder is often a good choice. Your information should also be well organized. Many people find using dividers or tabs helpful.

Press Kits Tell the Story

Press kits might be called media kits, promo kits, or press packs. Whatever they're called, if you're in the talent area of the industry, you're going to need one. A well-designed and well-conceived press kit can be an effective marketing and selling tool for anyone in the talent end of the music industry. It's another key element in your success if you are a musician, singer, songwriter, or other creative talent in the industry.

What's a press kit? Your press kit is a sales pitch. Done right, it's a chance to shine, to set yourself apart, and to get noticed.

Physically, it's a binder or folder that contains background material, promotional material, photos, and publicity to help market and publicize your act. Press kits are handy to give to anyone who needs information about your act. This includes:

◎ the media
◎ reporters

- editors
- journalists
- TV and radio producers
- talent coordinators
- column planters
- entertainment buyers
- club owners
- promoters
- agents
- music industry contacts
- record company executives
- music publishers
- producers
- entertainment and music attorneys
- others in the industry
- radio and music television contacts
- station music directors
- station program directors
- disc jockeys

How do you put together a press kit? Depending on where you are in your career and your financial resources, you can retain a publicist or publicity firm to handle the task or you might want to try your hand at putting together a press kit yourself.

What goes into a press kit? There are a variety of documents. You don't have to use each one every time. Tailor your press kit to the person to whom it's being sent. Here's a list to get you started.

Words from a Pro

If you're dealing with an unknown printer or company, ask to see samples of their work ahead of time. Then be sure to get a proof that you can check for errors and approve before your folders are printed.

Words from the Wise

When compiling your press kit, make sure that your contact information is on each and every piece of your kit. If you have a Web site, add that to each piece as well.

- biography (bio)
- fact sheet (one-page sheet giving key information on your act)
- press releases
- professional photos of act (8x10 glossies)
- press clippings
- reprints of articles and feature stories
- reviews
- testimonials
- preview video
- CDs or demo tape
- business cards
- quote sheets
- song list
- lyric sheets

Now that you have all the components of your press kit, what should you do with them? You have a few choices. Here are some to get you started:

- Go to the office supply store, purchase some attractive presentation folders, and put your information in them.
- Purchase plain presentation folders and design an attractive label to go on the front.
- Buy large presentation window envelopes, paste a color photo of your act in the envelope window, and put your information inside the envelope.
- Look for companies that specialize in designing and printing press kit

presentation folders and other marketing pieces. These usually can be located on the Internet.

◎ Have a graphic artist design press kit folders for you and have them printed.

It's important to remember that a press kit that can grab the right people's attention is worth its weight in gold because that ultimately is your goal. There are some areas where you just can't skimp when putting together your press kit.

Whatever type of packaging you choose, be aware that in the music industry you often only have one chance to make a first impression. Don't send anything out that doesn't look totally professional, or it stands the chance of getting tossed into a "look at it some day" pile. You want people to look at your press kit the moment they receive it. Use the best-designed press kit folder you can afford. When you make copies and reprints make sure they are clean and crisp.

Photos should be done by a professional. If you can find someone who does photography for entertainers and those in the music business, all the better. These pictures not only show who you are, but they will be the ones used in publicity and in the print media. Glossy black and whites are best for reproduction in newspapers. Once you get the photos you want to use, you can get them duplicated inexpensively. Make sure you have your name or the name of the act and contact information printed on the photos.

There are a couple different types of videos. Professional music videos, which you see on music television, are expensive to produce. If you can afford this and you're professionally ready for it, that's great, but if what you're trying to do is show agents, promoters, club owners, or other entertainment buyers what your act is like, consider a lower-priced alternative.

You might, for example, have a professional video producer shoot part of one of your live shows and then splice it attractively to make a great 10- or 15-minute preview video. Here's another idea that is usually a lot less expensive if you can make it work. If you perform at an event and the television news comes to cover it, all you have to do is speak to the producer or someone at the station and ask if you can buy the raw footage. Then just get it spliced into a 10-minute tape and get it duplicated. Generally, when television covers news, they film for a while, and then they edit what they have filmed for broadcast.

How can you get into a situation like this? One way is by volunteering to provide the entertainment to a major not-for-profit event in your community, which is usually covered by the media. While this shouldn't be your motivating reason for doing something nice, it is a great benefit. Another way is to offer to perform at a televised telethon. A third method is to take part in televised talent competitions. While you won't usually get a 10-minute tape, you generally can at least get a video of your performance.

If you are lucky enough to have industry professionals make positive comments about you or your music either verbally or in writing, you can use these by adding quote sheets to your press. Sometimes these comments are made on

---

★ **Words from the Wise**

If you don't have a professional-looking video, don't use one at all. Nothing is worse than a video that shakes up and down and sideways and doesn't present your act in a good light.

their own. Sometimes you have to solicit comments. Who do you ask? Industry professionals who know and like your work such as club owners, agents, producers, entertainment journalists, disc jockeys, music directors, program directors, and so on.

Put the quotes on a sheet under a heading like "Here's What They're Saying About (the name of your act)." Don't overwhelm people. Just choose a few selected quotes with the person's name and title. For example, "Amazing vocals,". . . Jim McMann, *Music Today.*

Take a look at the sample provided.

Here's What They're Saying About (Name of Act)

" _____ quote _____

_____," . . . name and title of person to whom the quote is attributed.

" _____ quote _____

_____," . . . name and title of person to whom the quote is attributed.

" _____ quote _____

_____," . . . name and title of person to whom the quote is attributed.

" _____ quote _____

_____," . . . name and title of person to whom the quote is attributed.

" _____ quote _____

_____," . . . name and title of person to whom the quote is attributed.

One thing we haven't covered yet is your logo. A logo is the artwork, picture, or graphic you create for your act's name so that people can look at and instantly identify with your act. A logo helps you create a consistent image.

Sometimes you can create them yourself. Other times an artistic family member or friend can do it. Often, you may need to go to a professional graphic artist to handle the task. If you have a logo associated with your act, use it on everything; every photo, press release, press kit, and marketing piece you send out. In this manner, every time someone sees the logo, they will think of your act.

If you have recorded a CD already, include it. If you don't have a CD and you're sending your information to a record label or agent, make sure you use a good quality, professionally duplicated demo tape or cassette showcasing your best work. Your demo should contain no more than three songs. Graphically pleasing labels should include the name of the act, the contents of the tape, and contact information.

Build a press kit that makes you and your act stand out from others and you will be that much closer to getting noticed.

Do you want to increase your chances of getting your press kit noticed? Whether you hand deliver it or mail it, don't put your press kit in the traditional manila envelope. Why? Because people in the music industry get tons and tons of mail. Most people send their information in manila envelopes because they are convenient. You want yours to stand out! You want yours to be noticed! Spend some time coming up with a different solution.

Remember the story I told you about my hot pink brochures? I sent those in hot pink envelopes . . . and that was way before hot pink was a hot color. Do you have to use hot pink?

Of course not, but try to find envelopes that are a little different. Maybe you want to use navy envelopes with gold trim. Perhaps you want to use one with a pattern. Visit office supply stores. Look through catalogs. Surf the net and find something different yet classy.

It's also a good idea to send a cover letter with your press kit introducing yourself and your act. When doing so, if at all possible, personalize your letter. As suggested with any cover letter, you stand a better chance of a good response if you send correspondence to a specific person and not just to News Editor or A&R Director.

Every Talent Needs a Bio

Whether you are a solo artist or part of a group, whether you're a singer, musician, songwriter, or any other creative talent in the entertainment industry, you are going to need a bio or biography. As in other marketing pieces, you have the option of retaining a professional publicist or publicity firm to write your bio or you can write it yourself. Whether it's for your press kit, your Web site, or any other opportunity that comes your way, a good bio can effectively tell your story.

Your bio will illustrate:

◎ who your act is
◎ what your act does
◎ why your act is special
◎ the history of your act

Remember, your bio isn't a resume. It doesn't have to be a book. It's going to be a one- to two-page story about your act. The more interesting you can make it, the better. Be creative when developing your bio, but as in your resume, don't lie. It will make you lose all credibility.

To write an effective bio, you are going to have to take some time to think about what is important. What is the act's name? Who are they? What do they do? Try to start off with an interesting fact or two that grabs the attention of the reader, and then go on to give some information on the act.

Here's a couple of examples of the first paragraph solo artists might use for their bios.

ROBIN MYERS

If all of Robin Myers' fans stood side by side, they would circle the world many times over. Robin is a dynamic, energetic, and charismatic singer, songwriter, and entertainer who took the world by storm five years ago. She has been going strong ever since.

LINCOLN TUNNEL

If you like R&B vocals, you'll love Lincoln Tunnel. The group is a five-member R&B vocal act that has generated a fan base from their home base of Detroit to Philadelphia, New York City, Atlanta, Los Angeles, and everywhere in between.

Now let's look at a complete bio a group might use, shown below.

Keep in mind that these are just samples. Your bio can be similar or totally different. Take some time working on it. When it's done, it's a good idea to give it to friends, family, and others in the music industry to review.

Get their comments and make corrections if necessary.

Print your bio on high-quality paper. It should be graphically pleasing to the eye and easy to read. As in all other pieces of your press kit, make sure your contact information is prominent.

THE BLINKS

The Blinks are here, and they're here to stay. The four-member country/pop group is celebrating their fourteenth anniversary, which is an amazing feat in the music business. The fact that the members of the group are all under 21 years old is even more amazing.

Hailing from Philadelphia, Mac Johnson, Jeremy Kerry, George Watson, and Donnie Bush make up the Blinks. The group started performing together when they were just six years old in a school talent show. After garnering first prize, beating older and more experienced students, the Blinks moved on to performing in other competitions in the Philadelphia and surrounding New Jersey areas.

Soon they were asked to play for parties and events. By the time they were in junior high school, they were performing concerts for schools and dances in the area. The Blinks were then discovered by legendary producer John Homes. It wasn't long before they were signed to Great Homes Records.

Their first single, "Lucky," written by group member Jeremy Kerry hit the *Billboard* charts with a bullet. While the tune never hit number one, their next four singles "We're Here," "Country Home," "Let's Have Fun," and "Let's Dance" all not only hit the number-one position but turned gold as well. Their CD, *The Blinks Are Here to Stay,* recently went platinum.

The Blinks stage show is an electrifying, energetic mix of pop and country that appeals to almost everyone. Ten minutes into every show, the entire audience is up on their feet dancing.

The group is starring in their first prime time special television special on CBS later this year. They have also appeared on *The Tonight Show with Jay Leno* and *The Late Show with David Letterman.*

"The Blinks are going to be a legendary musical act," said Blake Johnson, in the *Music Times* recently. "The Blinks are so hot, they sizzle," noted Wilson Edwards on his widely syndicated daily radio show.

The group is currently working on a new CD which is scheduled to be out later this year.

The Blinks are totally self-contained and travel with an eight-piece band. Three backup singers complete the show. Booking is done through Artists Booking Agency.

It's www. . . . Your Personal Web Address

If you're on the talent end of the industry, sooner or later, you're going to need a Web site. Why? Because the Internet is where it's at today. Your competition probably has a Web site, which means that you need one too! It's yet another of the key tools for your success and a marketing tool you really can't do without.

What can a Web site do for you? It can present you and your act to the world. Your act's bio, photos, appearances, recording, news, and more are right there with a simple click of the mouse. Whether you're trying to obtain a recording contract, more appearances and engagements, looking for a manager, an agent, creating new fans, or letting people know what you're doing, a Web site can help.

"A Web site? How do I put together a Web site?" you ask.

You can develop a Web site yourself, but you don't have to. If you want to, that's fine, but there are a number of easy-to-use Web site development programs and other options for you to explore.

You can hire a professional Web site developer or company to develop and manage your site. Many Internet service providers (ISPs) offer similar services. You might even have a friend or family member who wants to put together and manage your site.

How complicated is the whole process? Basically once you decide you want a Web site, you have to find a host (the person or company from whom you will *rent* Web space). You also will need to need to decide the name of your domain (your www._____.com) and then get it registered. If you're not using a professional Web designer and you don't want to do this on your own, your ISP usually can do this for you. How do you decide what your domain name should be? Make it simple and make it recognizable. You want to be able to say, "Check us out at www.ourband.com." You want to make it easy to remember and easy for people to find you.

Once that's done, you have to develop the content. What are you going to put on the site? What is your Web site going to look like? If you are using a professional Web site developer, he or she might give you some ideas. Also, surf the net and look at other sites until you find some you like. What do you like about each? Is it the design? The colors? The graphics? What do you want your home page to look like? What about links? There are many questions you have to answer, but once you get started, it's not difficult.

What do you need on your site? The possibilities are endless. Here are some ideas to get you started.

◎ your act's bio
◎ news
◎ photos
◎ your act's itinerary
◎ special events
◎ recordings
◎ press releases
◎ links to news stories which have appeared online
◎ mini-videos
◎ merchandise for sale (T-shirts, hats, CDs, and so on)
◎ contact information
◎ e-mail

Your Web site can be simple or elaborate as long as it showcases your act in a professional manner and accurately portrays your image.

Once you have your site up and running, use your Web address on everything. Emblazon it on your business cards, flyers, advertisements, CDs, stationary, and every other marketing and publicity piece.

Whether you're pursuing a career in the business or talent end of the industry, use every tool you can to help yourself attain success.

7

GETTING YOUR FOOT IN THE DOOR

Once you get in the door, you have a chance to sell yourself, sell your talent, and sell your products and services. The problem is that sometimes the hardest part is getting your foot in the door. Whether you simply walk in off the street to see someone or call to make an appointment, you often are faced with the same situation. You need to get past the receptionist, the secretary, or whoever the "gatekeeper" happens to be between you and the person with whom you want to speak.

We have already discussed the rejection often encountered by those in a quest for success in the music industry. We've also discussed why rejection should not be taken personally. However, to feel rejected when you didn't even get the chance to really be rejected because you couldn't get through to someone is quite another thing. It's not personal, but the secretary, receptionist, assistant, and even the person you're trying to reach often think of you and most other unsolicited callers as unwanted intruders who waste their time. It doesn't really matter whether you're trying to sell something, get a job, or get your act listened to; unless they can see what you can do for them, it's going to be hard to get through.

In reality you are trying to sell something. You're trying to sell *you* or *your music, your song,* or *your act.* You're trying to get a job or a chance for your talent. What you need to do, however, is try to not let them know exactly what you want. I am in no way telling you to lie or even stretch the truth. What I'm telling you to do is find a way to change their perception of you. Be creative.

The music industry is very competitive. Everyone wants to talk to the producer, the A&R director, the human resources director, the record company president, the club owner, or the potential manager or booking agent. Whether you want a career in talent or to work in the business end of the industry, you need to get past the gatekeeper so you can get your foot in the door. Before you rush in and find the door locked let's look at some possible keys to help you get in.

Getting Through on the Phone

Let's start with the phone. If your goal is to talk to a specific person or make an appointment, it's important to know that many high-level business people don't answer their own phone. Instead, they rely on secretaries, receptionists, or assistants to handle this task. And that's not even counting the dreaded voice mail.

You can always try the straightforward approach. Just call and ask to speak to the person you are looking for. If that works, you have your foot in the door. If not, it's time to get creative.

Let's look at a couple of scenarios and how they might play out.

Scenario 1
Secretary: Good afternoon, Best Records.

You: Hello, this is Bob Green. Can I please speak to Mr. Baxter?

Secretary: Does he know what this is in reference to?

You: No, I'm looking for a job and would like to see if I could set up an interview.

Secretary: I'm sorry, Mr. Baxter isn't looking for fill any positions at this time. Thank you for calling.

You: Thanks. Good-bye.

With that said, you're done. Is there something you could have said differently that might have led to a better ending? Let's look at another scenario.

Scenario 2
Secretary: Good afternoon, Best Records.

You: Is Mr. Baxter in?

Secretary: Who's calling?

You: Bob Green.

Secretary: May I ask what this is in reference to?

You: Yes, I was trying to set up an informational interview. Would Mr. Baxter be the person who handles this or would it be someone else at your company?
[Asking the question in this manner means that you stand a chance at the gatekeeper giving you

a specific name that you can call if Mr. Baxter is the wrong person.]

Secretary: Informational interview for what purpose?

You: I was interested in some information on a career at your record label. Would Mr. Baxter be the right person?
[Make sure you are pleasant. This helps the person answering the phone want to help you.]

Secretary: No, he doesn't handle that. You need to speak to Jen Jones in personnel. Would you like me to switch you?
[What you are really doing is helping her get you off the phone even if it means she is dumping you on someone else.]

You: Yes that would be great. What was your name?
[Try to make sure you get the name. In this manner, when you get transferred, the person answering at the other end will be more apt to help you.]

Secretary: Sue Morris.

You: Thanks for your help. I really appreciate it.

Secretary: I'll switch you now.

Jen Jones: Jen Jones, may I help you?

You: Hi Ms. Jones, Sue Morris in Mr. Baxter's office suggested you might be the right person for me to speak to. I'm interested in setting up an informational interview regarding the possibility of working with your company.

At this point, she probably will either say, "Sorry, we have no openings," ask you some additional questions, or set up an appointment. If she says, "Sorry, we have no openings at this time," say something like: "I understand. Would it be possible for me to send my resume for you to review and keep on file?" If this is the case, make sure you ask to whose name your information should be directed as well as getting the exact addresses and her extension.

· If she starts to question you about what type of job you are looking for make sure you have an answer prepared. Never say: "Oh, I don't care; any job would be fine" or "I just want to work in a record company to get to meet famous people."

Instead, have a definitive answer. For example: "I'm interested in working in the publicity or marketing departments. When I was still in school I worked on my school paper and also interned at a local radio station. I also have worked at a local newspaper and did a lot of their entertainment stories as well as in a hospital in the public relations department."

Have your calendar in front of you so that at this point, if she wants to set up an interview, you can make every effort to go with the time and date she suggests.

Scenario 3

Sometimes mentioning that you are looking for a job is not a good idea. Because jobs in record companies are so coveted, those already working there may not be that open about helping those on the outside.

Receptionist: Good afternoon, Best Records.

You: I'm working on a project involving careers in the music industry and was

---

⭐ Tip from the Top

Remember that skills are transferable. If you've done publicity for a hospital, a bank, or any other type of business, you can usually do publicity in the music business.

---

told your company was one of the best ones to talk to. Do you know who in your company I might speak to?

[Here is where it can get a little tricky. If you are very lucky, he or she will just put you through to someone in publicity, public relations, or human resources. If you're not so lucky, he or she will ask you questions.]

Receptionist: What type of project?

You need to be ready with a plausible answer. What you say, will, of course, depend on your situation. If you are in college, you can always say you are working on a project for school. If not, you can say you are doing research on career opportunities in the music industry. If you have writing skills, you might contact a local newspaper or magazine to see if they are interested in an article on careers in music. If you can't find someone to write for, you can always write a story on "spec." This means that if you write a story, you can send it in to an editor on speculation. They might take it and they might not. Don't think about money at this point. Your goal here is to get the "right people" to speak to you and get an appointment.

One of the interesting things about writing an article (whether on spec or on assignment) is that you can ask people questions and they will usually talk to you. They won't be looking at you like you're looking for a job. You have changed their perception about why you're talking to them. One of the most important bonuses of interviewing people about a career in the music industry is that you are making invaluable contacts. While it might be tempting, remember to use this opportunity to ask questions and network, not to sell yourself. After you write the article, you might call up one of the people you interviewed, perhaps the human resources director, and say something like, "You made the music business sound so interesting, I'd like to explore a career in the industry. Would it be possible to come in for an interview or to fill in an application?

What can you do if none of these scenarios work? The receptionist may not be very eager to help. He or she may have instructions on "not letting anyone through." It may be his or her job to block unsolicited callers and visitors from the boss. What can you do?

Here are a few ideas that might help. See if you can come up with some others.

◎ Try placing your call before regular business hours. Many executives and others you might want to talk to come in before the secretary or receptionist is scheduled to work. This is especially true in the music industry where record labels or other music industry executives on the West Coast want to do business with those working on the East Coast.

◎ Try placing your calls after traditional business hours when the secretary probably has left. The executives and others you want to reach generally don't punch a time clock and often work late. They also may be doing business with those on the other coast. More important, even if people utilize voice mail, they may pick up the phone themselves after hours in case their family is calling.

◎ Lunch hours are also a good time to attempt to get through to people. This is a little tricky. The executive may use voice mail during the lunch hour period or he or she may go out to lunch themselves. On the other hand, you might get lucky.

◎ Sometimes others in the office fill in for a receptionist and aren't sure what the procedure is or who everyone is. While you might not get through on the first shot, you might use this type of opportunity to get information. For example, you might ask for the person you want to speak to and when the substitute tells you he or she isn't in and asks if you want to leave a message, say something like, "I'm moving around a lot today. I'll try to call later. Is Mr. Brown ever in the office after 6:00 P.M.?" If the answer is yes, ask if you can have his direct extension in case the switchboard is closed.

Remember the three Ps to help you get through. You want to be:

◎ pleasant
◎ persistent
◎ positive

Always be pleasant. Aside from it being general good manners to be nice to others, being pleasant to gatekeepers is essential. Gatekeepers talk to their bosses and can let them know if you were annoying or obnoxious. When someone tells you their boss "never takes unsolicited calls or accepts unsolicited tunes," tell them you understand. Then ask what they suggest. Acknowledge objections, but try to come up with a solution.

Be persistent. Not getting through on the first try doesn't mean you shouldn't try again. Don't be annoying, don't be pushy, but don't give up. People like to help positive people. Don't moan and groan about how difficult your life is to the secretary. He or she will only want to get you off the phone.

Persistence and the Guilt Factor

Don't forget the guilt factor. If you consistently place calls to "Mr. Baxter" and each time his secretary tells you he is busy, unavailable, or will call you back and he doesn't, what should you do? Should you give up? Well, that's up to you. Be aware that persistence often pays off. In many cases, after a number of calls, you and the secretary will have built up a "relationship" of sorts. As long as you have been pleasant, he or she may feel "guilty" that you are such a nice person and his or her boss isn't calling you back. In these cases, the secretary may give you a tip on how to get through, tell you to send something in writing, or ask the boss to speak to you.

Voice mail is another obstacle you might have to deal with. This automated system is of-

ten more difficult to bypass than a human gatekeeper. Many people don't even bother answering their phone, instead letting their voice mail pick up the calls and then checking their messages when convenient.

Decide ahead of time what you're going to do if you get someone's voice mail. Try calling once to see what the person's message is. It might, for example, let you know that the person you're calling is out of town until Monday. What this will tell you is that if you are calling someone on a cold call, you should probably not call until Wednesday because they probably will be busy when they get back in town.

If the message says something to the effect of "I'm out of town, if you need to speak to me today, please call my cell phone" and then provides a phone number, don't. You don't *need* to speak to him or her; you *want* to. You are cold-calling a person who doesn't know you to ask for something. It is not generally a good idea to bother them outside the office.

If you call a few times and keep getting the voice mail, you're going to have to make your move. Leave a message something like this.

You: Hi, this is Sue Marks. My phone number is (123) 456-7890. I'd appreciate if you could give me a call at your convenience. I'll look forward to hearing from you. Have a great day.

If you don't hear back within a few days, try again.

You: Hi, Ms. Brooks. This is Sue Marks. (123) 456-7890. I called a few days ago. I was interested in discussing the possibility of your agency booking our act. I have a video and press kit that I'd like you to see. I look forward to hearing from you. Thanks.

★ Voice of Experience

While persistence can work, don't be annoying. Calling more than once a day or in most cases even more than once a week (unless you are given specific instructions by the secretary to do so) will put you on the annoying list.

You might not hear from Ms. Brooks herself, but one of her assistants might call you. What do you do if you don't get a call back? Call again. How many times should you call? That's hard to say. Persistence may pay off. Remember that the person on the other end may start feeling guilty that he or she is not calling you back and place that call.

Be prepared. When you get a call back, have your ducks in a row and be able to sell yourself. Practice ahead of time if need be and leave notes near your phone.

I suggest when making any of these calls that you block your phone number, so that no one knows who is calling. To permanently block your phone number from showing on the receiver's caller ID, call your local phone company. Most don't charge for this service. You can also block your phone number on a temporary basis by dialing *67 before making your call. Remember that as soon as you hang up, this service will be disabled, so you will need to do it for each call.

Getting Them to Call You

While persistence and patience in calling and trying to get past the receptionist is usually necessary, you may need something else, too. You want something to set you apart, so the busy executive, A&R director, or human resources director not only wants to see you but remembers you. You want them to give you a chance to sell yourself.

What can you do? Creativity to the rescue! The music industry is a creative industry in the first place, so you have a lot more latitude than you might in more straight-laced industries.

Your goal is to get the attention of the important person who can give you a chance to sell yourself. As I've discussed throughout this book, once you have their attention, it's up to you to convince them that they should work with you.

Let's look at some ideas that either I have personally used to get someone's attention in the music business and other industries or that others have told me worked in their quest to get a foot in the door. Use these ideas as a beginning, but then try to develop some more of your own.

My Personal Number-One Technique for Getting Someone to Call You

I am going to share my number-one technique for getting someone to call you. I have used this technique successfully over the years. I first tried this when I wanted to get a job in the music industry. Unfortunately, at that time, there was no book to help. There was no career coach. There was no one who really wanted to help.

I had tried all the traditional methods. I had tried calling. Most of the time, I couldn't get past the gatekeeper. When I did, no one called me back. I had tried sending out resumes. As I had just graduated college, I had no "real" experience. I didn't know anyone and didn't even know anyone who knew anyone. I needed a break. Here's what I did.

When I was younger my parents used to take raw eggs, blow out the contents, and then decorate the shells. The eggs popped into my mind, and I found a method to get people to call me back. Here's how it works.

Get a box of eggs. Extra-large or jumbo work well. While either white or brown eggs can be used, because of the coloration differences in brown eggs, start with white ones. Wash the raw eggs carefully with warm water. Dry the eggs. Hold one egg in your hand and using a large needle or pin, punch a small hole in the top of the egg. The top is the narrower end. Then, carefully punch a slightly larger hole in the other end of the egg. You might need to take the needle or pin and move it around in the hole to make it larger. Keep any pieces of shell that break off.

Now, take a straw and place it on the top hole of the egg. Holding the egg over a bowl, blow into the straw, blowing the contents of the egg out. This may take a couple of tries. Because of concerns with salmonella, don't put your mouth directly on the egg. Keep in mind that the bigger you have made the hole, the easier it will be to blow the contents out of the egg. However, you want the egg to look as "whole" as possible when you're done. The bigger the hole, the harder this is to accomplish.

After blowing the contents out of the egg, carefully rinse out the shell, letting warm water run through it. Get the egg as clean as possible. Shake the excess water out of the egg and leave it to dry thoroughly. Depending on the temperature and humidity when you are preparing the eggs, it might take a couple of days.

Do at least three eggs at one time in case one breaks or cracks at the next step. Keep a few extra eggs around for when you want to get someone's attention fast and don't have time to prepare new ones.

Next, go to your computer and type the words, "Getting the attention of a busy person is not easy. Now that I have yours, could you please take a moment to review my resume." You can customize the message to suit your purposes by including the name of the recipient if you have it or specifying your background sheet or demo recording if that's what you want them to consider. Then type your name and phone number.

Use a small font to keep the message to a line or two. Neatly cut out the strip of paper with your message. Roll the strip around a toothpick. Carefully, insert the toothpick with the strip of paper into the larger of the holes in the egg. Wiggle the toothpick around and slowly take the toothpick out of the egg. The strip of paper should now be in the shell.

Visit your local craft store and pick up a package of small moveable eyes, miniature plastic or felt shaped feet, and white glue. Glue the miniature feet to the bottom of the egg, covering the hole. Make sure you use the glue sparingly so none goes on your message. Now glue on two of the moving eyes making the egg look like a face.

Go back to your computer and type the following words: "BREAK OPEN THIS EGG FOR AN IMPORTANT MESSAGE." Print out the line and cut it into a strip. You might want to use bright-colored paper. Glue the strip to the bottom of the feet of the egg.

Now you're ready. Take the egg and place it in a small box that you have padded with cotton, bubble wrap, or foam. These eggs are very fragile, and you don't want the egg to break in transit! Wrap the egg-filled box in attractive wrapping paper and then bubble wrap to assure it won't move around. Put your resume (or background sheet) and a short cover letter in an envelope. Put it on the bottom of a sturdy mailing box. Put the egg box over it.

Make sure you use clean boxes and pack the egg as carefully as possible. Address the box. Make sure you include your return name and address, and then either mail it or hand deliver it to the office of the person you are trying to reach. Even if that person has a secretary opening his or her mail, the chances are good that the "gift" will be opened personally. In the event that a secretary opens the package, he or she will probably bring the egg into the boss to open.

So now the recipient has the egg in front of them. He or she will probably break it open, see the message, and glance at your resume. Here's the good news. By the time the person breaks open the egg, he or she won't even notice the hole on the bottom and usually has no idea how you got the message in there. Generally, people who have seen this think it is so neat, they want to know how you did it, and so they call you to ask. Once you have them on the phone, your job is to get an interview. You want to get into their office and meet with them. When you get that call, tell the recipient, you would be glad to show them how you did it; it's kind of complicated. Offer to show them how it is done and ask when they would like you to come in.

Voila, you have an appointment. Now all you have to do is sell yourself.

Is your letter sitting in a pile of hundreds of others asking permission to send a demo? Can't get a record company executive to listen to your demo? Are you having difficulties getting a booking agent to call you back? Do you want your resume to stick out amongst the hundreds that come in?

While I love the egg idea and have used it to obtain appointments, call backs, and to get noticed throughout my career, there are other ideas that work too. You might want to try a couple of these.

Have you ever considered using these simple items to help you succeed? If you haven't, perhaps now is the time.

◎ fortune cookies
◎ chocolate chip cookies
◎ candy bars
◎ mugs
◎ pizzas
◎ roses

Fortune Cookies

Almost no one can resist cracking open a fortune cookie to see what the "message" says. This can be good news for your music industry career.

Some fortune cookie companies make cookies similar to the ones you get in Chinese restaurants but with personalized messages inside. What could you say? That depends on what you are looking for. How about something like, "He or she who listens to the Crystal Star Demo will have good luck." Then list the contact number for the act. If, on the other hand, you're interested in having a human resources director at a record company review your resume and call you back, you might use a message like, "Human Resources Director who interviews Sean Block will have good luck for rest of day. Sean's lucky number: 111-222-3333."

Whatever message you choose, remember that you generally need to make all the messages the same or it gets very expensive to have the cookies made. You also need to either print cards on your computer or have cards printed professionally that read something to the effect of, "Getting the attention of a busy person is not easy. Now that I have yours, could you please take a moment to listen to our demo?" Or ask them to review your resume, review your press kit, or give you a call to set up an appointment. Make sure your name and phone number are on the card.

Put a couple of cookies with the card and your resume, press kit, demo or other material in a clean, attractive mailing box, and address it neatly. Make sure you address the box to someone specific. For example, don't address it to H.R. Department, AAA Records. Instead address it to Ms. Susan Green, Human Resources Director, AAA Records.

Now, while you might have heard of sending fortune cookies to get attention before, here's the twist. Send the same package of cookies, the card, and whatever else you sent (your demo, resume, or press kit) every day for two weeks. Every day, after the first day, also include a note that says, "Cookies for [Name of person] for Day 2," "Cookies for [Name of Person] for Day 3," and so on. At the end of the two-week period, stop. By now your recipient will probably have called you. If not, he or she will at least be expecting the cookies. So, if you don't hear from your recipient, feel free to call the office, identify yourself as the fortune cookie king or queen, and ask for an appointment.

This idea can be expensive, but if it gets you in the door and you can sell yourself, your idea, your music, or your song, it will more than pay for itself.

Another great idea that can really grab the attention of a busy music executive or anybody else for that matter is finding a company that makes gigantic fortune cookies with personalized messages. These cookies are often covered in chocolate, sprinkles, and all kinds of goodies and almost command people to see who sent it. Send these cookies with the same types of messages and supporting material as the others. The only difference is that if you choose to send the gigantic cookies, you only need to send one. If you don't get a call within the first week, feel free to call the recipient yourself.

Chocolate Chip Cookies

Chocolate chip cookies are a favorite of most people. Why not use that to your advantage? Go to the cookie kiosk at your local mall and

---

The Inside Scoop

To avoid potential problems with people who have allergies, do not send any food with nuts as an ingredient. Nothing can ruin your chances of getting a job better than the causing an allergic reaction in the person you're trying to impress.

---

order a gigantic pizza-sized cookie personalized with a few words asking for what you would like done. For example:

- ◎ "Please Review My Resume . . . John Jackson"
- ◎ "Please Listen To Our Demo. . . . The Diamond Crush"
- ◎ "Please Call Me For An Interview. . . . Joan Block"
- ◎ "You're Invited To Our Showcase". . . . The Miracle Makers

Keep your message short. You want the recipient to read it, not get overwhelmed. Generally, the cookies come boxed. Tape a copy of your resume or whatever you are sending to the inside of the box. If it is a demo, put it in an envelope, and tape it inside the top cover.

Write a short cover letter to your recipient stating that you hope he or she enjoys the cookie while reviewing your resume, listening to your demo, or giving you a call. Put this in an envelope with another copy of your resume, your demo, or other material. On the outside of the box, neatly tape a card with the message we discussed previously, stating, "Getting the attention of a busy person is not easy. Now that I have yours, would you please take a moment to review my resume?" Or ask them to listen to your demo, give you a call, or whatever you are

---

Words from the Wise

Make sure cookies are individually wrapped and factory sealed. Otherwise, some people may just toss them.

Voice of Experience

Do not try to save money by making the cookies yourself. In today's world, many people won't eat food if they don't know where it came from or that it was prepared by a commercial eatery.

hoping they will do. Make sure your name and phone number are on the card.

If the cookie company has a mail or delivery service, use it. Otherwise, mail or deliver the cookie yourself. You should get a call within a few days.

Candy Bars

There have been a number of studies that tout chocolate as a food that makes people happy. Keeping this in mind, you might want to use chocolate to grab someone's attention and move them to call you. Most people love chocolate and are happy to see it magically appear in their office. There are a number of different ways you can use chocolate to help your career.

- Buy a large chocolate bar. Carefully fold your resume or a letter stating what you would like accomplished and slip it into the wrapping of the chocolate bar.
- Buy a large, high-quality chocolate bar. Wrap the chocolate bar with your resume or the letter stating what you would like accomplished.
- There are companies that create personalized wrappings for chocolate bars. Use one to deliver your message.
- Create a wrapping on your computer, but if you do this, make sure you leave the original wrapping intact and cover it.

Whatever method you choose, put the candy bar in an attractive box, and attach the card with the message, "Getting the attention of a busy person is never easy. Now that I have yours, could you please take a moment to listen to my demo?" or review your resume or media kit or whatever you are asking. Add a cover letter and send it off.

Mugs

When was the last time you threw out a mug? Probably not for a while. How about using this idea to catch the attention of a potential employer, booking agent, record company executive, or manager? Depending on your career aspiration, have mugs printed with replicas of your business card, key points of your resume or background sheet along with your name and phone number, the name of your act and songs on your demo, the name of your act and places you have appeared along with your name and phone number, or even snippets of articles from the newspaper where your act has been mentioned along with your name and phone number.

Add in a small packet of gourmet or flavored coffee and perhaps an individually wrapped biscotti or cookie and, of course, the card with the message that states, "Getting the attention of a busy person is never easy. Now that I have yours, could you please take a moment to check out our media kit?" or whatever else you are requesting. Put the mug, a short cover letter, and your resume, background sheet, press kit, demo, or other material in a box and mail or deliver to your recipient.

Pizza

Want to make sure your resume, background sheet, or press kit gets attention or that your demo gets listened to? Have it delivered to your recipient with a fresh, hot pizza. This can be tricky but effective.

Here are some of the problems. To guarantee the pizza gets there with your information, you really need to be in the same geographic location as the company you're trying to reach. You will need to personally make sure that your information is placed in a good-quality sealed plastic bag and then taped to the inside cover of the pizza box. You also not only have to know the name of the person for this to be delivered to, but that he or she will be there the day you send it and doesn't have a lunch date. It's difficult to call an office where no one knows you and ask what time the recipient goes to lunch. So you are taking the risk that you will be sending a pizza to someone who isn't there. One way to get around this is by sending it in the late afternoon instead.

Make sure that you have the pizzeria tape on the card with the message about getting a busy person's attention on the front of the box, so even if the receptionist gets the pizza, he or she will know who it came from.

Roses

A last but very pricey way to get your recipient's attention is to have a dozen roses delivered to their office. No matter how many things you have tried with no response, there are very few people who will not place a thank-you call when they receive a dozen roses. Talk to the florist ahead of time to make sure that the roses are fragrant. Send the roses to your recipient with a card that simply says something to the effect of, "While you're enjoying the roses, please take a moment to review my resume sent under separate cover." Sign it "Sincerely hoping for an interview," and include your name and phone number.

It is imperative to send your information so it arrives on the same day or at the latest the next day, so the roses you sent are still fresh in the recipient's mind.

It's Who You Know

Breaking into the music industry can be difficult. Competition on both the talent and business side is keen. Thousands of talented people never make it; thousands of people are schooled in the music industry, yet never get past the door. Knowing someone who can get you in the door will most certainly help.

Before you say, "Me? I don't know anyone," stop and think. Are you sure? Might you know someone, anyone, even on a peripheral basis who might be able to give you a recommendation, make a call, or be willing to lend his or her name?

What about your mother's aunt's husband's friend's neighbor's boss? Sure it might be a stretch. But think hard. Who can you think of who might know someone who might be able to help? This is not the time to be shy. Call up your aunt. Explain what you're trying to do with your career. Then ask if she would be willing to talk to her husband's friend about talking to their neighbor about using their name to make an appointment with the neighbor's boss.

What if you don't have a relative who has a contact down the line? What about you local radio station? Do they have reps come in from the record companies? How about your newspaper? Is there someone on staff who deals with music entertainment? Might he or she have some contact with record companies, publicists, or A&R people?

The trick here is to think outside the box. If you can find someone who knows someone willing to help you to get your foot in the door, then all you will have to do is sell yourself. If someone does agree to lend their name, make a call, or help you in any manner, it's important to write thank-you notes immediately. These notes should be written whether or not you actually get an interview or set up a meeting.

If you do go on an interview or meeting or speak to the person in the music industry, it's also a good idea to either call or write another note letting your contact know what happened. For example, you might write something like this:

Dear Aunt Mary,

Thanks for helping me in my quest for a career in the music industry. I just wanted to let you know how things turned out after you so generously called Uncle Jim's friend for me.

I actually got an interview with the president at ABC Booking. He was very nice, but told me he had no openings for booking agent trainees. He did, however, keep my resume.

Two days later, I got a call from a management company he works with asking if I would be interested in coming in to interview for an opening for a position as an assistant. Guess what? I got the job! There's a lot of opportunity to learn there and the people in the office seemed nice.

Thanks so much for helping me get this opportunity. I sent Uncle Jim's friend, John Black, a note as well thanking him for his help. I'll keep you all posted on my success.

Yours truly,
(Your name here)

Meeting the Right People

You think and think and you can't come up with anyone you know with a connection to anyone at all in the music industry. What can you do? Sometimes you have to find your own contacts. You need to meet the right people. But how can you do this? The best way to meet the right people in the music industry is to be around people in the music industry. There are several possible ways you might do this.

To begin with, consider joining industry organizations, associations, and unions. Many of these organizations offer career guidance and support. They also may offer seminars, workshops, and other types of educational symposiums. Best of all, many have periodic meetings and annual conventions and conferences. All of these are treasure troves of possibilities to meet people in the industry. Some of them may be industry experts or insiders. Others may be just like you: people trying to get in and succeed. The important thing to remember is take advantage of every opportunity.

Workshops and seminars are great because not only can you make important contacts, but you can learn something valuable about the industry. Most of these events have question and answer periods built into the program. Take advantage of these. Stand up and ask a good question. Make yourself visible. Some seminars and workshops have break-out sessions to encourage people to get to know one another. Use these to your advantage as well. Walk around and talk to people. Don't be afraid to walk up to someone you don't know and start talking. Network, network, network!

After the session has ended, walk up, shake the moderator's hand and tell him or her how much you enjoyed the session, how much you learned, and how useful it will be in your career. This gives you the opportunity to ask for their business card, so that you have the correct spelling of the person's name, their address, and their phone number. This is very valuable information. Make sure you keep business cards in a safe

Words from a Pro

Don't just blend in with everyone else at a seminar or workshop. Make yourself visible and memorable in a positive way. Ask questions and participate when possible.

place. When you get home, send a short note stating that you were at the session they moderated, spoke to them afterwards, and just wanted to tell them again how much you enjoyed it. You might also ask, depending on their position, if it would be possible to set up an informational interview with them or if they could suggest who you might call to set up an appointment. If you don't hear back within a week, feel free to call up, identify yourself, and ask again.

One of the best ways to meet people in the industry is to attend industry or organization annual conventions. These events offer many opportunities you might not normally have to network and meet music industry insiders.

There is usually a charge to attend these conventions. Fee structures may vary. Sometimes there is one price for general admission to all events and entry to the trade show floor. Other times, there may be one price for entry just to the trade show floor and another price if you also want to take part in seminars and other events.

The cost of attending these conventions may be expensive. (Many industry trade organizations offer special prices for students. Make sure you ask ahead of time.) In addition to the fee to get in, if you don't live near the convention location, you might have to pay for airfare or other transportation as well as accommodations, meals, and incidentals. Is it worth it? If you can afford it, absolutely! If you want to meet people in the industry, these gatherings are the place to do it.

How do you find these events? It's easy. Look in the appendix of this book for industry associations in your area of interest. Find the phone number and call up and ask when and where the annual convention will be held. Better yet, go to the organization's Web site. Most groups put information about their conventions online. Read through industry publications such as *Billboard*. There is often a calendar of industry events or editorial or advertisements discussing upcoming functions.

Here are a few industry trade associations that regularly hold trade events as well as a number of music industry conferences.

- American Music Conference (AMC)
- Billboard Dance Music Summit
- Billboard Latin Music Conference and Awards
- Cutting Edge Music Business Conference
- Emerging Artists & Talent In Music (EATM)
- Independent Music Conference
- Millennium Music Conference
- Nashville Songwriters Association International (NSAI)
- National Association for Campus Activities (NACA)

- National Association of Music Merchandisers (NAMM)
- National Association of Recording Merchandisers (NARM)
- NEMO Music Showcase and Conference
- Radio and Records Convention

If you are making the investment to go to a convention or a conference, take full advantage of the opportunity. As we've discussed throughout this book, network, network, network! Some events to take part in or attend at conventions and conferences might include

- opening events
- keynote presentations
- educational seminars and workshops
- certification programs
- break sessions
- breakfast lunch and/or dinner events
- cocktail parties
- trade show exhibit areas
- career fairs

There's an art to attending conventions and using the experience to your best benefit. Remember that the people you meet are potential employers and new business contacts. Because this is the music industry, you have some leeway in how you dress, but remember, this is a business. This is your chance to make a good first

impression. Dress appropriately and neatly. Do not wear heavy perfume or cologne. There are some people who are allergic to the odor and who will walk away from you because they just can't take the smell.

One of the most important things to remember is not to get inebriated. If you want to have a drink or a glass of wine, that's probably okay, but don't over-drink. You want potential employers or people you want to do business with to know you're a good risk, not someone who drinks at every opportunity. Just because there is an open bar or someone else is paying does not mean you have to indulge.

This is one of those times that that you must have business cards. Bring them with you and give them out to everyone you can. You can never tell when someone remembers getting one and will give you a call. Collect cards as well. Then when you get home from the convention or trade show, you will have contact names to call or write regarding business or job possibilities.

Walk the trade show floor. Stop and talk to people at booths. They are usually more than willing to talk. This is a time to network and try to make contacts. Ask questions and listen to what people are saying. Ask for business cards and other literature.

You will probably be tempted to collect things at the trade show such as information, giveaways, trade magazines or newspapers, and CDs, and you might be worried about how you will get it all home. Instead of trying to stuff it all in your luggage, ship it back via FedEx, Airborne Express, or UPS. Many hotels hosting conventions have business centers where they will provide mailing boxes or envelopes as well as shipping services. They usually charge a fee. Unfortunately on occasion things get lost in transit. To assure you don't lose all your newly acquired contact information, try to keep the business cards you have collected with you instead of mailing them.

If you have writing skills, one great way of meeting people in the industry is to write articles, do reviews, or interview people for local, regional, or national periodicals or newspapers. How does this work? A great deal of it depends on your situation, where you live and what's happening in your area. If you're still in school, become involved with the school newspaper. Try to become the entertainment or music reporter. If you live in an area where you have a lot of musical entertainment events or concerts consider calling up your local newspaper or a regional magazine and see if they might be interested in a review of the show.

⭐ Words from a Pro

Remember that many of the people at the trade show need to pack up their stuff and travel home by plane. Don't overload them with your press kits, resumes, or CDs unless requested. They stand a good chance of getting lost or being left behind. Instead, wait until you get home and send your information with a short cover letter stating that you met at the convention.

Develop an angle or hook for a story on a singer, songwriter, or other musical act. For example, is the lead singer of a hot recording act the spokesperson of a national charity you're involved with on a local level? Did a leading record executive go to your alma mater? Is a major record label working on a campaign to stop teenage drug use? These are all angles or hooks you might use to entice a local or regional periodical let you do an article.

You probably will have to give them some samples of your writing and your background sheet or resume. You might also have to write on "spec" or speculation. What this means is that when you do the story they may or may not use it. If they do, they will pay you. If not, they won't.

Your goal here (unless you want to be an entertainment journalist) is not to make money (although that is nice.) Your goal is to be in situations where you have the opportunity to meet industry insiders. As an added bonus, you'll be meeting them on a different level than if you were looking for a job.

Press credentials give you access to promoters, managers, publicists, tour managers, and the acts themselves. Depending on the story you are working on, you might have the opportunity to speak to record company executives as well as other industry insiders.

Networking Basics

It's not always what you know, but sometimes who you know. With that in mind, I'm going once again to bring up the importance of networking, especially in the music industry. You can never tell who knows someone in some area of the industry, so it is essential to share your career dreams and aspirations with those around you. Someone you mention them to might just say, "My cousin is in the music business too."

Think it can't happen? Think again. A college student living in a small town called me one day and said, "I don't know anyone in the music industry. I can't make any contacts. No one who lives here could possibly know anyone in the music business."

"Have you told anyone what you want to do?" I asked.

It turns out that a good friend of her mom had a neighbor whose son was a big executive at one of the major music television stations. A few calls later, she snagged a great summer internship at a record label.

Knowing how important networking can be to your career in the music industry, let's talk about some networking basics.

The first thing you need to do is determine exactly who you know and who is part of your network. Then you need to get out and find more people to add to the list.

When working on your networking list, add the type of contact you consider each person. Primary contacts are people you know: your family members, teachers, friends, and neighbors. Secondary contacts are individuals referred to you by others. These would include, for instance, a friend of a friend, your aunt's neighbor, your attorney's sister, and so on.

You might also want to note whether you consider each person a close, medium, or distant relationship. Close, for example, would be family, friends, employers, and current teachers. Medium would be people you talk to and see frequently such as your dentist, attorney, or your UPS, FedEx, or mail delivery person. Distant would include people you talk to and see infrequently or those you have just met or have met just once or twice.

Here's an example.

It would be great to have a network full of people in the music industry. However, that may not be the case. That does not mean, though, that other people can't be helpful. Your network may include a variety of people from all walks of life. These may include

- family members
- friends
- friends of friends
- coworkers and colleagues
- teachers or professors
- your doctor and dentist
- your pharmacist
- your mail carrier
- your hairstylist
- your personal trainer
- your priest, pastor, or rabbi
- members of your congregation
- UPS, FedEx, airborne, or other delivery person
- your auto mechanic
- your attorney
- the server at the local diner or coffee shop
- bank tellers from your local bank
- entertainment reporter from local newspaper
- disc jockey from local radio station
- your neighbors
- friends of your relatives
- business associates of your relatives
- people you work with on volunteer not-for-profit boards and civic groups

Now look at your list. Do you see how large your network really is? Virtually everyone you come in contact with during the day can become part of your network. Just keep adding people to your list.

Networking Worksheet

Name	Relationship/ Position	Type of Contact (Primary or Secondary)	Closeness of Contact (Close, Medium, or Distant)
Mary Jones	Former Music Teacher	Primary	Medium
Bill Baker	Bank Teller	Primary	Distant
Bob	UPS Delivery Person	Primary	Medium
Matt Rodgers	Newspaper Reporter	Secondary	Distant
Gina	Sister-in-law	Primary	Close
Dr. Castina	Dentist	Primary	Medium
Rob Secra	Attorney	Primary	Medium
George J	Disc Jockey	Secondary	Distant
Jill Thomas	Receptionist at radio station	Primary	Medium

Expanding Your Network

How can you expand your network? There are a number of ways. Networking events are an excellent way to meet people. Industry networking events are, of course, the best to attend, but don't count out nonindustry events. For example, your local chamber of commerce may have specific networking programs designed to help business people in the community meet and "network" with each other. In case you're thinking that no one in the music business will be there, remember two things: First, as we've discussed, you don't know who people know. People you meet may know others who are in the industry. Second, no matter how small your area, you never really know who is involved in

what. For all you know, someone in your area may be

◎ an investor in a recording act
◎ a lawyer who represents someone in the music industry
◎ the dentist of someone in the music business
◎ the personal physician of someone in the music business
◎ the tailor to industry executives
◎ the caterer at arenas or concert halls in your region

If you're under the impression that everyone who has a client, a friend, or a relative in the music industry talks about it and brags, you

Networking Worksheet			
Name	Relationship/ Position	Type of Contact (Primary or Secondary)	Closeness of Contact (Close, Medium, or Distant)

couldn't be more mistaken. Many people just don't think their business is someone else's. Others may not want to drop names. It might not be until someone like you says, "I wish I knew someone in the music business" that someone else brings their own network into the picture.

Civic and other not-for-profit groups also have a variety of events that are great for networking. Whether you go to a regular meeting or attend a charity auction, cocktail party, or large gala to benefit a not-for-profit, you will generally find business people in the community you might not know. As an added bonus, many larger not-for-profit events also have media coverage, meaning that you have the opportunity to add media people to your network.

Those who take advantage of every opportunity to meet new people will have the largest networks. The idea in building a network is to go out of your comfort zone. If you just stay with people you know and are comfortable with, you won't have the opportunity to get to know others. You want to continually meet new people; after all, you never know who knows whom.

Networking Savvy

You are learning how to build your network. However, the largest network in the world will be useless unless you know how to take full advantage of it. So let's talk a little about how you're going to use the network you are building.

Previously, we discussed the difference between skills and talents. Networking is a skill. You don't have to be born with it. You can acquire the skill to network, practice, and improve. What that means is that if you practice networking, you can get better at it, and it can pay off big in your career!

Get out. Go to new places. Meet new people. The trick here is when you're in a situation where there are new people, don't be afraid to walk up to them, shake their hand, and talk to them. People can't read your mind, so it's imperative to tell them about your career goals, dreams, and aspirations.

Because of the mystique surrounding the music industry, people will generally find your choice of careers interesting. And if they are involved or have any contact in the industry at all, they will usually say something like, "Oh, that's neat; my cousin works at one of the major labels," or "My accountant was just telling me he handles a couple of recording acts."

When you meet new people, listen to them. Focus on what they're saying. Ask questions. Be interested in what they are telling you. You can never tell when the next person you talk to is the one who will be able to help you open the door or vice versa.

If you're shy, even the thought of networking may be very difficult for you. However, it is essential to make yourself do it anyway. Successful networking can pay off big. It can mean the difference between getting in the industry or not, between success and failure. Isn't it worth the effort?

Just meeting people isn't enough. Whether you meet the president of a major record label, a successful music publisher, or anyone to add to your network, the idea is to try to develop the relationship further. Just having a story to tell about who you know is not enough. Arrange a follow-up meeting, send a note or letter, or make a phone call. The more you take advantage of every opportunity, the closer you will be to getting what you want.

A good way to network is to volunteer. I've mentioned attending not-for-profit events and civic meetings to expand your network, but how about volunteering to work with a not-for-profit or civic group?

I can imagine you saying, "When? I'm so busy now, I don't have enough time to do anything."

Make the time. It will be worth it.

Why? People will see you on a different level. They won't see you as someone looking for a job or trying to succeed as a performer. Generally, people talk about their volunteer work to friends, family, business associates, and other colleagues. This means that when someone is speaking to someone else, they might mention in passing that one of the people they are working with on their event or project is trying to get into the music business or is trying to succeed as a singer. Anyone they mention it to is a potential secondary networking contact. Those people, in turn, may mention it to someone else. Eventually, someone involved in the music industry might hear about you. Another reason is people will see that you have a good work ethic. Treat volunteer projects as you would work projects. Do what you say you are going to do, and do it in a timely manner.

This also gives you the opportunity to demonstrate skills and talents people might not otherwise know you have. Can you do publicity? Can you write? How about organizing things? Do you get along well with others? What better way to illustrate your skills than utilizing them by putting together an event, publicizing it, or coordinating other volunteers. Are you trying to get exposure as a singer, songwriter, or with some other type of talent? What better opportunity to showcase your songwriting talents than writing the opening tune for a not-for-profit's

The Inside Scoop
Volunteer to do projects that no one else wants to do, and you will immediately become more visible.

Tip from the Coach
While volunteering is good for networking, don't get involved with too many organizations. Depending on your schedule, one, two, or even three is probably fine. Anything more than that, and you're on the road to burnout.

big event? How about volunteering to perform at the event gratis? No, you won't get paid, but you will have great exposure and possibly get some media attention.

Best of all, you can use this activity on your resume. While volunteer experiences don't take the place of work experience, they certainly can fill out a resume short of it. Don't just go to meetings. Participate fully in the organization. That way, you'll not only be helping others; you'll be adding to your network.

Where can you volunteer? Pretty much any not-for-profit or civic organization is a possibility. The one thing you should remember, however, is to volunteer only for organizations whose causes you believe in. Here are some ideas to get you started.

- community theaters
- hospital auxiliaries
- parent teacher association (PTA) or parent teacher organization (PTO)
- colleges or universities
- public schools
- private schools
- professional organizations
- libraries
- children's organizations
- civic groups
- political organizations

To make the most of every networking opportunity, it's essential for people to remember you. Keep a supply of your business cards with you all the time. Don't be stingy with them. Give them out freely to everyone. That way, your name and number will be close at hand if needed. Make sure you ask for cards in return. If people don't have them, ask for their contact information.

Try to keep in contact with people on your network on a regular basis. Of course, you can't call everyone every day, but try to set up a schedule of sorts to do some positive networking every day. For example, you might decide to call one person every day on your networking list. Depending on the situation, you can say you are calling to touch base, keep in contact, or see how they are doing. Ask how they have been or talk about something you might have in common or they might think is interesting. You might also decide that once a week, you will try to call someone and set up a lunch or coffee date.

Be on the lookout for stories, articles, or other tidbits of information that might be of interest to people in your network. Clip them out and send them with a short note saying you saw the story and thought they might be interested. If you hear of something they might be interested in, call them. The idea is to keep in contact with people in your network and stay visible.

Keep track of the contacts in your network. You can use the sample sheet provided, a card file using index cards, or a database or contact software program on your computer. Include as

much information as you have about each person. People like when you remember them and their interests. It makes you stand out.

Then use your networking contact list. For example, a few days before someone's birthday, send him or her a card. If you know someone collects old guitars, for example, and you see an article on old guitars, clip it out and send it. Don't be a pest, but keep in contact. People in sales have been using this technique for years. It works for them, and it will help you as well.

You might want to use some of the items here and then add information as it comes up. You don't have to ask people for all this information the first time you meet them. Just add it when you get it.

- ◎ person's name
- ◎ address
- ◎ phone number
- ◎ e-mail address
- ◎ Web address (URL)
- ◎ birthday
- ◎ when and where you met them
- ◎ occupation
- ◎ hobbies
- ◎ spouse's (or significant other's) name
- ◎ children's names
- ◎ type of dog and dog name
- ◎ cat's name
- ◎ honors
- ◎ things they collect
- ◎ any other interesting facts

Networking Contact Information Sheet

Name
_____

Business Address
_____

Business Phone
_____

Home Address
_____

Home Phone
_____

E-mail Address
_____

Web Address (URL)
_____

Birthday
_____

Anniversary
_____

Where and When Met
_____

Spouse or Significant Other's Name
_____

Children's Name(s)
_____

Dog Breed and Name
_____

Cat Breed and Name
_____

Hobbies
_____

Interests
_____

Things Collected
_____

Honors
_____

Awards
_____

Interesting Facts

Networking and Nerve

Successful networking will give you credibility and a rapport with people in the industry. But networking sometimes takes nerve, especially if you're not naturally outgoing. You have to push yourself to get out and meet people, talk to them, tell them what you are interested in doing, and stay in contact. On occasion, you may have to ask people if they will help you, ask for recommendations, ask for references, and so on. Don't let the fear of doing what you need to do stop you from doing it. Just remember that the result of all your effort will be not only entry into a career you want but a shot at success.

Here are some things that might take some nerve but will pay off in your quest for the career you want in the music industry.

- ◎ Ask people (in conversation) if they know anyone in the music industry.
- ◎ If you know someone who knows someone in the industry, ask if they will call them for you. If that isn't an option, ask if you can use their name as a reference when calling or writing for an appointment. When you are referred by someone, it gives you credibility.
- ◎ Ask for letters of recommendation.
- ◎ Ask for letters of reference.
- ◎ Ask specific people in your network if you can use their name as references on job applications. Make sure that you tell someone when you think they will be called.

As long as you're pleasant, there is nothing wrong with asking for help. Just remember that while people can help you get your foot in the door, you are going to have to sell yourself once the door is open.

Networking is a two-way street. While it might be hard for you to imagine at this moment, someone might want you to help them in some part of their career. Reciprocate and reciprocate graciously. As a matter of fact, if you see or know someone you might be able to help even in a small way, don't wait for them to ask—offer your help.

Making and Using Contacts in the Music Industry

If you are interested in the talent end of the industry, make additional contacts in that area. Make contact with people who can help push your songs, book you, manage you, or just help you get your foot in the door and advance your career.

How can you catch the attention of people like this? Think creatively. We discussed volunteering to write a song for an upcoming not-for-profit organization event, and we talked about volunteering to provide the talent (gratis) for an event. Look for every opportunity. Do you see classes offered in songwriting? Workshops on various aspects of the music industry? Seminars on performing? Take them! Aside from learning something, you can never tell who you might meet there.

Workshops where people in the industry critique your work are especially useful. In the event that someone doesn't like your work, don't let it get to you. He or she is only one person. Use these opportunities to hone your craft and talent. Use them also to meet others in the industry.

Words from a Pro

Copyright all songs before letting anyone outside of your family listen to them. Catchy tunes often stick in people's heads. It's not uncommon for people to inadvertently think that *they* came up with a song. A copyright will protect you.

Be on the lookout for contests and competitions. They're great for exposure. If they are televised, even on a local basis, all the better. Make sure you get a tape even if you have to buy one. If the local television news covers an event and you don't tape it yourself, call them up and ask how you can get a copy. If the news happens to film you and only uses a few seconds or a minute, see if you can buy the raw tape footage that they didn't use.

Many television and cable stations are now hosting television shows showcasing talent. If you are ready, consider applying. Shows such as *Star Search* and *American Idol* can give you major exposure and have already spawned a number of top recording stars. If you are talented and lucky, you could be one of them.

Don't forget talent showcases. In the music industry, these are opportunities to display your talent. While we will discuss these in more depth later, you should be aware of the opportunities these offer to both meet industry insiders and gain exposure. Showcases may be sponsored by a variety of music industry organizations, trade associations, or other businesses. Sometimes a manager or other business associate may put together a showcase for you, inviting industry professionals such as agents, concert promoters, producers, and record company executives. In some cases, you may even want to showcase yourself. If you hear of a showcase for another act and you have the opportunity to attend, you should do so. While it's fine to pick up business cards while you're there and network, don't try to overshadow the act or acts that are showcased. While every showcase or competition might not end up in a contract, the idea is to find places to go and opportunities to explore where you have the chance to meet industry insiders.

Finding a Mentor or Advocate

Mentors and advocates can help guide and boost your career. A mentor or advocate in the music industry also often provides you valuable contacts that, as you now know, are essential to your success. The best mentors and advocates are supportive individuals who help move your career to the next level.

Can't figure out why anyone would help you? Many people like to help others. It makes them feel good and makes them feel important. How do you find a mentor? Look for someone who is successful and ask. Sound simple? It is simple. The difficult part is finding just the right person or persons.

While someone in the music business would be ideal, don't let that exclude those outside the industry. Depending on the area of the industry in which you are interested, you might look to

◎ booking agents
◎ managers
◎ musicians
◎ singers

Tip from the Coach

If someone asks you to be their mentor or asks for your help and you can offer it, say yes. As a matter of fact, if you see someone you might be able to help, do just that. You might think that you don't even have your own career on track or you don't have time. You might be tempted to say no. Think again. You are expecting someone to help you. Do the same for someone else. There is no better feeling than helping someone else. And while you shouldn't help someone for the sole purpose of helping yourself, remember that you can often open doors for yourself, while opening them for someone else.

- attorneys
- other businesspeople
- music teachers
- club owners
- radio station personnel
- bankers
- media people
- friends
- relatives
- teachers

Sometimes you don't even have to ask. In many cases, a person may see your potential and offer advice. They may not call it mentoring, but with any luck, that's what it turns into. Time is a valuable commodity, especially to busy people. Be gracious when someone helps you or even tries to help. Make sure you say thank you to

anyone and everyone who shares his or her time, expertise, or advice. And don't forget to ask them if there is any way you can return the favor.

> ## ★ Words from the Wise
> It is not uncommon to run into someone who doesn't want to help you. This may be for any number of reasons ranging from they really don't know how they can help or they don't have time in their schedule or they think that if they help you in your career, it puts their position at risk. If you do ask someone to be your mentor and he or she says no, just let it go. Look for someone else. The opposite of having a great mentor is having someone in your life who is sabotaging your career.

8

THE INTERVIEW

Getting the Interview

One of the keys to getting the job you want is the interview. The interview is your chance to shine. During an interview, you can show what can't be illustrated on paper. This is the time your personality and talents can be showcased. In the music industry, where more people want to get in than there are jobs, obtaining an interview and excelling in the meeting can help get you the job you want.

If you do it right, the interview can help make you irresistible. It is your chance to persuade the interviewer to hire you. It is your main shot at showing why you would be better than anyone else; why hiring you would benefit the company; why not hiring you would be a big mistake. So let's take some time to discuss how to get that all-important meeting.

There are many ways to land job interviews. Some of these include

- responding to advertisements
- recommendations from friends, relatives, or colleagues
- making cold calls
- writing letters
- working with executive search firms, recruiters, or headhunters
- working with employment agencies
- attending job and career fairs
- finding the jobs that have not been advertised (the hidden job market)

Responding to an advertisement is probably the most common approach people take to obtaining a job interview. Where can you look for ads for jobs in the music industry? Depending on the exact type of job you're looking for, here are some possibilities:

- trade magazines (*Billboard, Radio and Records,* and others)
- music industry periodicals and newspapers
- music business–oriented Web sites (record label sites and music industry sites)
- daily newspapers (While positions may be located throughout the country, the majority of major record label jobs which are advertised will be located in major music capitals such as Los Angeles, New York City, and Nashville. Indies may be located almost anyplace.)
- Sunday newspapers (Sunday newspapers generally have the greatest number of classified ads.)
- weekly newspapers

159

Now let's say you open the paper or a trade magazine or even see an advertisement on the Web that looks like this:

RECORD LABEL seeking the following positions: Director of Public Relations, Administrative Assistant to A&R exec, Artist Relations Staffer, and Marketing Exec. For consideration for these positions either fax resume to (111) 222-3333, e-mail to record@recordlabel.com or mail to PO Box 111, Record Label Town, NY 11111.

Once you see the ad, you get excited. You have been looking for a job just like one of these. You can't wait to send your resume.

Want a reality check? There may be hundreds of other people who can't wait either. Here's the good news. With a little planning, you can increase your chances of getting an interview from the classified or display ad, and as we've just discussed, this is your key to the job.

Your resume and cover letter need to stand out. Your resume needs to generate an interview.

You should be aware of the life of a resume after you send it out in response to a classified ad. Where does it go? Who reads it? That depends. In some companies, usually smaller ones, your resume and cover letter may go to the person who will be hiring you. It may go to that person's secretary or administrative assistant. This might be the case, for example, if you're re-

plying to an ad for a job in a small recording studio or a smaller music industry public relations firm. In some companies, usually larger ones, your resume and cover letter may go to a hiring manager or human resources director. This would probably occur if you're answering an ad for a position at a midsized to larger record label or large booking agency. If you are replying to an advertisement placed by an employment agency, your response will generally go to the person at the employment agency responsible for that client and job.

In any of these cases, however, your resume may take other paths. Depending on the specific job and company, your response may go through executive recruiters, screening services, clerks, or even receptionists. Whoever the original screener of resumes turns out to be, he or she will have the initial job of reviewing the information to make sure that it fits the profile of what is needed. But that doesn't mean that if you don't have the exact requirements you should not apply for a job.

The trick is to tailor your resume as much as possible to the specific job and write a great cover letter. For example, let's say the job requirements for a position at a record label in the publicity department look something like this:

Creative, enthusiastic individual with strong organization skills. Excellent verbal and writing skills. Ability to work without direct supervision. Minimum requirements include bachelor's degree and four years' experience in the music industry.

Now let's say that while you are creative and enthusiastic and have excellent verbal and writing skills, you don't have four years' experience working in the music industry. Should you not apply for the job? If you want it, go for it.

Here is what you need to know. When you are working on your resume and your cover letter in response to an ad, remember that skills are transferable. Skills for specific areas might need to be fine-tuned, but sales skills are sales skills, writing skills are writing skills, and public relations skills are public relations skills. Stress what you have done successfully, not what you haven't done.

Whoever your resume and cover letter go to, you want to increase your chances of it being looked at and passed on to the pile of resumes from people who will ultimately end up getting called for an interview. Whoever the screener of the resumes is, he or she will probably pass over anything that doesn't look neat and well thought out or anything where there are obvious errors.

What can you do? First, go over your resume. Make sure it is perfect. Make sure it is neat. Make sure it is tailored to the job you are going after. If you are going to mail it, make sure it's printed on high-quality paper.

Human resources departments dealing with entertainment-oriented companies often receives hundreds of responses to ads. While most people use white paper, consider using off-white or even a different color such as light blue or light mauve. You want your resume to look sophisticated and classy but still stand out in a professional way. Of course, the color of the paper will not change the content of your resume, but it will at least help your resume get noticed in the first place.

If the advertisement directs you in a specific method of responding to the ad, use that method. For example, if the ad instructs applicants to fax their resumes, fax it. If it says to e-mail your resume, use e-mail and pay attention to whether the ad specifies sending the file as an attachment or in the body of your e-mail. The company may have a procedure for screening job applicants.

If given the option of methods of responding, which should you use? Each method has its pros and cons.

- E-mail
  - On the pro side, e-mail is one of the quickest methods of responding to ads. Many companies utilize the e-mail method.
  - On the con side, you are really never assured someone gets what you sent, and even if they do, you're not sure that it won't be inadvertently deleted. Another concern is making sure that the resume you sent reaches the recipient in the form in which you sent it. If you are using a common word processing program and the same platform (Mac or PC) as the recipient, you probably won't have a problem. If you are using a Mac and the recipient is using a PC, you might.
- Fax
  - On the pro side, faxing can get your resume where it's going almost instantaneously.

- On the con side, if the recipient is using an old-fashioned fax, the paper quality might not be great. The good news is that most companies now use plain paper faxes.
- Mailing or shipping (USPS, FedEx, Airborne, UPS, and so on)
  - On the pro side, you can send your resume on high-quality paper so you know what it is going to look like when it arrives. You can also send any supporting materials that might help you get the coveted interview. You can send it with an option to have someone sign for it when it arrives so you definitely know when it arrived.
  - On the con side, it may take time to arrive by mail. One of the ways to get past this problem is to send it overnight or two-day express. It will cost more, but you will have control over when it arrives.

When is the best time to send your response to an ad in order to have the best chance at getting an interview? If you send your resume right away, it might arrive with a pile of hundreds of others, yet, if you wait too long, the company might have already found a candidate and stopped seriously looking at new resumes.

Many people procrastinate, so if you can send in your response immediately, such as the

Tip from the Coach

If faxing any documents, remember to use the "fine" option on your fax machine. While this may take a bit longer to send, the recipients will get a better copy.

The Inside Scoop

If mailing your resume and cover letter, use an envelope large enough to fit the paper so you don't have to fold it. That way, it comes in flat and looks neat when it arrives.

day the ad is published or the very next morning, it will probably be one of the first ones in. At that time, the screener will be reading through just a few responses. If yours stands out, it stands a good chance of being put into the "initial interview pile."

If you can't respond immediately, wait two or three days so your resume doesn't arrive with the big pile of other responses. Once again, your goal is to increase your chances of your resume not being passed over.

When you are trying to land an interview through a recommendation from friends or colleagues, cold calls, letters, executive search firms, recruiters, headhunters, employment agencies, people you met at job fairs, or through other networking events, or any aspect of the hidden job market, the timing of sending a resume is essential. In these cases, you want the people receiving your information to remember that someone said it was coming, so send it as soon as possible. This is not the time to procrastinate. If you do, you might lose the opportunity to set up that all-important meeting.

Persistence is the word to remember when trying to get an interview. If you are responding to an advertisement and you don't hear back within a week or two, call to see what is happening. If after you call the first time, you don't hear back after another week or so (unless you've been specifically given a time frame), call back again. Don't be obnoxious and don't be a pain, but call.

If you're shy, you're going to have to get over it. Write a script ahead of time to help you. Don't read directly from the script, but practice so it becomes second nature. For example: "Hello, this is Harry Woods. I replied to an advertisement you placed in the paper for the marketing exec position at your label. I was wondering who I could speak with to find out about the status of the position?"

When you get to the correct person, you might have to reiterate your purpose in calling. Then you might ask, "Do you know when interviewing is starting? Will all applicants be notified one way or the other? Is it possible to tell me whether I'm on the list to be contacted?" Don't be afraid to try to get as much information as possible, once again making sure you are being pleasant.

Remember that becoming friendly with the secretary or receptionist is a good thing. These people are on the inside and can provide you with a wealth of information.

Be aware that there is a way that you can get your resume looked at, obtain an interview, and beat the competition out of the dream job you want in the music industry. Remember that we discussed the hidden job market? We know that some jobs are not advertised. Following this theory, all you have to do is contact the company and land the job you want *before* it is advertised.

"How?" you ask.

Take a chance. Make a call or write a letter and ask. You might even stop in and talk to the human resources department. There is nothing that says you have to wait to see an ad in the paper. Call up and ask to speak to the human resources department or hiring manager. Write a script ahead of time so you know exactly what you want to say. Ask for the hiring manager or

---

Words from the Wise

Don't be in such a rush to get your resume out that you make errors or don't produce a neat and tailored resume. If you're not ready, send your information out in a few days instead.

---

human resources department. Ask about job openings. Make sure you have an idea of what you want to do and convey it to the person you are talking to.

If you are told there are no openings or you are told that they don't speak to people unsolicited, which is often the case at record companies, be persistent. Ask if you can forward a resume to keep on file. In many cases, they will agree to get you off the phone. Ask for the name of the person to whom you should direct your resume; then ask for the address and fax number. Thank the person you spoke to and make sure you get their name.

Now here's a neat trick. Fax your resume. Send it with a cover letter that states that a hard copy will be coming via mail. Why fax it? Did you know that when you fax documents to a company they generally are delivered directly to the desk of the person you are sending them to? They don't go through the mailroom, where they might be dumped in a general inbox. They don't sit around for a day. They are generally delivered immediately.

So now that your resume is in the hands of the powers that be, it's your job to call up, make sure they received it, and try as hard as you can to set up an interview. The individual's secretary might try to put you off. Don't be deterred. Thank her or him and say you understand his or her position. Say you're going to call in a week or so after the boss has had a chance to review your material. Send your information out in hard copy immediately. Wait a week or so and call back. Remember that persistence pays off.

Sometimes you might reach someone who tells you that "if they weren't so busy, they'd be glad to meet with you." They might tell you when their workload lightens or a project is done, they will schedule an interview. You could say thank you and let it go. Or you could tell them that you understand that they're busy. All you are asking for is 10 minutes and not a minute longer. You'll even bring a stopwatch and coffee if they want.

⭐ Tip from the Coach

When I was first trying to get into the music business, I knew a young man who was a comedian. He wasn't a very good comedian, but he said he was a comedian and did have a good number of jobs, so I guess he was a comedian. During this time, I was trying to land interviews with everyone I could so I could get my own dream job in the music industry.

I had made contact with a booking agent I had called and developed a business relationship with. Every week I'd call, and every week he would tell me to call him back. It wasn't going anywhere, but at least someone was taking my calls. This went on for about three or four months.

One day when I called, the owner got on the phone and said, "Do you know Joe Black? [Not his real name.] He said he has worked up in your area."

I said, "Yes, he works as a comedian."

"What do you know about him?" he asked.

"Well, he's not a great comedian, but he seems to keep getting jobs. He's booking himself," I replied.

"That's interesting," he said. "He has called me over twenty-five times looking for a job as an agent. What do you think?"

I was wondering why he was asking my opinion, because I had yet to get into his office myself. "If he can book himself, he can probably do a great job for your agency," I said. "You have great clients. I bet he would do a good job."

"Thanks," he said, "I might just do that."

"What about me?" I asked.

"I still can't think of where you might fit in," he said. "Why don't you give me a call in a couple of weeks."

I waited a couple of weeks, called back and asked to speak to the owner.

"Hello," he said. "Guess who's standing next to me?"

He had hired Joe Black the comedian to work as an agent in his office.

"He had no experience, outside of booking himself," the agent said. "But I figured if he was as persistent making calls for our clients as he was trying to get a job, he'd work out for us. Why don't you come in and talk when you have a chance. I don't have anything, but maybe I can give you some ideas."

I immediately said that I had been planning a trip to the booking agent's city the next week. We set up an appointment.

Did the agent ever have a job for me? No, but while in his office, he introduced me to some of the clients he was booking, who introduced me to some other people who later turned out to be clients of mine when I opened up a public relations business. The moral of the story is that networking and persistence always pay off.

Guarantee them that 10 minutes after you get in the door, you will stand up to leave.

If you're convincing, you might land an interview. If you do, remember to bring that stopwatch. Introduce yourself, put the stopwatch down on the desk in front of you, and present your skills. You must practice this before you get there. Give the highlights of your resume and how hiring you would benefit the company. When your 10 minutes are up, thank the person you are meeting with for their time and give them your resume, any supporting materials you have brought with you, and your business card. Then leave. If you are asked to stay, by all means, stay and continue the meeting. One way or the other, write a note thanking them for their time.

If you have sold yourself or your idea for a position in the company, someone may just get back to you. Once again, feel free to call in a week or two to follow up.

The Interview Process

You got the call. You landed an interview. Now what? The interview is an integral part of getting the job you want. There are a number of different types of interviews. Depending on the company and the job, you might be asked to go on one or more interviews ranging from initial or screening interviews to interviews with department heads or supervisors you will be working with.

Things to Bring

Once you get the call for an interview, what's your next step? Let's start with what you should bring to the interview.

◎ copies of your resume (While they probably have copies of your resume, they might have misplaced it or you might want to refer to it.)

◎ letters of reference (Even though people have given you letters of reference, make sure you let them know you are using them.)

◎ references (When interviewing for jobs, you often need to fill in job applications that ask for both professional and personal references. Ask before you use people as references. Make sure they are prepared to give you a good reference. Then when you go for an interview, call the people on your reference list and give them the heads-up on your job hunting activities.)

◎ a portfolio of your work (Refer to Chapter 6 to learn how to develop your professional portfolio.)

◎ business cards (Refer to Chapter 6 learn more about business cards.)

You want to look as professional as possible, so don't throw your materials into a paper bag or a sloppy knapsack. At the very least, put your information into a large envelope or folder to carry into the interview. A professional-looking briefcase or portfolio is probably the best way to hold your information.

Your Interviewing Wardrobe

You've landed an interview, but what do you wear? Remember that while you might see people in the music industry wearing micro-mini skirts, ripped jeans, midriff tops, sneakers, and skin-tight pants and T-shirts, they are not the ones going for the job. The music business is just that—a business.

First, here's a list of what *not* to wear:

◎ sneakers
◎ flip-flops
◎ sandals
◎ micro-mini skirts or dresses

- very tight or very low dresses or tops
- jeans of any kind
- ripped jeans or T-shirts
- midriff tops
- skin-tight pants or leggings
- very baggy pants
- sweatshirts
- work-out clothes
- heavy perfume, men's cologne, or aftershave lotion
- very heavy makeup
- flashy jewelry (this includes nose rings, lip rings, and other flamboyant piercings)

What you *should* wear:

Men
- dark suit
- dark sports jacket, button-down shirt, tie, and trousers

Women
- suit
- dress with jacket
- skirt with blouse and jacket
- pumps or other closed-toe shoes

Interview Environments

In most cases, interviews are held in office environments. If you are asked if you want coffee, tea, soda, or any type of food, my advice is to abstain. This is not the time you want to accidentally spill coffee, inadvertently make a weird noise drinking soda, or get sugar from a donut on your fingers when you need to shake hands.

In some cases, however, you may be interviewed over a meal. Whether it is breakfast, lunch, or dinner, it is usually best to order something simple and light. This is not the time to order anything that can slurp, slide, or otherwise mess you up. Soups, messy sauces, fried chicken, ribs, or anything that you have to eat with your hands would be a bad choice. Nothing can ruin your confidence during an interview worse than a big blob of sauce accidentally dropping on your shirt—except if you cut into something and it splashes onto your interviewer's suit. Eating should be your last priority. Use this time to present your attributes, tell your story, and ask intelligent questions.

This is also not the time to order an alcoholic beverage. Even if the interviewer orders a drink, abstain. You want to be at the top of your game. If, however, the interviewer orders dessert and coffee or tea, do so as well. That way he or she isn't eating alone and you have a few more minutes to make yourself shine.

A company may invite you to participate in a meal interview to see how you will act in social situations. They might want to check out your table manners or whether you keep your elbows on the table or talk with your mouth full. They might want to see whether you drink to excess or how you make conversation. They might want to know if you will embarrass them, if you can handle pressure, or how you interact with others. They might want you to get comfortable so they can see the true you. If you are prepared ahead of time, you will do fine. Just remember this isn't a social meal. You are being scrutinized. Be on your toes.

Words from the Wise
Never ask for a doggie bag at an interview meal. I've seen it happen and I've heard the interviewers talking about it in a negative manner two weeks later.

During the meal, pepper the conversation with questions about the company and the job. Don't be afraid to say you're excited about the possibility, you think you would be an asset to the company, and you hope they agree. Make eye contact with those at the table. When the interviewer stands up after the meal, the interview is generally over. Stand up, thank the interviewer or interviewers for the meal, tell them you look forward to hearing from them, shake everyone's hand, and then leave.

Many companies preinterview or do partial interviews on the phone. This might be to prescreen people without bringing them into the office. Other times it might happen if, for example, you live in the Midwest and a record company in Los Angeles is interested in your resume. Whatever the reason, be prepared. If the company has scheduled a phone interview ahead of time, make sure your "space" is prepared so you can do your best.

Here are some ideas:

◎ Have your phone in a quiet location. People yelling, a loud television, or music in the background is not helpful in this situation.
◎ Have a pad of paper and a few pens to write down the name of the people you are speaking to, take notes, and jot down questions as you think of them.

◎ Have a copy of your resume near you. Your interviewer may refer to information on your resume. If it's close, you won't have to fumble for words.
◎ Prepare questions to ask in case you are asked whether you have any.
◎ Prepare answers for questions that you might be asked: Why do you want to work for us? What can you bring to the company? What type of experience do you have?

Timing is everything in an interview. Whatever you do, don't be late. If you can't get to an interview on time, chances are you won't get to a job on time. On the other hand, you don't want to be an hour early.

Try to time your arrival so you get there about 15 minutes before your scheduled time. When you arrive, tell the receptionist your name and who your appointment is with. When you are directed to go into the interview, walk in, smile sincerely, shake hands with the interviewer or interviewers, and sit down. Look around the office. Does the interviewer have a photo of children on the desk? Is there any personalization in the office? Does it look like the interviewer is into golf, or fishing, or some other hobby? Do you have something in common? You might say something like:

"What beautiful children."
"Is golf one of your passions too?"
"Do you go deep sea fishing?"

> ### ★ Tip from the Top
>
> If you have an extreme emergency and absolutely must be late, call and try to re-schedule your appointment. Do not attempt to arrive late and come up with an excuse when you get there.

Try to make the interviewer comfortable with you before the questions start.

Interview Questions

What might you be asked? The music business is like every other business. You will probably be asked a slew of general questions and then, depending on the job, some questions specific to your skills and talent.

◎ Why should we hire you?
   ▫ This is a common question. Think about the answers ahead of time. Practice saying them out loud so you feel comfortable. For example, "I believe I would be an asset to the label. I have the qualifications. I'm a team player, and this is the type of career I really want to pursue. I'm a hard worker, a quick study, and I'll help you achieve your goals."

◎ What makes you more qualified than other candidates?
   ▫ Another common question. How about saying something like, "I believe my experience working as an intern while in college gave me a fuller understanding of how a label works. I brought my portfolio so you can actually see some of the projects I worked on."

◎ Where do you see yourself in five years?
   ▫ Do not say, "Sitting in your chair" or "In your chair." People in every business are paranoid that someone is going to take their job. In the music industry, many worry that younger people will take their place, so don't even joke about it. Instead, think about the question ahead of time. It's meant to find out what your aspirations are. Do you have direction? One answer might be, "I hope to be a successful member of this company. I've always respected this label and the artists it represents, and I would love to think that I can have a long career here."

◎ What are your strengths?
   ▫ Be confident but not cocky when answering this one. Toot your horn, but don't be boastful. Practice ahead of time reciting what your greatest strengths, talents, and skills are. "I'm passionate about what I do. I love working at something I'm passionate about. That's one of the main reasons I applied for this position. Let's see; I also have great organizational skills, I'm a people person, and I'm a really good communicator. I pride myself on being able to solve problems quickly, efficiently, and successfully."

◎ Where are your weaknesses?
   ▫ We all have weaknesses. This is not the time to share them. Be creative. "My greatest weakness is also one of my strengths. I'm a workaholic. I don't like leaving a project undone. I have a hard time understanding how

someone cannot do a great job when they love what they do."

◎ Why did you leave your last job?
  ▫ Be careful answering this one. If you were fired, simply say you were let go. Don't go into the politics. Don't say anything bad about your former job, company, or boss. If you were laid off, simply say you were laid off, or, if it's true, that you were one of the newer employees and unfortunately that's how the layoff process worked. You might add that you were very sorry to leave because you really enjoyed working there, but on the positive side, you now are free to apply for this position. If you quit, simply say the job was not challenging and you wanted to work in a position where you could create a career. Never lie. The music industry is small. You can never tell when your former boss knows the person interviewing you. In the same vein, never say anything bad about anyone or any other company. The boss you had yesterday might end up moving over to your new company and being your new boss. It is not unheard of in the industry.

◎ Why do you want to work in the music business?
  ▫ Interviewers in the music industry want to make sure you're not a groupie. It's okay to be a fan. Do not say you want to make a lot of money. Do not say you want free records. You might say something like you've been interested in the music industry for many years. You understand that even the music industry is a business and you thought you'd create a career in a business that was such an interesting and expanding industry.

◎ Do you like music?
  ▫ The answer here should be yes. Do not say, "I can take it or leave it." The answer here is, "Yes, I love music. I have always especially loved jazz [or country or whatever you really love]."

◎ Who's your favorite artist or band?

◎ Are you a team player?
  ▫ Companies want you to be a team player, so the answer is, "Yes, it's one of my strengths."

◎ Do you need supervision?
  ▫ You want to appear as confident and capable as possible. "I work well with limited supervision," is one good answer. "Once I know my responsibilities, I have always been able to fulfill them," is another.

◎ Are you free to travel?
  ▫ You might be required to travel for some jobs. A publicist at a record label may need to go on the road. A marketing executive might need to travel to various locations. A&R people often travel to check out new talent. Be honest here. If the job you are applying for requires travel and that is a problem, now is the time to straighten it out. You might ask how often travel will be required and if is scheduled ahead of time.

◎ Will working overtime, nights, or on weekends be a problem?
  ▫ The answer they are looking for is no. A good answer here is if the project requires it, you will be

available but only if that is not a problem for you. Don't be afraid to ask how much overtime is anticipated or what situations would require working nights or weekends.

◎ Do you get along well with others?
  ▫ The answer they are looking for is yes. Do not provide any stories about times when you didn't.

◎ What type of music do you listen to at home?
  ▫ You are going for a job in the music business. Hopefully, you like music. Have an answer ready. It's a pretty normal question that gets thrown in at interviews in music-oriented companies.

◎ Every now and then, you get a weird question or one that you just don't expect. If you could be a car, what type of car would you be and why? If you were an animal, what animal would you be? If you could have dinner with anyone alive or dead, who would it be? These questions generally are just meant to throw you off balance and see how you react.
  ▫ Stay calm and focused. Be creative, but try not to come up with any answer that is too weird.

◎ An interviewer might ask what was the last book you read, what newspapers you read, what television shows are your favorites, or if you read the trades.
  ▫ Be honest. If your answer is related to the music business, all the better.

◎ What type of salary are you looking for?
  ▫ This is going to be discussed in detail, but what you should know now is that this is an important matter. You don't want to get locked into

---

⭐ Tip from the Top

Try not to discuss salary at the beginning of the interview. Instead, wait until you hear all the particulars about the job and you have given them a chance to see how great you are.

---

a number before you know exactly what you will be responsible for. You might say something to the effect of, "I'm looking for a fair salary for the job. I really would like to know more about the responsibilities before I come up with a range. What is the range, by the way?" You might turn the tables and say something like, "I was interested in knowing what the salary range was for this position." This poses the question back to the interviewer.

What Can't They Ask You?

Some questions are illegal for interviewers to ask. For example, they aren't permitted to ask you anything about your age, unless they are making sure you are over 18. They aren't supposed to ask you about marriage, children, or relationships. Interviewers are not supposed to ask you about your race, color, religion, or national origin. If an interviewer does ask an illegal question, in most cases it is not on purpose. He or she just might not know that it shouldn't be asked.

Your demeanor in responding to such questions can affect the direction of the interview. If you don't mind answering, by all means do so. If answering bothers you, try to point the questions in another direction, such as back to your skills and talents. If you are unable to do so, simply indicate in a nonthreatening, nonconfrontational manner that those types of questions are not supposed to be asked in interviews.

What You Might Want to Ask

Just because you're the one being interviewed doesn't mean you shouldn't ask questions. You want to appear confident. You want to portray someone who can fit in with others comfortably. You want to ask great questions. Depending on the specific job, here are some ideas.

◎ What happened to the last person who held this job? Were they promoted or did they leave? (You want to know whose shoes you're filling.)

◎ Does the company promote from within as a rule or look outside? (This is important because companies that promote from within are good companies to build a career with.)

◎ Is there a lot of longevity of employees here? (Employees who stay for a length of time generally are happy with the company.)

◎ Is there a lot of laughing in the workplace? (If there is, it means a less stressed environment.)

◎ How will I be evaluated? Are there periodic reviews? (You want to know how and when you will know if you are doing well in your supervisor's eyes.)

◎ How do your measure success on the job? By that I mean, how can I do a great job for you? (You want to know what your employer expects from employees.)

◎ What are the options for advancement in this position? (This illustrates that you are interested in staying with the company.)

◎ To whom will I report? What will my general responsibilities be? (You want to know exactly what your work experience and duties will be like.)

Feel free to ask any questions you want answered. Don't, however, ask questions like, "How many famous people will I meet?" "Do I get free records?" "Do I get free tickets to concerts?" and so on. You don't want to appear like a groupie. You want to come across as a professional who wants to work in the music industry. And while it's fine to ask questions, don't chatter incessantly. You want to give the interviewer time to ask you questions and see how you shine.

It's normal to be nervous during an interview. Relax as much as you can. If you go in prepared and answer the questions you're asked, you should do fine. If things are going well, somewhere during the interview, salary will come up.

Salary and Compensation

As much as you want a job in the music industry, you're not going to work for free. Compensation may be discussed generally at the interview or may be discussed in full. A lot has to do with the specific job. One way or another, salary will generally come up sometime during your interview. Unless your interviewer brings up salary at the beginning of an interview, you should not. If you feel an interview is close to ending and another interview has not been scheduled, feel free to bring it up when asked if you have any questions.

A simple question such as "What is the salary range for the job?" will usually start the ball rolling. Depending on the specific job, your interviewer may tell you exactly what the salary and benefits are or may just give you a range. In many cases, salary and compensation packages are only ironed out after the actual job offer is made.

Let's say you are offered a job and a compensation package. What do you do if you're not happy with the salary? What about the benefits? Can you negotiate? You certainly can try. Sometimes you can negotiate better terms for salary, better benefits, or both. A lot of it depends on how much they want you, how much of an asset you will be, and what they can afford.

When negotiating, speak in a calm, well-modulated voice. Do not make threats. State your case and see if you can meet in the middle. If you can't negotiate a higher salary, perhaps you can negotiate extra vacation days. Depending on the company and specific job, compensation may include salary, vacation days, sick days, health insurance, stock options, pension plans, or a variety of other things. Some very high-level jobs in the music industry provide company cars, entertainment allowances, and more. When negotiating, look at the whole package.

You might do some research ahead of time to see what similar types of jobs are paying. Information on compensation may also have been in the original advertisement you answered. General salary ranges on many jobs in the music industry may also be located in *Career Opportunities in the Music Industry* (Checkmark Books, 2004).

Whatever you do in your quest to get a job in the music business, don't undersell yourself. Many people are so desperate to get into the music indus-

try that they take jobs for almost anything. Some come up with salary requirements far below what the company might be willing to offer.

Things to Remember

To give yourself every advantage in acing the interview, there are a few things you should know. First of all, practice ahead of time. Ask friends or family members for their help in setting up practice interviews. You want to get comfortable answering questions without sounding as though you're reading from a script.

Many people go on real "practice interviews." These involve going on interviewers for jobs you might not want in order to get experience in interview situations. Some people think it isn't right to waste an interviewer's time. On the other hand, you can never tell when you might be offered a job that you originally didn't plan on taking but that turns out to be something you want.

Here are some other things to remember to help you land an offer.

◎ If you don't have confidence in yourself, neither will anyone else. No matter how nervous you are, project a confident and positive attitude.

◎ The one who looks and sounds most qualified has the best chance of getting the job. Don't answer questions in monosyllables. Explain your answers using relevant experience. What does that mean? If you're asked if you have good organizational skills, for example, you might say something like, "Yes, I have great organizational skills. When I was an intern at the radio station, I developed a system for organizing all the names and information about people who had entered their promotions. We

---

⭐ **The Inside Scoop**

Accepting a job offer below your perceived salary "comfort level" often results in your resenting your company and coworkers and, even worse, whittles away at your self-worth.

then used the names to send out station newsletters for new station promotions. I was reading *Billboard* during my coffee break and read about a couple stations selling the list to their advertisers, so I suggested it to the advertising director. I have a letter in my portfolio from the advertising director indicating the increase in revenue from just that technique." Use your experiences in both your work and personal life to reinforce your skills, talents, and abilities when answering questions.

◎ Try to develop a rapport with your interviewer. If your interviewer likes you, he or she will often overlook less than perfect skills because you seem like a better candidate.

◎ Smile and make sure you have good posture. It makes you look more successful.

◎ Be attentive. Listen to what the interviewer is saying. If he or she asks a question that you don't understand, politely ask for an explanation.

◎ Turn off your cell phone and beeper before you go into the interview.

◎ When you see the interview coming to a close, make sure you ask when a decision will be made and if you will be contacted either way.

◎ When the interview comes to a close, stand up, thank the interviewer, and then leave.

◎ While you're trying for a job in the music business, remember that it is just that—a business. Act accordingly.

Here are some things you should not do:

◎ Don't smoke before you go into your interview.

◎ Don't chew gum during your interview.

◎ Don't be late.

◎ Don't talk negatively about past bosses, jobs, or companies.

◎ Don't say, "Uh-huh" or "Don't know" or other similar things. It doesn't sound professional and suggests that you have poor communication skills.

◎ Don't wear heavy perfume or men's cologne before going on an interview. You can never tell if the interviewer is allergic to various odors.

◎ Don't interrupt the interviewer.

◎ While you certainly can ask questions, don't try to dominate the conversation to try to "look smart."

◎ Don't drop names. People in the music industry frown on this.

Thank-You Notes

It's always a good idea to send a note thanking the person who interviewed you for his or her time. Think a thank-you note is useless? Think again. Take a look at some of the things a thank-you note can do for you:

◎ show that you are courteous and have good manners

◎ show that you are professional

◎ give you one more shot at reminding the interviewer who you are

◎ show that you are truly interested in the job

◎ illustrate that you have good written communication skills

◎ give you a chance to briefly discuss something that you thought was important yet forgot to bring up during the interview

◎ help you stand out from other job applicants who didn't send a thank-you note

Try to send thank-you notes within 24 hours of your interview. You can handwrite or type them. While it's acceptable to e-mail or fax them, I suggest mailing.

What should the letter say? It can simply say thank you or it can be longer. For example:

> Dear Mr. Garofalo:
>
> Thanks for taking the time to interview me yesterday for the assistant marketing director position at your record label. As I indicated during our meeting, I am sure the experience I gained handling marketing for a national record chain will transfer well to the record label.
>
> I feel that I would be a good match for the job and an asset to the label. I look forward to hearing from you and hope that I am able to help with the push to make the artists on your label number one!
>
> Thanks once again.
>
> > Sincerely yours,
> > Gene Handy

> Dear Ms. Green:
>
> While I was excited when I heard there was a job opportunity as a booking agent trainee at your company, I was absolutely thrilled about the possibilities after speaking to you. Thank you so much for taking the time not only to interview me but also to explain all the intricacies of your agency. You made me feel as though I would fit right in.
>
> I look forward to hearing from you about your choice of candidates for the position and am truly hoping that it's me.
>
> Thanks again.
>
> > Sincerely,
> > Gina Hastings

Waiting for an Answer

You've gone through the interview for the job you want. You've done everything you can do. Now what? Unfortunately, now you have to wait for an answer. Are you the chosen candidate? Hopefully, you are.

If you haven't heard back in a week or so (unless you were given a specific date when an applicant would be chosen), call and ask the status of the job. If you are told that they haven't made a decision, ask when a good time to call back would be.

If you are told that a decision has been made and it's not you, say thank you, tell them you appreciate the consideration, and request that your resume be kept on file for the future. You might just get a call before you know it. If the company is large, such as a record label or major agency, ask if other positions are available and how you should go about applying if you are interested.

If your phone rings and you got the job, congratulations! Welcome to a great job in the music industry. Once you get a call telling you that you are the candidate they want, depending on the situation, they will either make an offer on the phone or you will have to go to the company to discuss your compensation package. If an offer is made on the phone, you have every right to ask if you can think about it and get back to them in 24 hours. If you are satisfied with the offer as it is, you can accept it.

Depending on the job, you may be required to sign an employment contract. Read the agreement thoroughly and make sure that you are comfortable signing it. If there is anything you don't understand, ask. Don't just sign without reading. You want to know what you are agreeing to.

9

Marketing Yourself for Success

What Marketing Can Do for You

How badly do you want success? Do you know that there's a way to increase your chances to get what you want? Do you want to know the inside track on becoming successful and getting what you want? It's simple; all you have to do is market yourself.

Every successful product, event, and person utilizes marketing strategies in some manner. This includes everything from new toys, hot trends, blockbuster movies, top TV shows, hot CDs, music videos, and mega-superstars. You can do the same thing for yourself!

If you need proof of this, look at any of the major popular music stars on the charts now. Sure they can sing, but a great deal of their celebrity status comes from marketing. You don't even have to look at contemporary stars. Look at Elvis Presley. His popularity began in the 1950s and spanned through 1977, when he died. Today, his estate is worth more than on the day he died. Why? The people in charge of his estate are masters of marketing.

Thousands of people want to be musicians, singers, and songwriters. Some make it, and some don't. Is it all talent? A lot of it has to do with talent, but that is not everything. Thousands of talented musicians, singers, and songwriters

haven't made it, so what is the key to success? As we've discussed, in addition to talent, probably a lot of it has to do with luck and being in the right place at the right time. The other factor that seems to set one artist apart from another is the way they were marketed.

Whether you are seeking a career on the business end of the industry or in the talent area, marketing can help you become one of the hottest commodities around.

What is marketing? On the most basic level, marketing is finding markets and avenues to sell products or services. In this case, you are the product. The buyers are employers if you are looking for a traditional job or fans, managers, booking agents, and so on if you are a performer.

To be successful, you not only want to be the product; you want to be the brand. Look at Nabisco, Kelloggs, McDonalds, and Disney. Look at Donald Trump, a master marketer who understands this concept. He branded himself. He continues to illustrate to people how he can fill their needs. Then he finds new needs he can fill. If you're savvy, you can do the same.

If you know or can determine what you can do for an employer or what can help them, you can market yourself to illustrate how you can fill those needs. If you can sell and market yourself effectively, you can succeed in your career; you can push yourself to the next level and you can get what you want.

Is there a secret to this? No, there really isn't a secret, but it does take some work. In the end, however, the payoff will be worth it.

Do you want to be the one who gets the job? Marketing can help. Want to make yourself visible so potential employers will see you as desirable? Marketing can help. Do you want to set yourself apart from other job candidates? Guess what? Marketing can help. It can also distinguish you from other employees. If you have marketed yourself effectively, when promotions, raises, or in-house openings are on the horizon, your name will come up. Marketing can give you credibility and open the door to new opportunities.

If you're pursuing a career on the talent end of the industry, marketing is just as important. Do you want to stand out from every other singer, musician, and songwriter? You know what you have to do. Market yourself. Do you want to become more visible? Get the attention of the media? Do you want to get the attention of agents, managers, labels, promoters, and other important people? Do you want to open up the door to new opportunities? Do you want to become a star? Market yourself!

"Okay," you're saying. "I get it. I need to market myself. But how?"

That's what we're going to talk about now. To begin with, understand that in order to market yourself or your act effectively, you are going to have to do what every good marketer does. You're going to have to develop your product, perform market research, and assess the product and the marketplace. Now let's get busy.

The Five Ps of Marketing and How They Relate to Your Career

There are five Ps to marketing, whether you're marketing a hot new restaurant, your career, your music, your act, or anything else. They are

◎ product
◎ price
◎ positioning
◎ promotion
◎ packaging

Let's look at how these Ps relate to your career.

◎ *Product:* In this case, as I just mentioned, the product is *you.* "Me," you say. "How am I a product?" You are a package complete with your physical self, skills, ideas, and talents. If you're on the talent end of the industry, your product might also include your act, your songs, your music, and your creativity.

◎ *Price:* Price is the compensation you receive for your work. As you are aware, there can be a huge range of possible earnings for any one job. On the talent end of the industry, there can be an even greater range. One singer might be paid $100 to perform for an evening. Another may command thousands. Your goal in marketing yourself is to sell your talents, skills, and anything else you have to offer for the best possible compensation.

◎ *Positioning:* What positioning means in this context is developing and creating innovative methods to fill the needs of one or more employers, record companies, fans, or other potential clients. It also means differentiating yourself and/or your talent from other competitors. Depending on your career area, this might mean differentiating yourself from other employees, singers, songwriters, musicians, bands, and so on.

◎ *Promotion:* Promotion is the promotion and implementation of methods that make you or your act visible in a positive manner.

◎ *Packaging:* Packaging is the way you present yourself or your act.

Putting Together Your Package

Now that we know how the five Ps of marketing are related to your career, let's discuss a little more about putting together your package.

The more you know about your product (you), the easier it is to market and sell it. It's also essential to know as much as possible about the markets to which you are trying to sell. What do you have to offer that a potential buyer (employer) needs? If you can illustrate to a market (employer) that you are the package that can fill their needs, you stand a good chance to turn the market into a buyer.

Assess what you have to offer as well as what you think an employer needs. We've already discussed self-assessment in Chapter 4. Now review your skills and your talents to help you determine how they can be used to fill the needs of your target markets.

While all the Ps of marketing are important, packaging is one of the easiest to change. It's something you have control over.

How important is packaging? Very! Good packaging can make a product more appealing and more enticing and make you want it. Not convinced? Think about the last time you went to the store. Did you reach for the name-brand

products more often than the bargain brand? Not convinced? How many times have you been in a bakery or at a party and chosen the beautifully decorated deserts over the simple un-iced cake? Packaging can make a difference—a big difference—in your career. If you package yourself or your act effectively, people will want it.

Want to know a secret? Many job candidates in every industry are passed over before they get very far in the process because they simply don't understand how to package themselves. What does this mean to you? It means that if you get the concept, you're ahead of the game. In a competitive industry such as music, this can give you the edge. Knowing that a marketing campaign utilizes packaging to help sell products means that you want to package yourself as well as you can. You want potential employers, record labels, managers, agents, and others to see you in the most positive manner possible. You want to illustrate that you have what it takes to fill their needs. So what does your personal package include?

People base their first impression of you largely on your appearance. Whether you are going for an interview for a hot job in the music industry or currently working and trying to move up the career ladder, appearance is always important.

It might seem elementary, but let's go over the elements of your appearance. Personal grooming is essential. What does that mean?

Words from a Pro
Even if you are interviewing for an entry-level job, dress professionally. You want your interviewer to see that you are looking for a career, not just a job.

Words from the Wise

Strong perfume, cologne, and after-shave often make people not want to be near you. Many people are allergic to strong odors. Many just can't stand the smell. You don't want to be known as the one who wears that stinky stuff. If you wear scents, go light.

◎ Your hair should be clean and neatly styled.

◎ You should be showered with no body odor.

◎ Your nails should be clean. If you polish them, make sure that your polish isn't chipped.

◎ If you are a man, you should be freshly shaved, and mustaches and beards should be neatly styled.

◎ If you are a woman, your makeup should look natural and not overdone.

◎ Your breath should be clean and fresh.

Good grooming is important whether you're on the talent end of the industry or the business end. Of course, there might be situations in the talent or performance areas of the business where you are building a specific type of image and some of these points don't apply.

Now let's discuss your attire. This advice is more appropriate for the business end of the industry. Attire on the performance or talent end will probably be different, especially if you're on stage.

It's important whether you're interviewing, in a networking situation, or already on the job to dress appropriately. What's appropriate? Good question.

Remembering that the music industry is a business, you want to look professional, but like other creative fields, the music industry is often more fashion conscious and accepting of fashion trends than other industries. This means you might have more leeway in the dress code at a job at a record label or other music industry business than, for example, a job at a bank or an insurance company. Mini-skirts are not appropriate for working in a lawyer's office, but they might be acceptable at a label. Similarly, jeans might not be appropriate for working at a book publishing house, but they might be very appropriate at a recording studio or a music publisher.

Always dress to impress. Employers want to see that you will not only fit in but that you will not embarrass them when representing the company. So what should you do? What should you wear?

If you are going on an interview, dress professionally. If you're a man, you can never go wrong in a suit and tie or a pair of dress slacks with a jacket, dress shirt, and tie. Women might wear a suit, a professional-looking dress, a skirt and jacket, or a skirt and blouse. Once you're hired, learn the company dress policy. It's okay to ask. No matter what the policy is, observe what everyone else is wearing. If the policy is casual and everyone is still dressed in business attire, dress in business attire.

Tip from the Top

Here's a tip for career advancement. Check out what the higher-ups are wearing and emulate them. If you dress like you're already successful, not only you will feel more successful, but you will set yourself apart in a positive way in your superior's eyes.

Your communication skills, both verbal and written, are yet another part of your package. What you say and how you say it can mean the difference between success and failure in getting a job or succeeding at one you already have. You want to sound articulate, polished, strong, and confident.

Do you ever wonder how others hear you? Consider using a tape recorder, recording yourself speaking, and then playing it back.

Is this scary? It can be if you've never heard yourself. Here's what to remember. No matter what you think you sound like, it probably isn't that bad. You are probably your own worst critic.

When you play back your voice, listen to your speech pattern. You might, for example, find that you are constantly saying "uh" or "uh-huh." You might find that your voice sounds nasal or high pitched or that you talk too quickly. If you're not happy with the way you sound, there are exercises you can do to practice to change your pitch, modulation, and speech pattern.

Because you can't take words back into your mouth after you say them, here are some *don'ts* to follow when speaking.

◎ Don't use off-color language.
◎ Don't swear or curse.
◎ Don't tell jokes or stories that have either sexual or racial undertones or innuendoes.
◎ Don't interrupt others when they are speaking.

Voice of Experience

If you're not sure whether you should say something, don't say it.

◎ Don't use poor grammar or slang.
◎ Don't use words like *ain't*.

We've discussed your verbal communication skills; now let's discuss the importance of your written communication skills. Here's the deal: Whatever your career choice, you need at least basic written communication skills. You need to be able to compose simple letters, memos, and reports. If you are uncomfortable with your writing skills, either pick up a book to help improve them or consider taking a basic writing class at a local school or college.

Your body language can tell people a lot about you. The way you carry yourself can show others how you feel about yourself. We've all seen people in passing who are hunched over or look uninterested or just look like they don't care. Would you want one of them working for *you?* Generally, neither do most employers.

What does your body language illustrate? Does it show that you are confident? That you are happy to be where you are? Do you make eye contact when you're speaking to someone? Are you smiling? What about your demeanor? Common courtesy is mandatory in your life and your career. Polite expressions such as "please," "thank you," "excuse me," and "pardon me" will not go unnoticed.

Your personality traits are another part of your package. No one wants to be around a whiner, a sad sack, or people who complain constantly. You want to illustrate that you are calm, happy, well balanced, and have a positive attitude. You want to show that you can deal effectively with others, are a team player, and can deal with problems and stress effectively. You might be surprised to know that in many cases employers will lean toward hiring someone with a bubbly, positive, and energetic personality over one with better skills who seems negative and less well balanced.

Last but not least in your package are your skills and talents. These are the things that make you special. What's the difference between skills and talents?

Skills can be learned or acquired. Talents are things you are born with and can be embellished. Your personal package includes both.

What you must do is package the product so the buyer wants it. In this case, the product is you and the buyer is a potential employer, manager, agent, or fan. Now you know what goes into your package, and you're going to work on putting together your best possible package. What's next?

Marketing Yourself like a Pro and Making Yourself Visible

How can you market yourself? If you're like many people, you might be embarrassed to promote yourself, embarrassed to talk about your accomplishments, and embarrassed to bring them to the attention of others. This feeling probably comes from childhood when you were taught "it isn't nice to brag."

It's time to change your thinking. It's time to toot your own horn! If you do this correctly, you won't be bragging; you will simply be taking a step to make yourself visible. Want to know the payoff? You can move your career in a positive

Tip from the Coach

Be positive about yourself and don't be self-deprecating, even in a joking manner. Many people start doing this because they want the person with whom they are speaking to say, "No you're not." The truth is, when you're self-deprecating you will start believing it and so will the people with whom you are speaking.

direction quicker. Career success can be yours, but you need to work at it.

Visibility is important in every aspect of business and the music industry is no exception. Whether you want to make it on the talent end of the industry or the business side, visibility can help you attain your goals. What can visibility do for you?

To start with, it can help set you apart from others who might have similar skills and talents.

How can you make yourself visible?

◎ Tell people what you are doing.
◎ Tell people what you are *trying* to do.
◎ Share your dreams.
◎ Live your dreams.
◎ Send out press releases.
◎ Toot your own horn.
◎ Make it happen.

When you make yourself visible, you will gain visibility in the workplace, the community, the media, and more. This is essential to getting what you want and what you deserve in your career, whether it's the brand-new job you want in the music business, a promotion pushing you up the career ladder, or your shot at success as a performer.

We'll discuss how you can tell people what you're doing without bragging later, but first, let's discuss when it's appropriate to toot your own horn. Here are some situations:

◎ when you get a new job
◎ when you get a promotion
◎ when you sign a record deal
◎ when you are awarded a gold or platinum record
◎ when you go on tour
◎ when you sign an agreement with a booking or management agency
◎ when you have a special appearance scheduled

- when you are going to be (or have already appeared) on television or radio
- when you sign a song publishing agreement
- when someone records your song
- when you have a major accomplishment
- when you receive an honor or an award
- when you chair an event
- when you graduate from school, college, or a training program
- when you obtain professional certification
- when you work with a not-for-profit organization on a project

And the list goes on. The idea isn't only to make people aware of your accomplishments but to make yourself visible in a positive manner. These are the reasons you would toot your own horn, but how do you do it? Well, you could shout your news from a rooftop or walk around with a sign, but that probably wouldn't be very effective.

One of the best ways to get the most bang for your buck is by utilizing the media.

"I don't have money for an ad," you say.

Well, here's the good news. You don't have to take out an ad. You can use publicity. Newspapers, magazines, and periodicals need stories to fill their pages. Similarly, television and radio need to fill airspace as well. If you do it right, your story can be among the ones filling that space, and it will cost you next to nothing.

Tip from the Top

A press release is not an ad. Ads cost money. There is no charge to send press releases to the media. Press releases are used by the media to develop stories or are edited slightly or published as is.

Words from a Pro

Many of the stories you read in newspapers and magazines or hear on the radio or television are the direct result of press releases. Don't make the mistake of not sending out press releases because you think the media won't be interested.

How do you get your news to the media? The easiest way is by sending out press or news releases.

Developing and writing press releases is discussed in depth in a later section. Generally, however, press releases are composed of answering the five Ws:

- Who
  - Who are you writing about?
- What
  - What is happening or has happened?
- When
  - When did it happen or is it happening?
- Where
  - Where is it happening or has it happened?
- Why
  - Why is it happening or why is it noteworthy or relevant?

While it would be nice for everyone to have their own personal press agent, this usually isn't the case. You are going to have to be your own publicist. To market yourself, you'll have to find opportunities to issue press releases, develop them, and send them out. You want your name to be visible in a positive manner as often as possible.

Let's look at an example. Let's say Jim Pennington is a singer, songwriter, and musician. He has recently heard that the local school systems are planning to cut music programs out of the school budget.

"So what?" you say. "I'm not even in school now."

Well, neither is Jim Pennington, but he remembered how school music programs helped him when he was younger. It bothered him that others wouldn't have the same types of opportunities. So Jim decided to do something. He decided to launch a campaign letting people know about the negative repercussions of cutting these programs. In the process, he is becoming visible for doing something good as well as getting his name and music out there.

In order to help get the word out, Jim would send out a press release like this:

**NEWS FROM
JIM PENNINGTON**
PO Box 222
Some City, NY 11111
Media: For additional information, contact Jim Pennington, 222-222-2222
For Immediate Release:
Pennington Snagged By

Jim Pennington of Some City, New York, will be a guest on WAAB's popular *Paul Hudson Show* on Tuesday, September 6 at 8:00 P.M. He will be discussing the importance of keeping music programs in the school system.

Local school systems in four districts have recently announced that due to budgetary problems, they are considering cutting music programs. This would include elective music classes as well as band, chorus, and all after-school music activities.

Pennington has launched a campaign to help let people know the importance of music to youngsters in school. "My high school music teacher was the one who told me I could actually have a career in the music industry," noted Pennington. "Before that everyone told me it was a pipe dream." He continued, "High school band, singing in chorus, all the extracurricular music activities . . . that's what started me off. I want every youngster to have the same opportunities I had."

A talented songwriter, singer, and musician, Pennington has penned more than 100 songs. One of his tunes, "I'm A Winner," was just recorded by up-and-coming artists Joyous Bench. Pennington, who regularly appears at clubs around the tristate area, will be recording his own CD later this year.

According to Pennington, studies indicate that school music programs help children in a number of ways, including developing self-esteem, self-worth, and self-confidence. Pennington said that the studies also illustrated that music helped youngsters excel in math, English, and a number of other subject areas.

The appearance on Paul Hudson's show will kick off the campaign to stop the cutting of music programs in the schools. Pennington will be speaking to local school boards, acting as MC at a number of upcoming rallies, and taking part in a full-fledged media campaign. He will also be appearing at a benefit concert next month aimed to help raise awareness of the problems associated with lack of music education in the school system.

"My dream was to work in the music industry," said Pennington. "I am extremely lucky to be living my dream. I want every youngster to have the same benefits I did."

What does this press release do? In addition to publicizing Pennington's appearance, it gets his name in the news. It gets his message out. It exposes his career accomplishments and helps keep him in the pubic eye in a positive way. By Pennington using this avenue to market himself, he is putting himself in a different light from those who are not doing so.

Make sure your press releases look professional by printing them on press or news release stationary. Always have someone else read them not only for errors but to make sure they make sense. This can easily be created on your computer. Have the words "News" or "News From" or something to that effect someplace on the stationary so the media is aware it is a press release. Also make sure to include your contact information. This is essential in case the media wants to call to ask questions about your release. In many instances, the media just uses the press release as a beginning for an article. Once you pique their interest, they use the press release as background and write their own story.

So, you've developed a press release. Now what? Whether it's about getting a promotion, being named employee of the month, signing a contract, or anything else, developing and

Words from the Wise

Remember that just because you send a press release doesn't mean it will get into the publication. Small local publications are likely to eventually use your press releases. Larger publications are more discriminatory. Do not call up media and insist that they use your release. This will make you look like an amateur, and they will probably ignore your releases from that day forward.

The Inside Scoop

Always be ready for the media. Keep stock paragraphs on your computer so you can turn out press releases quickly when needed. You might want to keep stock press releases and bios on hand so you're always ready when the media calls. Make it easier to issue press releases by setting up sheets of labels. That way, when you're ready to send out a mailing, you need only stick labels on envelopes.

writing a great press release is just the first step. Once that's done, you have to get the releases to the media.

How do you do this? You have a few options. You can print the press releases and then send or fax them to the media or you can e-mail them. Either way, it's essential to put together a media list so you can reach the correct people. Look around your area. Get the names of your local media. Then find regional media. If your stories warrant it, national or trade media should also be included. Don't forget any Web or online publications.

Call up each and ask who press releases should be directed toward. Sometimes it will be a specific person. Sometimes it may just be "News Editor." Then get their contact information. Put together a database consisting of the name of the publication or station, contact name or names, address, phone, and fax numbers, e-mail, and any other pertinent information. You might, for example, find out the publication's deadline. The deadline is the day you need to get the information to the publication so that your news can be considered for the next issue.

Send your press releases to all applicable publications and stations. The idea with press releases is to send them consistently. Keep in

> ### ★ Tip from the Top
>
> If you're e-mailing press releases, find out what format they accept ahead of time. If you're sending out printed press releases, you might also call to find out what font is preferred. Many smaller publications just scan your release, and certain fonts scan better.

mind that while you don't want to write a press release about *nothing,* anytime you have *anything* noteworthy for which to send out a press release, you should.

Becoming an Expert

Want another idea to make yourself visible? Become an expert. You probably already are an expert in one or more areas either in or out of the music industry. Now it's time for you to exploit it.

Many people are used to the things they know well. They don't give enough credence to being great at them. It's time to forget that type of thinking!

One of the wonderful things about being an expert in any given area is that people will seek you out. Everyone knows how to do something better than others. You have to figure out what it is.

"Okay," you say. "You're right. Let's say I'm an expert cook. But what does that have to do with the music business?"

It might have nothing to do with the music business on the surface. However, if it can help you gain some positive attention and visibility, it will give you another avenue to get your story out. This will help you achieve the career success you desire. So with that in mind, it has everything to do with it.

Let's begin by determining where your expertise is. Sit down with a piece of paper and

spend some time thinking about what you can do better than anyone else in or out of the music business. What subject or area do you know more about than most? Do you volunteer in an interesting area?

Need some help? Can't think of what your expertise is? Here are some ideas to get you started.

◎ Are you a gourmet cook?
◎ Do you bake the best brownies?
◎ Are you a trivia expert?
◎ Are you a master gardener?
◎ Can you speak more than one language fluently?
◎ Do you love to shop?
◎ Do you know how to coordinate just the right outfit?
◎ Are you an expert at organizing?
◎ Do you know how to write great songs?
◎ Do you know how to write great press releases?
◎ Do you know how to pack a suitcase better than most people?
◎ Are you an expert organizer?
◎ Do you know how to arrange flowers?
◎ Are you an expert in building things?
◎ Are you a great fund-raiser?
◎ Do you volunteer teaching people to read?
◎ Do you know about helping children with special needs?
◎ Do you have special skills or talents that others don't?

Are you getting the idea? You can be an expert in almost any area. The way in which you exploit it can make a difference in your career.

You want to get your name out there. You want to draw positive attention to yourself. You want others to know what you can do. That way, you can market yourself in the areas in which you are interested.

Find ways to get your name and your story out there. How? Developing and sending out press releases is one way, but what else can you do?

You can become known for your expertise by talking about it. How? Most areas have civic or other not-for-profit groups that hold meetings. These groups often look for people to speak at their meetings. You can contact the president of the board or the executive director to find out who sets up the meeting speakers. In some areas, the chamber of commerce also puts together speaker lists.

You might be asking yourself, "Unless I'm a rocket scientist, why would any group want to hear me speak about anything? What would anyone want to know about me knowing how to pack a suitcase?" or "Why would anyone be interested in my organizing ability?"

Here's the answer: They might not, *unless* you tailor your presentations to their needs. If you create a presentation from which others can learn something useful or interesting, they usually will. For example, if you're speaking to a group of business people, you might do a presentation about "The Stress Free Bag: Packing Easily For Business Trips," "Organize Your Career, Organize Your Life," "Helping Children In Need," or "Making Money In Music." Whatever your subject matter is when you speak in front of a group, whether it be 20 or 2000 people, you will gain visibility. When you are introduced, the host of the event will often mention information about your background to the audience. Make sure you always have a short paragraph or two with you to make it easy for the emcee to present the information you want to convey.

For example, based on information you provide, the emcee might introduce you like this: "Good evening, folks. Our dinner speaker tonight is Mary Lear. Mary will be speaking about how you can make your life easier by organizing things. Mary has to organize her life creatively, or she would never get anything done. While she is currently working full time as an administrative assistant at WFAB radio, she is also fitting us in between singing appearances at some of the local nightclubs in town. Let's give a warm welcome to Mary Lear."

As you can see, Mary is getting exposure, which is an asset to her career at the radio station. More important, people at her presentation might just stop by one of the local clubs to hear her sing. One of these people just might be connected to the music industry.

On a local level, you will do most of these types of presentations for no fee. The benefit of increased visibility, however, will usually be well worth it. When you are scheduled to do a presentation, make sure you send out press releases announcing your speech. If it was a noteworthy event, you might also send out a release after the event as well. Many organizations will also call the media to promote the occasion. Sometimes the media will call you for an interview before the event. Take advantage of every opportunity.

It's exciting once you start getting publicity. Take advantage of this too. Keep clippings of all the stories from the print media. Make copies. If you have appeared or have been interviewed on television or radio, get clips. Keep these for your portfolio. Every amount of positive exposure will help set you apart from others and help you market yourself to career success.

"Oh, no," you say. "I'm not getting up to speak in public."

> ## ★ Words from a Pro
> The media works on very tight deadlines. If they call you, get back to them immediately, or you might lose out.

If you don't feel comfortable speaking in public, you don't have to. Use any of these ideas to get you started and then find ways you are comfortable in marketing yourself.

More Strategies to Market and Promote Yourself

If you aren't comfortable speaking in public, how about writing an article on your area of expertise instead? Or how about writing an article on life as an up-and-coming singer or songwriter? You might also consider writing articles or columns for newspaper or magazines on a given subject. The idea once again is to keep your name in the public's eye in a positive manner.

How do you get your articles in print? Call the editor of the publication you are interested in writing for and ask! Tell them what you want to do, and offer to send your background sheet, resume, or bio and a sample. Small or local publications might not pay very much. Don't get hung up on money. You are not doing this for cash. You are doing it to get your name and your story before the public.

If you are a good writer, like writing, are already working in a music-oriented company, and want to move up the career ladder, think about offering to put together a periodical column for your company's newsletter. They don't have one? Offer to put one together. Why? It will bring you visibility. You will have opportunities to meet and converse with higher-ups that you might not otherwise speak with.

Consider doing this even if you're not currently working in a music-oriented company.

"I'm just here until I get the job at the record company," you say.

True, but while you're there, why wouldn't you want to excel? As we've discussed, you can never tell who knows who. Someone in your company reading your newsletter might just mention that they don't know why you're editing the newsletter as a special project when you really want to work in the music industry. Coincidentally, they might just be saying it to someone who knows someone in the music industry. Think it can't happen? It can.

Don't forget to tell media editors about your expertise. You can call them or send a short note. Ask that they put you on a list of experts for your specific area if they are working on a story that relates to your subject.

Remember that if you don't make the call or write the note, no one will know what you have to offer. You have to sometimes be assertive (in a nice way) to get things moving.

Consider teaching a class, giving a workshop, or facilitating a seminar in your area of expertise. Everyone wants to learn how to do something new, and you might be just the person to give them that chance. Every opportunity for you is an opportunity to become visible and move your career forward. Can you give someone the basics of songwriting? Offer to teach a class at a local college or school. What a great way to get your name out if you're a songwriter! Have you been booking your band yourself? Offer to teach a class about managing a performing group for a local school.

The Inside Scoop

Don't get caught up in the theory that if you help someone do something or learn how to do something, it will in some way take away opportunities from you. Help others when you can.

What can your expertise do for you? It will get your name out there. It will give you credibility, and it will give you visibility. Of course, when you're at meetings or speaking to the media, it's up to you to network. Tell people what you do. Tell people what you want to do. Give out cards.

Join professional associations and volunteer to be on committees or to chair events that they sponsor. Similarly, join civic groups and not-for profit organizations volunteering to work on one or two of their projects.

"I don't have time," you say.

Make time. Volunteering, especially when you chair a committee or work on a project, is one of the best ways to get your name out there, obtain visibility, and network.

Here's an idea that most people are afraid of trying. Offer to be a guest on radio, cable, and television station news, variety, and information shows.

"Who would want me?" you ask.

You can never tell. If you don't ask, no one will even know you exist in many instances.

Check out the programming to see where you might fit. Then send your bio with a letter to the producer, indicating that you're available to speak in a specific subject area. Pitch an idea. A producer just might take you up on it.

Here's a sample pitch letter to get you started.

Terry Lewis-Producer
WAAA-Radio
Everyone Is Talking Show
PO Box 111
Anytown, NY 22222

Dear Ms. Lewis:

As far back as I can remember, I have wanted to work in the music industry. I know that it is a dream many have. I got lucky. Last summer I landed an internship at Millionaire Booking Agency. When I graduated college, I was offered a job as an administrative assistant to one of the top agents at the company. I have recently moved and been promoted to a position as an assistant agent.

I would love to share some of my stories with your listeners. I believe that the subject matter fits well into your show's format.

I have included my background sheet for your review. Please let me know if you require additional information.

I look forward to hearing from you.

Sincerely,
Gina Hastings

Wait a week or so after sending the letter. If you don't hear back, call the producer and ask if he or she is interested. If there is no interest, say thank you, and ask if your background sheet can be kept on file.

Remember that people talk to each other so that every person you speak in front of who reads an article about you, who hears you on radio, or sees you on television has the potential of speaking to other people who might then speak to others.

As we've discussed, networking is one of the best ways to get a job, get a promotion, and advance your career. If you're on the talent end of the industry, the same concept applies. Even if your expertise is something totally not involved in the music industry, you can use your expertise to boost your career.

Now, if your expertise happens to be something related to the music business, that's even better. What might that be? You might be an expert in getting publicity. You might have expertise in getting gigs. You might even be an expert in getting into the music industry. Whatever your expertise, exploit it and it will help your career move forward.

More Marketing Techniques to Get You Noticed

Many charities and not-for-profit groups sponsor charity auctions. If you're a performer and looking for a way to get noticed, here's an idea: Donate your services.

"What's in it for me?" you ask.

Aside from doing some good for a worthwhile organization, you probably can get a ton of exposure. There are a couple ways to do it. You can offer to perform gratis at the event or you can donate your services for the auction. What's that mean? Depending on what your talent is, you could, for example, donate a one- or two-hour concert to the winning bidder. If your act is a band, you might donate the entertainment for the winning bidder's event. Most people bidding at these type of auctions are con-

nected to the community and its businesses in some manner. You will be building goodwill. You will be opening up new markets for your act and have opportunities to network.

Here's another idea that can get you noticed: A feature story in a newspaper or magazines. How do you get one of these? Well, everyone wants a story about them or their product or service, so you have to develop an angle to catch their attention. Then contact a few editors and see if you can get one of them to bite. Before you call anyone, however, think out your strategy. What is your angle? Why are you the person someone should talk to or do a story on? Why would the story be interesting or unique or entertaining to the reader.

How do you develop an angle? Come up with something unique that you do or are planning to do. What is the unique part of your package? Were you the runner up in a talent competition? Everyone wants to talk to the winner. How about giving the story from the one who didn't win?

Send a letter with your idea, a background sheet or bio, and press kit if you have one. Wait a week and then call the editor you sent your information to. Ask if he or she received your information. (There is always a chance it is lost, if only on the reporter's desk.) If the answer is no, offer to send it again and start the process one more time. Sometimes you get lucky. Your angle might be just what an editor was looking for or they might need to fill in a space with a story.

Opening the Door to New Opportunities

If you keep on doing the same old thing, things might change on their own, but they probably

⭐ Tip from the Top

Many people lose out because they just don't follow up. They either feel like a nuisance or feel that they are being a pain. No matter how awkward and uncomfortable you feel, follow up on things you are working on. Be polite, but call to see what's happening.

won't. It's important when trying to create a more successful career to find ways to open the door to new opportunities. Start by moving out of your comfort zone even if it's just a little way. Find new places to go, new people to meet, and new things to do. You are the number-one factor in creating your success.

Try to begin looking at things that happen as new opportunities to make other things happen. If you train yourself to think of how you can use opportunities to help you instead of hinder you, things often start looking up.

Do you want to be around negative people who think nothing is going right, people who think they are losers? Probably not. Well neither does anyone else. Market yourself as a winner, even if you are still a winner in training. The old adage "misery loves company" is true. One problem people often have in their career and life is that they hang around other people who are depressed or think that they're not doing well. Remember that negative energy attracts negative results, so here's your choice. You can either stay with the negative energy, help change the negative energy, or move yourself near positive energy. Which choice do you want to make?

Work on developing new relationships with positive people. Cultivate new business relationships. When doing that, don't forget cultivating a business relationship with the media. How? Go to events where the media is present. Go to chamber of commerce meetings, not-for-profit

Tip from the Coach

If you don't think you're worth something, usually neither will anyone else. In the same vein, if you don't think you're the best, neither will anyone else. Maintain a positive attitude illustrating that you are marketing the best.

organization events, charity functions, entertainment events, meetings, and other occasions.

Walk up, extend your hand, and introduce yourself. Give out your business cards. Engage in conversation. If the reporter writes an interesting story, drop him or her a note saying you enjoyed it. If a newscaster does something special, drop a note telling him or her. The media is just like the rest of us. They appreciate validation.

Don't just be a user. One of the best ways to develop a relationship with the media or anybody else is to be a resource. Help them when you can.

Want to close the door to opportunity? Whine, complain, and be a generally negative person who no one wants to be near. Want the doors to opportunity to fly open? Whatever level you are at, more doors will open if you're pleasant, enthusiastic, and professional.

Dreams can come true. They can happen to you or happen to someone else. If you want it bad enough and market yourself effectively, you will be the winner.

10

SUCCEEDING IN THE WORKPLACE

Learning As You Go

Once you've got the job, what can you do to increase your chances of success and turn your job in the career of your dreams? Lots of people have jobs, but you don't just want a job. You want a great career! To move up the career ladder, you have to do more than is expected of you and put some extra effort into getting what you want.

Once you get your foot in the door of the music industry, do what you can to get to the top. You want to create your perfect career. Getting a job is a job in itself. However, just because you've been hired doesn't mean your work is done. It's essential once you get in to learn as you go. If you look at some of the most successful people, in all aspects of life and business, you'll see that they continue the learning process throughout their life. If you want to succeed, you'll do the same.

Learning is a necessary skill for personal and career growth and advancement. Many think that your ability to learn is linked to your success in life. This doesn't necessarily mean going back to school or taking traditional classes, although sometimes that's a good idea. In many cases, it means life learning. What's life learning? Basically, it's learning that occurs through life experiences. It's learning that occurs when you talk to people, watch others do things, work, experience things, go places, watch television, listen to the radio, hear others talking, or almost anything else. Every experience you have is a potential learning opportunity.

Not only that, but almost everyone you talk to can be a teacher. If you're open to it, you can usually learn something from almost everyone you come in contact with.

"What do you mean?" you ask.

Look for opportunities. Be interested. Everything you learn might not be fascinating, but it might be helpful; maybe not today or tomorrow, but in the future. Sometimes you might learn something work related, sometimes not. It doesn't matter. Use what you can. File the rest away until needed.

How do you learn all this stuff? Observe what people say or do in passing. Sometimes

> ### Tip from the Coach
> While success does sometimes just fly in the window, it always helps to at least open the window first.

you might see that someone has a skill you want to master. Don't be afraid to ask them how to do something. Whether it's simple or complicated, most people are flattered when someone recognizes they're good at something and asks for their help.

Challenge yourself to learn something new every day. Not only will it help improve your total package, but it will make you feel better about yourself. Whether it's a new word, new skill, new way to do something, or even a new way to deal better with people, just continue to learn as you go.

How else can you continue to learn? Take advantage of internships, formal and informal education, company training programs, and volunteer opportunities. Many companies in and out of the music industry have formal volunteer programs. If yours does, take advantage of it. If yours doesn't, you might want to get your company involved in one.

What can you learn? The possibilities are endless. You might learn a new skill or a better way to get along with others. You might learn how to coordinate events or run organizations. You might learn almost anything. And as a bonus, if you volunteer effectively, you might obtain some important visibility.

Don't discount books as a learning tool. Are you an administrative assistant at a record label, but yearn to work as a recording engineer? Look for a book. Read more about it. See if it's a career area you want to pursue. Interested in learn-

ing more about doing publicity? Find a book. Need help in improving your correspondence and letter writing skills? Check out some books for ideas. Want to make sure you're up on the lingo of the music biz? There are tons of books on the music industry. The more you read, the more you'll know. Books often hold the answer to many of your questions. They give you the opportunity to explore opportunities.

Trade journals offer numerous possibilities as well. They'll keep you up to date on industry trends and let you know about industry problems and solutions. What else can you find in the trades? Advertisements for job openings, notices for trade events, and current news. There are a number of trade publications in the music industry, but probably the biggest one is *Billboard*. If you can't find a copy in your workplace, pick up a copy on a regular basis at the newsstand and read it.

How about workshops, seminars, and other courses? In addition to learning new skills in or out of the music industry, there are a number of benefits to going to these. First, you'll have the opportunity to meet other people interested in the same subject area as you. If you're attending classes or seminars about the music industry, you'll also be able to network with people. Instructors, facilitators, and even other students in the class are all potential contacts who might be instrumental in your career.

If you continue to navigate your way through formal and informal learning experiences throughout your life and career, you will be rewarded with success and satisfaction.

Workplace Politics

To succeed in your career in the music industry, it's essential to learn how to deal effectively with some of the challenging workplace situations you'll encounter. Workplace politics are a part of life. The real trick to dealing with them is trying to stay out of them. No matter which side you take in an office dispute, you're going to be wrong. You can never tell who the winner or loser will be, so try to stay neutral and just worry about doing your job. Is this easy? No. But for your own sake, you have to try.

Will keeping out of it work all the time? Probably not, and therein lies the problem. There's an old adage that says the workplace is a jungle. Unfortunately, that's sometimes true.

If you think you're going to encounter politics only in the office, think again. You'll run into them on the talent end of the industry too. In fact, politics are probably part of every area of life, from your personal relationships to family to work. With this in mind, let's learn more about them.

Why are politics in the workplace? Much of it comes from jealousy. Someone might think

you have a better chance at a promotion or are better at your job than they are at theirs. Someone might think you slighted them. Believe it not, someone just might not like you. In any business setting, there are people who vie for more recognition, feel the need to prove themselves right all the time, or just want to get ahead.

There really is nothing you can do about workplace politics except stay out of them to the best of your ability.

When office politics do come into play, they can be in a number of forms, some of which are obvious and some which are not.

Office Gossip

Workplace gossip is a common form of office politics. Anyone who has held a job has probably seen it and perhaps even participated in it in some form. Have you? Well, forget the moral or ethical issues. Gossip can hurt your career.

Here's a good rule of thumb. Never, ever say anything about anyone that you wouldn't mind them hearing and knowing it came from you. If you think you can believe someone who says, "Oh, you can tell me; it's confidential," you're wrong.

"But she's my best friend," you say. "I trust her with my life."

It doesn't matter. Your friend might be perfectly trustworthy, but trust is not always the problem. Sometimes people slip and repeat things during a conversation. Other times a person might tell someone else whom they trust what you said and ask him or her to keep it confidential, but then that person tells another person, and so it goes down the line. Eventually, the person telling the story doesn't even know it's supposed to be confidential and might even mention it to a good friend or colleague of the person everyone has been gossiping about.

The reason people gossip is because it makes them feel like part of a group. It can make you feel like you're smarter or know something other people don't. Most of the time, however, you don't even know if what you're gossiping about is true, yet once a gossip session gets started, it's difficult to stop.

Most people are good at heart. After gossiping about someone else, they often feel bad. It might just be a twinge of conscience, but it's there. Is it worth it? No. Worse than that, it's safe to assume that if you are gossiping about others, they are gossiping about you.

How do you rise above this? Keep your distance. People generally respect that you don't want to be involved. Don't start any gossip, and if someone starts gossiping around you, just don't get involved.

How do you handle the conversation?

Suppose someone says to you, "Did you hear that the boss got so drunk, and he fell over at the party?"

You respond, "No. Have you tasted that great new flavored coffee at the coffee shop?"

They might want to keep the conversation going and say, "Yeah, it's great. You should have seen the boss. I don't know how he can show his face around here."

All you have to do is either change the subject again or say, "I made a decision a long time ago not to get involved in office gossip. It can only get me in trouble."

Every now and then, you hear through the grapevine that people are gossiping about you. It's not a good feeling, but you might have to deal with it. What do you do? You have a few options.

◎ You can ignore it.
◎ You can confront the person or people gossiping about you.

◎ You can start gossiping about the person or people gossiping about you.

What's your best choice? Well, it's definitely not gossiping about the person gossiping about you. Ignoring the gossip might be your best choice, except that suppressing your feelings of betrayal and anger can be stressful. So how about confronting the person or people gossiping about you? If you're certain about who has been spreading the gossip and you can do this calmly and professionally, it often resolves the situation.

Whatever you do, don't have a public confrontation and don't confront a group. Instead, wait until the person is alone. Calmly approach him or her and say something like this:

"Bill, I didn't want to bring this up in front of anyone else, because I didn't want to embarrass you, but I've heard that you've been talking to others in the office about my performance and discussing my personal life. I've always had respect for you, so I really questioned the people who told me it was happening. I'd just like to know if it's true."

At this point, Bill probably will be embarrassed and claim that he doesn't know what you're talking about. He might ask you who mentioned it. Don't give out any names. It's better to let him start questioning the trust of all the people he's been talking to. While he might tell a couple of people you confronted him on the gossip subject, Bill will probably find someone else to gossip about in the future.

In the music industry, office gossip may often lead to bigger problems. Depending on your work environment, you might be privy to private stories about singers, musicians, bands, or other prominent people. They might call the office with problems on the road; you might hear about bands breaking up or personal problems between their members; or you might be privy to contract negotiations.

Here's the deal. Office gossip is bad enough, but gossip regarding those in the music industry or any other part of the entertainment industry often gets to the media and can get totally blown out of proportion. Gossiping about what happens in the office, what you hear, or what you know (even if it is true) can ruin your career, especially if it leads to embarrassment for powerful people.

It's essential to your success in the industry not to spread rumors in the office or out. Don't talk about the inside information you have whether it's good or bad. Don't be surprised if friends and family pump you for information on a musical artist, megastar, or other popular performer whom they know you work with. Learn to simply say, "Sorry, that's confidential."

Workplace Romance

One of the most common office politics situations you might encounter is dating a coworker,

Words from the Wise

Working in the music industry, you might be approached by a news or tabloid reporter who offers money or gifts for a story or information about a specific artist or group associated with your company. Remember one thing: Your loyalty is to the company paying you. Aside from it being ethically wrong to divulge confidential or personal information to the public, you stand a good chance of ruining your career by doing so. No matter how much you are assured your words will be quoted from an anonymous source, your conversation will remain confidential, or any other such promises, say no. Don't even consider giving up any information. If you sell out, someone will eventually find out about it, and no one in the industry will ever trust you again.

supervisor, or client of the company. Should you? Shouldn't you?

This is a delicate situation. Many people think that workplace romances are bad news all around. They can be. However, when you're working eight or more hours a day, your coworkers are the people you spend the most time with. These are the people you see every day, and you often have things in common with them. These are people who want to work in the music industry just like you do, enjoy working in the music industry just like you do, and probably are looking forward to a long career in the music industry just like you are. So, it's not uncommon for office romances to develop.

Are there problems? Yes. Can you work around them? Well, sometimes you can and sometimes you can't. It all depends on the specific situation.

As long as you're dating, things might be great, but what happens if you break up? The answer is that the situation often becomes quite uncomfortable. People take sides. You or your ex might not be able to work together effectively. It may get very stressful even for your other coworkers, so stressful that you or your supervisor might decide it would be better if you left the company. Is it worth it? Only you can answer the question.

Another thing to consider is that others in your workplace may be uncomfortable when coworkers date. They may feel that the dating couple has little secrets or that they keep others out of the loop. If the two of you are constantly whispering to each other, holding hands, or hugging and kissing each other, it might annoy your coworkers.

Is there a way around it? Sometimes. A lot of this has to do with your personality and the personality of the coworker you're dating.

Can you keep things professional? If so, you might be able to swing it. But if you're not positive you can manage a professional attitude when you're dating and if you break up, this type of relationship might be a problem that can jeopardize your career.

Workplace romances can be easier to deal with and less trouble for all involved if you date someone in another department instead of the one in which you work. You still have to act professionally, but it is usually less uncomfortable.

A real problem might develop if you start dating a supervisor. While there are relationships like this that work, be aware that most don't work. If you break up, you are then faced with working with an ex-boyfriend or ex-girlfriend who now holds your career in his or her hands. Is it worth it? Once again, you have to decide. Be aware that dating a supervisor or boss will most likely cause gossip. You might be accused of not working as hard as everyone else. If you get a promotion or a raise, many will think it's because of your relationship.

"I don't care what people say or think," you say.

That's fine, but if it gets in the way of your career, you might think differently. For such a large industry, the music business is still a small world. Your reputation will follow you, so think before you act.

What about dating clients of the company? In normal situations, dating your clients is often

a problem. Dating clients in the music business is often an even bigger problem. Want to really ruin your music career fast? Start dating a client. There are so many scenarios here for what can go wrong that it's hard to zero in on one.

There are a lot of not-so-famous people in the music business, and there are also a lot of famous ones. If you're working at a record label, booking agency, entertainment publicity firm, studio, club, venue, or other music company, there's a good chance you'll have contact with recording artists, singers, musicians, and other entertainers. It's very flattering when a rock star or a recording artist asks you out. It might be hard to turn down. What you have to ask yourself is whether the date or relationship is worth your job. If it is, by all means go for it. If not, think long and hard before getting involved in the relationship.

"What's wrong with it?" you ask.

Clients are the people who make your company money. Anything that stands in the way of that or complicates it will be a problem to your employer.

"But I can keep it professional," you say.

Any problems that arise between the client and your company or with the client in general will probably be blamed on your relationship. Is it fair? No, but unfortunately not everything is fair. Your relationship with a client puts you in a position where you might become a convenient scapegoat when business goes badly.

Want to hear another thing that's not fair? If you're a female and you start dating one of the

Words from the Wise
Do not get into a relationship with a boss or supervisor thinking that it will improve your career. In many cases, it does just the opposite.

> ### ⭐ Tip from the Coach
>
> There's no question that there is a tremendous amount of money to be made in the music industry. Top record label execs, successful songwriters, and major recording artists make big bucks. It's very easy to start comparing your earnings with those of others and feeling sorry for yourself. Try not to compare yourself, your job, or your earnings to anyone else. Instead of concentrating on what "they're making," try to concentrate on how you can get there.

company's male clients, you might be classified as a groupie. Is it fair? No. Is it true? Probably not. But it doesn't matter. That's what people might say about you.

Money, Money, Money

How upset would you be if you found out that a coworker who had a job similar to yours was making more money than you? Probably pretty upset. Whether it's what you're making, your coworker is making, or someone else is making, money is often a problem in the workplace. Why? Because everyone wants to earn more. No matter how much money people are paid for a job, they don't think they're getting enough. If they hear someone is getting paid better than they are, it understandably upsets them.

Here's the deal. If you know you're making more than someone else, keep it to yourself. If you're making less than someone else, keep it to yourself. No matter what your earnings are, keep it to yourself. Don't discuss your earnings with coworkers. The only people in the workplace you should discuss your earnings with are the human resources department and your supervisors.

Why would one person be earning more than another in a similar position? There might be a number of reasons. Compensation for many positions is negotiated, and the person might be a better negotiator. He or she might have more experience, more education, seniority, or different skills.

"But it's frustrating," you say.

Worry about your own job. Don't waste time comparing yourself to your coworkers. Definitely don't whine about it in your workplace. It will get on people's nerves.

What can you do? Make sure you are visible in a positive way. Make sure you're doing a great job. If you're already doing a great job, try to do a better job. Keep notes on projects you've successfully completed, ideas you've suggested that are being used, and things you are doing to make the company better. When it's time for a job review, you'll have the ammunition to not only ask for but get the compensation you deserve.

> ### ⭐ Words from a Pro
>
> Do you like to be around negative people? Probably not. Well, neither does anyone else. We all have bad days when we complain and whine that nothing is going right. The problem comes when it occurs constantly. If you want to succeed in your career, try to limit the negativity, at least around your colleagues. Although they say misery loves company, in reality people won't want to be around you after a while. Eventually, they'll start to avoid you.
>
> On the other hand, most people like to be around positive people who make them smile and laugh. If you can do this, you'll have an edge over others.

Dealing with Colleagues

Whatever area of the music industry you choose to work in, you're going to be dealing with others. Whether they are superiors, subordinates, or colleagues, the way you deal with people you work with will affect your opportunities, your chances of success, and your future.

Many people treat colleagues and superiors well yet treat subordinates with less respect. One of the interesting things about the music business is that career progression doesn't always follow a normal pattern. That means that with the right set of circumstances someone might jump a number of rungs up the career ladder quicker than expected. The result could be someone who is a subordinate might technically become either a colleague or even a superior. It's essential to treat everyone with whom you come into contact with dignity and respect. Aside from showing common courtesy, you can never tell when the person making you coffee today will be at a desk making a decision about your future.

Want to know a secret about dealing effectively with people? If you can sincerely make every person you come in contact with feel special, you will have it made. How do you do this? There are a number of ways.

When someone does or says something intelligent or comes up with a good idea, you might tell him or her. For example, "That was a great idea you had at the meeting, Keo. You always come up with interesting ways to solve problems."

Sometimes you might want to send a short note instead. For example:

Maria,
    While I'm sure you're ecstatic that the press conference is over, I hope you know how im-

pressed everyone was with the event. You handled the coordination like a seasoned pro. No one would ever have guessed that this was the first one you ever put together.

    Everything was perfect. But the real coup was getting the story on every major television station. You did a great job. I'm glad we're on the same team.

                                            Tony

Everyone likes a cheerleader. At home, you have family. In your personal life, you have friends. If you can be a cheerleader to others in the workplace, it often helps to excel yourself.

Never be phony and always be sincere. Look for little things that people do or say as well. "That's a great tie, John." "Nice suit, Amy. You always look so put together." Notice that you're complimenting others; you're not supposed to be self-deprecating. You don't want to make yourself look bad; you want others to look good. For example, you wouldn't say, "Nice suite, Amy. You always look so put together. I couldn't coordinate a suite and blouse if I tried." Or "Great job on the press conference. I never could have coordinated an event like that."

The idea is to build people up so they feel good about themselves. When you can do that, people like to be around you, they gain self-confidence and pass it on to others. One of them might be you. Best of all, you will start to look like a leader—a very important image when you're attempting to move up the career ladder.

Tip from the Coach

In an attempt to build themselves up, many try to tear others down. Unfortunately, it usually has the opposite effect.

Dealing with Superiors

While you are ultimately in charge of your career, superiors are the people who can help either move it along or hold it back. Try to develop a good working relationship with your superiors. A good boss can help you succeed in your present job as well as in your future career.

One of the mistakes many people make in the workplace is looking at their bosses as the enemy. They get a mind-set of *us* against *them.* Worse than that, they sit around and boss-bash with other colleagues.

Want to better your chances of success at your job? Make your boss look good. How do you do that?

◎ Don't boss-bash.
◎ Speak positively about your boss to others.
◎ Do your work.
◎ Cooperate in the office.
◎ If you see something that needs to be done, offer to do it.
◎ Volunteer to help with incomplete projects.
◎ Ask if he or she needs help.

"But what if my boss is a jerk?" you ask. It's still in your best interest to make him or her look good. Believe it or not, it will make you look good.

While we're on the subject, let's discuss bad bosses. With any luck, your boss will be a great person who loves his or her job and always wanted to be in the music industry just like you. But every now and then, you just might run into a bad boss.

He or she might be a jerk, a fool, an idiot.

"I could do a better job than him or her," you say. Well, you might be able to but not if you can't learn to deal so you still have a job. In many cases, your boss has already proven him or herself to the company and is therefore more of a commodity than you are at this point. So just how do you deal with a bad boss and come out on top?

Let's first go over a list of *don'ts*:

◎ Don't be confrontational. This will usually only infuriate your boss.
◎ Don't shout or curse. Even if you're right, you will look wrong.
◎ Don't talk about your boss to coworkers. You can never tell who is who's best friend or who is telling your boss exactly what you're saying.
◎ Don't send e-mails to people from your office about things your boss does or says.
◎ Don't talk about your boss to clients.
◎ Don't cry in your workplace. No matter how mad your boss makes you, keep your composure until you're alone. If you have to, bite your lip, pinch yourself, or do whatever you have to do to keep the tears under control.

Now let's go over a list of *dos* that might help.

◎ Do a good job. It's hard to argue with someone who has done what they are supposed to do.
◎ Keep a paper trail. Keep notes when your boss asks you to do things and when you've done them. Keep notes regarding calls that have been made, dates, times, and so on. Keep a running list of projects you've completed successfully. Do this as a matter of course. Keep it to yourself. If you need something to jog your memory, you can refer to it.
◎ Wait until no one is under a time constraint to finish something and ask

your boss if you can speak to him or her. Then say you'd like to clear the air. Ask what suggestions he or she can give you to do a better job.

◎ Think long and hard before you decide to leave. If your boss is as much of a jerk as you think, perhaps he or she will find a new job or be promoted.

No matter what type of boss you have, learning to communicate with him or her is essential. If you think just because you're both in the music business that you both will be thinking the same, you're probably wrong. Everyone has a different communication style, and it's up to you to determine what his or hers is.

Does your boss like to communicate through e-mail? Some companies today communicate almost totally through e-mail. Everything from the daily "Good morning" until "See you tomorrow" and everything in between will be in your inbox. If this is the way it is at your office, get used to it. E-mail will be your communication style. The good thing about it is you pretty much have a record of everything.

Other bosses communicate mainly on paper. He or she may give you direction, tell you what's happening, or ask for things via typed or handwritten notes. Sometimes communications may be in formal memos formal, other times informal or even on sticky notes.

> **Words from the Wise**
> Do not put anything in e-mail that you wouldn't mind someone else reading. No matter what anyone tells you, e-mail is not confidential. Furthermore, be aware that in many situations your e-mails, private or business, may be classified as company property. This means management may have the right to access your e-mail.

> **Tip from the Top**
> Check out your company's policy on private e-mail. Be aware that in many situations, private e-mails are not allowed.

A great deal of the business in the music industry is done by phone. Good phone etiquette is essential. If you or your boss is on the road or you are dealing with clients, the phone may be a major communications tool. Learn how to use it effectively.

It's important to realize that you have a choice in your career. You can sit there and hope things happen or you can make them happen. You can either be passive or proactive. To succeed in your career, proactive is usually a better choice.

You can go to work and let your boss tell you what to do, or you can do that little bit extra, share your dreams and aspirations, and work toward your goals. Your boss and supervisors can help you make it happen.

Ethics, Morals, and More

We all have our own set of ethics and morals. They help guide us on what we think is right and wrong. In your career, you may be faced with situations where a person or group of people want you to do something you know or feel is wrong. In return for doing it, you may be promised financial gain or career advancement.

Would you do it? "Well," you might say. "That depends on what I'd have to do and what I'd get." Here's the deal. No matter what anyone wants you to do, if you know it's wrong, even if you only think it might be wrong, it probably is a bad idea.

"But they told me no one would know," you say. Most people are not very good at

> ### Tip from the Top
> If you carry a personal cell phone, set it to the vibrate mode while in the office. Getting constant calls from friends in the office even on your cell phone is inappropriate.

keeping secrets, and if they get caught, you're going down too. If you're just getting started in your career, you might be looking at ending it for a few dollars. If you're already into your career, are you really prepared to lose everything you worked that hard to get?

"But they told me if I did this or did that, they'd remember me when promotions came up," you say. But how do you know someone isn't testing you to see what your morals are? And exactly what are you planning on doing after you do whatever the person asked you to do and he or she doesn't give you the promotion? Report them? Probably not.

Throughout this book, we've discussed how small the music industry is. Everyone important knows everyone else important. Do you really want to take a chance doing something stupid? Probably not.

How do you get out of doing something you don't want to do? You might simply say something like, "My dream was to work in this industry. I am not about to mess it up for something like this." Or "No can do. Sorry." How about, "Sorry, I'm not comfortable with that."

But what do you do if a supervisor wants you to do something unethical? How do you handle that? You can try any of the lines above, but if your job is on the line, you have a bigger problem to deal with. In cases like this, document as much as you can. Then, if you have no other choice, go to human resources or a higher supervisor.

"What do I do if I see something going on around me?" you say. "What if I'm not involved but I see a supervisor or coworker stealing or doing something to that effect? Then what?" This is a tough one as well. No one likes a tattle-tale, but if something major is going on, you have a decision to make. Do you say something? Bring it to the attention of a higher up? Mention it to the alleged thief or wrongdoer? Or just make sure you're not involved and say nothing?

Hopefully at the time, you'll make the right choice. It generally will depend on the position you hold, your responsibilities, and the alleged crime. It's a difficult decision. If you decide to say something, be very sure that you are absolutely, positively positive about your information.

Accountability

No one is perfect. We all make mistakes. No matter how careful anyone is, things happen. Accept the fact that sometime in your career you are going to make one too. In many cases, it's not the mistake itself that causes the problem but the way we deal with it.

The best way to deal with it is to take responsibility, apologize, try to fix it, and go on. Be sincere. Simply say something like, "I'm sorry; I made a mistake. I'm going to try to fix it and will make sure it doesn't happen again." With that said, it's very difficult for anyone to argue with you.

If, on the other hand, you start explaining mitigating circumstances, blame your coworkers, your secretary, your boss, or make excuses, others get on the defensive. Similarly, when you're wrong, just admit it and go on. "I was wrong about the marketing campaign. You were right. Good thing we're a team." People will respect you, you'll look more professional, and you'll have a lot less turmoil in your life.

Okay, you're taking credit for your mistakes, but what happens if one of your subordinates makes a mistake and you're blamed or you're the one who looks like you're unprepared? Let's say you are at the management office of one of the label's new artists. You are showing them the new press kit the publicity department developed. As you look inside, you realize that the artist's new bio is missing. What do you do? Blame your assistant? Blame your secretary?

The management team probably doesn't care or want to know if you have an incompetent staff. It's not their problem. The best thing to do in these types of situations is also to acknowledge the problem, apologize, and see what you can do to fix it. "I'm sorry. I should have checked to make sure all the components of the press kit were here in the package before I left. I must have inadvertently left out the bio. My mistake. Would you mind if I call my office while you're reviewing the rest of the package and have them fax over a copy? I'll get you a hard copy by the end of the day." The result? What could have been a major faux pas is now just a minor inconvenience that no one will probably even remember.

In work as in life, many people's first thoughts when there is a problem is to cover themselves. So when things go wrong, most people are busy reacting or coming up with excuses.

Here's something to remember. The most successful people don't come up with excuses. Instead, when something goes wrong, their first thoughts are how to fix the problem, mitigate any damages, and get things back to normal. If you can do this and remain cool in a crisis, it will enhance your position at your company.

Time, Time Management, and Organization

Here's something to think about. Every person in this world, no matter who they are, has the same 24 hours a day. It doesn't matter who you are or what your job is. You don't get more time during the day if you're young, older, or in between. You don't get more time if you're a millionaire or you're making minimum wage. With that in mind, it's important to manage your time wisely.

To start with, let's deal with your workday. Try to get in to work a little earlier than you're expected. It's easier to get the day started when you're not rushing. On occasion, you might also want to stay late. Why? Because when superiors see you bolting at five o'clock (or whenever your day ends), it looks as though you're not really interested in your job.

The Inside Scoop

Many execs in the music industry either get in early or stay late to compensate for the East Coast/West Coast time difference of the music industry. The time period before everyone else gets in or after everyone has left the office is usually less formal and less stressed. If you make it a habit to come in when the big brass comes in and leave when they leave, you will become visible in a higher manner to higher ups. More than that, however, you will often have the opportunity to ask a question, make a comment, or offer a suggestion. If someone questions you about what you're doing at work so early, simply say something like, "Preparing for the day ahead," "Getting some project started before it gets busy," or "Finishing up a few things so I can devote tomorrow to new projects."

Another thing to keep in mind is that the music industry is often bicoastal. This means is that if you're working in New York, you may still need to deal with people in Los Angeles or visa versa. Generally, that means that there is a three-hour time difference. If you're dealing with business associates oversees, there are various time differences to deal with as well.

Depending on your specific position in the music industry, you may have to "work" at concerts, on the road, at press conferences, recording studios, or other nontraditional workplace locations. Those who dreamed about a career in the industry generally look at these situations as perks of the job.

No matter what your career choice in the music industry, to be successful, you will need to learn to prioritize your tasks. How do you know what's important?

If your boss needs it now, it's important. If you promised to do something, it's important. If things need to get done, they're important. Let's say your department is working on marketing a CD about to hit the charts. You are in charge of confirming store and radio appearances. Another of your tasks is updating the media list. Still another is looking for a venue for a press party the label will be holding in eight months. What would you do first? Probably confirm store and radio appearances because that is timely, then look for the venue, and then update the media list. Of course, if you are instructed to do something by your boss first, that probably would take precedence. Generally, what you need to do is determine what is most important and do it first. Do things that you have promised to do as well.

The more organized you are, the easier it will be for you to manage your time. Make lists of things you need to do. You might want to

> ⭐ **Words from the Wise**
> Don't get so caught up in wanting to be liked or promising to do something you really don't have time to get done. Doing so will just put you under pressure.

keep a master list and then a daily list of things you need to do. You might also want a third list of deadlines that need to be met. Just making lists won't do it. Checking them to make sure things that you needed to do actually got done is the key.

Here's an example of the beginnings of a master list. Use it to get started on yours.

- ◎ Call Rob B. to set up appointment.
- ◎ Update media lists.
- ◎ Contact accounting department to make sure checks were cut for photographer and graphic artists.
- ◎ Contact travel agent to confirm airline reservations for Ms. Lyons.
- ◎ Do out-of-pocket expense report.
- ◎ Get cell numbers for band's management team.
- ◎ Talk to Bob regarding press passes.
- ◎ Call radio stations to confirm next week's interviews.
- ◎ Make sure advertisements are running in *Billboard.*
- ◎ Call *Music Today* to get tape of show.
- ◎ Attend marketing staff meeting Friday.
- ◎ Meet with management team to discuss new bio for acts.
- ◎ Lunch with Nick C., Monday, 1 P.M.
- ◎ Work on budget.
- ◎ Budget meeting April 10, 4 P.M.
- ◎ Complete budget, due May 15.

Writing things down is essential for most people. Don't depend on your memory or anyone else's. Whatever your job in the industry, it will be filled with lot of details, things that need to get done, and just stuff in general. The more successful you get, the busier you will be, and the more things you'll have to remember.

Want to be really organized? Keep a notebook where you jot things down. Date each page so you have a reference point for later. Then make notes. Like what?

- The dates people called and the gist of the conversation.
- The dates you call people and the reason you called.
- Notes on meetings you attend. Then when someone says something like, "Gee, I don't remember whether we said May 9," you have it.
- Names of people you meet.
- Things that happened during the day.

After you get used to keeping the notebook, it will become a valuable resource. You might, for example, remember someone calling you six months ago. "What was his name?" you ask yourself. "I wish I knew his name." Voila. Just look in your notebook.

Find Ways to Garner Positive Attention in the Workplace

Find ways to garner positive attention in the workplace so when the job you're interested in becomes available, you are the one your superiors think about. Don't turn down opportunities just because they're not exactly what you had in mind. Instead, use opportunities that present themselves as a way to get your foot in the door.

Let's say, for example, your ultimate career goal is to be an artist and repertoire director. While you interviewed for a job in the A&R department, you were offered a position working in the publicity department. Should you take it or should you wait until you are offered a job in the department of your choice? Getting your foot in the door at the record label is your immediate goal, so unless you have another job at another label lined up, taking one offered would probably be a good idea. Once in, take action. How?

Start by doing the job you have been hired to do. If you're working in the publicity department, be the best you can be in that department. Don't complain that you really don't want to be there. Learn as much as you can. You can never have too much knowledge. Keep your eye out for projects that need to be done and then offer to handle them. Will you be doing more work? Probably, but this makes good career sense. Offering to do extra projects gives you career visibility, helps you learn new skills, and gives you the opportunity to meet new people. Additionally, once you complete the project successfully, it's a great leverage to use down the line when seeking a promotion or raise.

What else can you do? Get to know people in other departments. Volunteer to run a company event. Is the company having a picnic or holiday party? Offer to be on the committee. Does your company have an employee newsletter? Become involved. That way, you get to

Tip from the Top
The best projects to volunteer for are those no one else wants to do. Those give you the most visibility in the workplace.

know lots of people from lots of departments and they get to know you. If your company doesn't have an employee newsletter, offer to help develop one.

Why should you do all this extra work? Because it will help get you where you want to be. Get to know the inner workings of your company. Make contacts in the A&R department, the marketing department, the president's office. You want execs at your company to know who you are, so that when an opening occurs, you stand a better chance of them considering you.

Of course, when volunteering to do things, don't ever let your own work slide. It's imperative to look like you can do it all, do it with ease, do it well, and do it with a smile.

How will anyone know what you want? You don't want to walk up to everyone and say, "I'd like to volunteer to take this project because I read in a book it can get me out of this job and into the one I really want." You must create relationships where you can talk to people on various levels at your company.

For example, it might be a bad idea to just go knocking on the president's office door to shoot the breeze, but you might feel comfortable calling to make an appointment to do a short interview for an employee newsletter. You probably wouldn't knock on the door of the A&R director at the label to say, "Hi, I really wanted to work in this department," but you might have a conversation with him or her regarding an employee event you're working on. That gives you a chance to say something like, "It's so nice to finally talk to you. I had originally interviewed for a job in this department because I thought my talents would be put to good use here, but I was really happy to work in the publicity department as well." Those two sentences can plant the seed in the A&R director's mind. When an opening arises, he or she might think about you and ask if you would be interested.

A Few Other Things

It's important to realize that while of course you want to succeed in the workplace, everything you do may not be successful. Every idea you have may not work. Every project you do may not turn out perfectly. Things take time. None of these situations mean that you are a failure. What they mean simply is that you need to work on them a little bit more.

Be aware that success is often built on the back of little failures. Take a look, for example, at some of the top recording acts, singers, or songwriters. No matter what you read, most were not overnight successes. Most had a string of rejections and failures before they got where they were going. Eventually, after keeping at it, they got a contract, made a great CD, and had a hit tune.

Those on the business end of the industry often follow the same pattern. Managers and booking agents may handle a number of acts before one makes it big. Sometimes these same people believed so strongly in an act that they worked with them for a long time period and then, one day, success!

Countless record execs have turned down the next Elvis Presley, Rolling Stones, Madonna, Beyonce, or Usher only to have a different exec pick them up and hit gold.

Most successful people have a number of key traits in common. They have a willingness to take risks, a determination that cannot be undone, and usually an amazing amount of confidence in themselves and their ideas.

Can they fail? Sure. But they might also succeed and they usually do. What does this have to do with you? If you learn from the success of others, you can be successful too. If you emulate successful people, you, too, can be on the road to success.

Don't be so afraid of getting things right that you don't take a chance at doing them a better way or a different way. Don't get so comfortable in your current job that you're afraid to move to a new position, take a promotion, or accept a new job or new responsibilities. If you want to succeed in the workplace, your career, and your life, be confident and be willing to take risks. Be determined that you know what you want and how to get it, and you will.

11

SUCCEEDING ON THE TALENT END
OF THE INDUSTRY

How many times have you been at a concert and wished you were the one on stage? How many times have you turned on the radio and wished it was your CD everyone was listening to and requesting? How many times have you heard a song and wished it was the one you wrote?

While wishing certainly can't hurt, you need to take some positive actions to help you succeed on the talent end of the music industry. It's no secret that the industry is competitive, but why shouldn't you be the one on top? No matter how talented you are, remember that talent is only one aspect of success in the music industry. Fully understanding the business is just as important.

This section will explain some things that might help aspiring musicians or performers move ahead on the talent end of the industry. Those interested in a career in the business area should read this section to better understand some of the issues facing the talent. Knowledge is power, and having this information can help make you a more powerful force in the music industry.

Breaking Into the Music Business

Do you live, breathe, and play music? Is it something you love to do? I'm assuming you do, or

you wouldn't be reading this book. Is it something you want to do as a vocation instead of an avocation? If so, there's an important fact you need to remember. The music business is just that: a business. It's crucial to your success in any music career that you understand this. The music business is a business and needs to be treated as such.

Yes, it can be fun; it can be exciting; and it can be glamorous, but in the end, it is business. In order to succeed, you need to act in a professional manner. How can you be professional? Simply put, remember that you're not an amateur. Present yourself professionally. If you say you're going to be someplace, be there. If you say you're going to call somebody, call them. Most important, be on time for everything. There is nothing worse for your career than being known as the act that is always late.

Professionalism doesn't only mean the way you act. It also encompasses how you present yourself and your act. Are you ready to step on stage now? Are you ready to make it? Is your stage show together? Is it perfect? What about your material? Have you worked out all the kinks? Do you have a professional sounding demo? What about a press kit with a bio and photos? If you want industry professionals to take you seriously, make sure everything you do is professional.

"We're talented," you say. "Isn't that all anyone is really interested in anyway? What difference does it make if we're not all that professional right now? Talent is what they're looking for."

True, talent is what industry professionals are looking for, but it's not that simple. Here's the deal. There are a lot of talented singers, musicians, and songwriters. Give yourself the best shot possible. You don't want someone to say, "What a great voice, but I hear he doesn't show up for every show." You want your stage show, your bio, your press kits, and your demo to stand out from others. Even if you're not a professional yet, you want it to appear that you are.

What else should you know? To give yourself the best chances at success in the music industry, learn as much as possible about the business. Knowledge is power. The more you know, the more you can help yourself in your quest for success.

Even though your ultimate goal is to succeed on the talent end of the industry, it is imperative to learn everything you can about the business end. You've already started by reading this book. Don't stop here. Read everything you can about the business. Go to the library or the book store and find books on the music industry. Find books on artists who have made it. Read trade publications. Find other magazines and periodicals with articles on the recording industry, the music business, and artists. Scour the Internet for information.

"But I'm busy," you say. "I spend every spare moment practicing and working on our show. I don't have time to read books and magazines and scour the Internet."

Make time. If you just find one thing in a book or magazine or on the Internet that you

---

Tip from the Top
The more you know about the industry, the less of a chance that someone will try to take advantage of you. Learn something new every opportunity you get.

---

can use or one thing that you can relate to your career, it will be worth it. And don't stop there. Take classes, workshops, and seminars, both in your talent and craft and in the business end of the industry. Why? You will gain valuable information, learn new skills, and have the opportunity to network and make important contacts. And that is what can help you on the talent end of the industry.

Moving Up and Taking the Next Step

What's your next move if you have a group together and you're ready to take the next step? What's your next move if you're a singer or a musician? What do you do if you're a prolific songwriter with a box full of lyrics and music you've written? How do you move from amateur to pro? Take stock and get ready.

Is your music great? Do you have great songs? What about your stage show? Is it polished and professional? Can you perform a set without wondering what song is next? Does your show flow smoothly? Do you have stage presence? Do you exude charisma?

"Stage show? Stage presence? Charisma? Huh? What do mean?" you ask.

Let's discuss this aspect of your career for a bit. Think about some of the successful acts you love watching in concert. What's their stage show like? Do the singers just stand there? Does the band just play their instruments looking

> ### ⭐ Tip from the Coach
>
> If you don't have access to a camcorder, you often can rent one at a reasonable cost.

bored? Probably not. What do you look like on stage? Do you want to know?

Here's an idea. Next time you do a show, have a friend videotape your performance. If you don't have a show scheduled, videotape your rehearsal. Then watch the video. If you're part of a group, have everyone watch it. It's often difficult to see yourself without being overly critical. Don't be hard on yourself. That's not the point. What you want to do is watch to see how you look to others when you're on stage.

Are you just standing in front of a microphone singing your songs? Are your eyes closed when you're singing? Are you making eye contact with the audience? Are you gazing up while playing the drums or looking down at the floor while playing the guitar? Are you smiling and having fun, or does it look like being on stage is a chore?

Once you see what you look like to your audience, decide if you want to change anything. What should you try? Every performer is different. What works for one might not work for another. You have to be comfortable. Try interacting with the audience. Talk to them. Banter a bit. Have fun. Don't just stand there. Move around and be active. Develop unique segments of your show that you become known for; fans will hear about these signature segments and wait for them when they see you perform. Experiment with different things to see what works. If something works, great. If not, come up with other ideas.

You might add some dance steps or have audience participation. Maybe you want your fans to sing a chorus along with your group. What you want to do is make sure your audience is entertained. You want them to have fun, and you want them to look forward to the opportunity to see you again. Take some time to develop your stage show. Whatever you choose, it doesn't necessarily have to *look* like it's staged, but you want your show to look polished.

Whether you're a solo artist or part of a group, it's imperative to develop a rehearsal schedule so every show you have will be as tight as possible. Every appearance is important. Every appearance is an opportunity.

A mistake many acts make is thinking they can put their show together on stage. What happens is they get what they feel is an unimportant gig at a small club or a school. The night of the gig, everyone just stumbles in thinking it isn't a big deal, so no one prepares. Unfortunately, that could be the night someone who can help your career shows up. Maybe it's a disc jockey or someone from the media. Maybe it's someone who has a brother or sister in the industry. You can never tell who will be in the audience, so always put on the best show you can.

Getting the Gigs

A lot of singers and musicians want to perform live. It's one of the ways musical talent can generate income. Competition can be fierce. Whether you are just starting out or you have a hit record, you're competing for the public's entertainment dollars.

There are basically two main ways to get gigs. You can go out looking for them, or you can wait until they come to you. Whether you're booking the gigs yourself or booking them through an agent, if you want your calendar to be full, you're going to have to be proactive. If you're just starting out, you probably are going to be booking your own gigs. Are you ready to be your own booking agent? It means you have to find ways to get engagements, negotiate fees, and deal with contracts. As your career moves ahead, you may begin dealing with agents. Either way, the goal is to get more engagements, better engagements, and higher fees. You want to move out of your local market and find ways to reach more lucrative major markets.

How do you do that? It's going to depend to a great extent on where you are in your career, but generally marketing and promotion have a lot to do with it. Let's briefly review the relationship between marketing and booking engagements. Marketing can open doors for you. Why? Because all successful companies use marketing to sell products, and you need to look at yourself or your act as a product. Done correctly, marketing can tell your story, differentiate you from other acts, and convince potential talent buyers why they should hire you instead of another act. The result of good marketing in this case will be the booking or the selling of your live performances.

A major component of marketing is promotion. While it is useful at any level of your career, if you're just starting out or you don't have anyone else working on the task, self-promotion can help dramatically. How do you do this? Once again, there are many options. Whatever you choose, you want to create as much buzz about yourself (or your act) as possible. You want your act's name to be as prominent as possible before the public. That way, when people have entertainment needs, they might think of your act.

Unless you are signed to an agent on an exclusive basis and have someone working on this for you, create a list of potential talent buyers to target. The people included on this list will depend on where you are in your career.

Let's look at a few possibilities to get you started.

- booking agents
- bar owners
- casino entertainment buyers
- chambers of commerce
- civic groups
- club owners and entertainment bookers
- coffee houses
- college/university directors of activities
- college and university student unions
- convention center directors
- convention planners
- corporate party planners
- corporations and other business human resource directors
- cruise ship–line entertainment directors
- destination-management companies
- dinner-club entertainment directors or owners
- exposition managers
- fair and festival entertainment directors or talent bookers
- governmental agencies
- high school and junior high school administrative offices
- hotels and motels owners and entertainment bookers
- not-for-profit organizations
- radio station general managers, music directors, promotion directors
- record labels
- resort entertainment directors, entertainment bookers, or marketing directors
- television station general managers, human resource directors, marketing directors

◎ trade association executive directors
◎ trade show directors
◎ wedding planners

You might look over this list and say things like, "We don't want to play in a high school. We're beyond that." "We're not going to go on a cruise ship. One of our members gets seasick." "Why would a newspaper want us to perform?" or "We're not playing a wedding. We are not a wedding band. We're artists."

Don't limit your opportunities before you get an engagement. You can always turn down a job you don't want, but you can never tell how an opportunity may act as a springboard to something else. For example, just because you're sending information to a high school doesn't necessarily mean that the high school will book you. The person receiving your information at the school may, however, be in charge of a fundraiser where they need a specific type of act, and you just might fit the bill.

Back to your list of potential talent buyers. What do you send them? Remember that press kit/promo package we talked about? You're go-

ing to start by sending that. If you have a preview video and/or a CD, send that as well. You also want to send a list of your act's engagements. That way, people can check you out. Word of mouth and personal recommendations are the best advertising you can get.

Don't just stop at one mailing. Send mailings to potential buyers on a regular basis so your act's name is constantly in front of them.

Send out an updated engagement list every month with a flyer. How about developing a one-page newsletter showcasing your act? Fact sheets highlighting your news, accomplishments, and other items of interest are also good ideas. If you have T-shirts, CDs, calendars, or any other promotional items, you might want to send them with your information on occasion.

Don't always send the same exact mailings, or people will start throwing out your mail before they open it. Try to be creative while maintaining some consistency. One act I know always sends a list of interesting facts along with their information. Another sends monthly engagements on a calendar that also contains better-known as well as obscure special days of that month (for example, National Ice Cream Day, National Eat a Bagel Day, National Smile Day, and so on). It's neat to look at, so most people always open it. As a matter of fact, people start to look forward to getting it.

Keep sending your information and your updates. The more people see your name, the better the possibility they will remember you when they need talent. Having your act's name out there will give you an advantage over other acts who don't actively promote themselves.

In addition to sending promotional material through the mail, create an e-mail list. Why? Because e-mail is instant and less expensive than mailing information on paper. You don't want to

---

⭐ Tip from the Top

Keep a card file noting the date you called potential talent buyers, what their response was, and any other information you might pick up during the conversation. For example, the first time you call, the potential buyer may say in passing, "I'm swamped here; we're in the middle of remodeling the club." The next time you call, you might ask, "Last time I spoke to you, the club was being remodeled. How did it go?" Then go on to your sales pitch.

Words from a Pro

A mailing list and e-mail list might also be used to build a fan base. Fans are a very valuable asset to musical artists. Don't ever think that your fans can't get you engagements. They often are the first people who suggest you.

create spam, but if you're performing someplace or if you have big news, you want to tell people.

Remember when creating your potential buyers list to include people outside of your local area. Enlarge your market bit by bit until you're in new and larger market. Once you get gigs in your home area, look for jobs 50 or 100 miles away. Some of your fans from the local area will show up for support, and you'll gain new ones. After you've developed a fan base there, move on to other markets and do the same thing.

Now that you've introduced your act to potential talent buyers with your information, do you just sit back and wait for them to call you? Well, you can, but it's not a very effective approach. What do you do? Booking engagements is selling your product, so get on the phone and call your potential buyers. Creating a personal contact with potential buyers often makes the difference between them booking your act or not. Why? Because you're putting a voice to your material. When you get on the phone, you can sell yourself better than just some print information.

It might take a few calls, but that's okay. Persistence often pays off. How do you do it? See if you can generate interest.

"What do I say?" you ask.

Try something like this:

"Hi, this is Mark Charles. I'm representing the MC Group. We're a six-member, rock-

oriented, self-contained act. We have some open dates the last two weeks in February that we're trying to fill in, and I was wondering if you might need some entertainment during that time. We've been packing the clubs we've been playing and our fan base is expanding. I'd be glad to overnight our CD and our press kit."

The person on other end may say no, but they may say yes and request your press kit. They might also ask for references or where else you played, or they might ask about your fee. Be prepared.

If you have really good sales skills, you might just make a list of potential places where you would like to be booked and personally go visit the club managers, owners, or promoters. Instead of saying you're the best (which you probably are), simply tell them about the size of your fan base, how your act brings in people, and how you please the crowd.

Club owners might be cautious when hiring an act they don't know. How can you get around this? Network, network, network! You'll have an easier time if someone the club owner knows recommends you or will vouch for you. Who do you know that the club owner knows? How about the band who played there last week? What about a waiter or waitress? How about the club owner's lawyer or accountant?

What are some other ways to get gigs? Many acts advertise their services. Where should you

The Inside Scoop

If your plan is to personally visit club owners and other potential talent buyers, make sure you do so at times when they tend to be less busy. During the week is better than weekends. Midday is better than evening.

advertise? That depends to a great extent on where you are in your career and where you're trying to go. Many newer or local acts advertise in the local newspaper or the local entertainment media. Established acts as well as lesser-known acts often place ads in entertainment directories.

If you live in an area where there are a number of entertainment venues, consider renting a billboard. I've seen a number of up-and-coming acts use billboards to successfully fill up their calendar.

"Aren't billboards expensive?" you ask.

They can be, depending on the location and the billboard company's rates, but they can also be worth the investment.

A few months after mentioning this strategy at a seminar, I received a call from one of the attendees. He thanked me for the idea and told me how his act not only used it but built on it and wanted to share their method of making it affordable with other acts.

The act located an empty billboard. They called up to check the price and found that they just couldn't afford it. While talking to the owner of the billboard company, the band member mentioned why they wanted it so badly. Coin-

cidentally, the owner of the billboard company was president of the local chamber of commerce. He also had a daughter who was getting married who was looking for a band to play at the wedding. He asked if the group had any references. They did. He asked where they were performing next and came to check them out. To make a long story short, they worked out a barter deal.

While the group generally performed mostly originally material, they had started out doing cover music and agreed to play for the wedding. They also agreed to do a number of fundraising concerts for the chamber of commerce. In exchange for performing for no fee, the group not only got use of the billboard for a year, but the owner agreed to paint it as well. Within a couple of months from the time the billboard went up, the act was booked solid.

Being in the right place at the right time also helped. A recording group driving through late at night saw the billboard as they were coming into town to play and thought it was a unique advertising gimmick. As luck would have it, the local act was playing in the club of the hotel where the recording act was staying. They noticed the name of the act on the hotel marquee and stopped in to see them as they were finishing up their set.

Within the next two weeks, the recording act had called the local act and asked if they wanted to go on tour with them as an opening act. Will that happen to every act? Probably not, but if you get creative, you can never tell what opportunities will present themselves.

Does booking yourself seem like a lot of work? Well, it is. At the beginning of your career, there might not be anything you can do about it. Your goal, however, should be to have agents book you. You're still going to have to

---

⭐ ## Words from the Wise

If you are considering using a billboard, remember that people are driving by quickly and only have a very short time to read what's on the sign. Design your billboard with a good picture of your act, your contact phone number, and perhaps the genre of music. For example, "Ask For . . . Sparkling Diamonds. . . . Your Favorite Country Act 111-222-3333" or "Company Town . . . R&B You Love 222-333-4444."

promote yourself, but you can cut out a lot of the work.

Booking agents match acts with the venues or promoters who need the talent. They generally represent a number of acts. Very large agencies may represent hundreds of acts, some exclusively, some on a nonexclusive basis. It's important to understand that just because you have an agent doesn't necessarily mean you will get tons of engagements. You need to create a good working relationship with your agent. Call them weekly. Tell them what you're doing and ask how they're doing securing you engagements.

Always be cordial, polite, and professional to agents. Try to develop a friendly business relationship. This is important for a number of reasons. When a club calls looking for a certain type of act, the agent has a choice. He or she can probably recommend five or six acts similar to yours on the agency roster. If you've developed a good relationship with the agent and he or she knows you have a good act and that you're professional, it increases your chances of being recommended for the gig.

Agents face the same challenges you would if you were booking yourself; they need to find venues and promoters who are looking for talent. The difference is that booking is their business. They aren't trying to work on their act at the same time. They aren't looking for a new guitarist. Booking is their main concentration. Agents also have contacts that you might not have. They deal with clubs, promoters, and talent bookers on a daily basis. Booking agents may get regular calls from talent bookers, club owners, or promoters in search of talent to fill their entertainment needs. They also spend their days on the phone placing calls to clubs, promoters, and venues trying to secure engagements for artists on their roster.

Who pays the booking agent? Generally, the artist pays. Booking agents receive a percentage of the fee the artist is paid for the engagement. Percentages vary, but it will generally be between 10 percent and 20 percent of the total fee.

Some agents ask their acts to sign an exclusivity agreement. This means that other agents must go through your agent in order to book you. In these cases, no matter who secures an engagement, even if it's you, the agency gets their cut. If you don't have an exclusivity agreement, you can work with any number of agents, and whoever gets you the gig gets the commission.

How do you get agents? There are a number of ways. You can send a letter along with your press kit/promo package to various agencies and then follow up with phone calls. You might make an appointment to meet an agent and discuss the possibilities. Many agents are also on the lookout for talent. If you are making noise in the industry, agents might even approach you. If you're on the cusp of signing a record deal, they will often call you when they hear about the pending deal.

In addition to not having to book yourself, there are a number of advantages to using agents. Generally, if you're going through an agency, clubs will be less likely to try to rip you

Tip from the Top

Don't sign a long-term exclusive contract with a booking agency unless they have proven themselves to you. If you do and they aren't booking any engagements for your act and you find it necessary to use other agents, you will still have to pay your exclusive agent commissions throughout the duration of the agreement.

> ### ⭐ The Inside Scoop
>
> A good way to get noticed by agents, talent buyers, and labels is by taking part in talent showcases. If you're offered the opportunity to participate in a showcase, grab it. If you're not offered the opportunity, you might consider putting together your own showcase. To do this, rent out a club on an off night for a couple of hours; arrange for some hors d'oeuvres; send invitations to agents, talent buyers, labels, and the media; put out press kits, demos, videos, business cards; and play your best set ever. In many situations, if you pay for light food service or the bar is open, you won't even have to pay for the room.

off or not pay you your fee. Agents are also usually better negotiators than artists.

Are agents worth the money? They are if they can help get you more engagements with higher fees than you can get yourself.

What should you look for in agents? You want to work with people who are excited about your act and your career. You want people who believe in you.

What else? You want agents who are respected in the industry.

Are you better off with a larger agency or a smaller one? There are pros and cons on each side. A larger agency might send you on tour with one of their more popular acts helping to catapult your career. On the other hand, they might be too large to give much attention to their lesser-known acts. A smaller agency may not have as much clout, but they might put a lot more time into your career. Look at the roster of each agency that might represent you. Talk to some of their artists. See what they say before you make a decision.

Before we go too far, let's discuss one of the most important matters connected with performing—how you set your fees. How do you decide how much you're worth? This is a very difficult question for most artists. Do you charge what the other people are charging at your career level? Do you charge more because you feel you're worth more? Do you charge less because if you do, you might get more gigs? In many cases, especially when you're starting out, your agent will help you set fees.

Here's the deal. You have to decide what you're worth. You have to decide what the market will bear, and you have to decide what you'll accept. You also have to decide when you're willing to cut your fee. Flexibility is often the name of the game.

I know a number of former chart-topping recording artists who are still popular yet not currently on the charts. They might have a set a fee of $25,000 per show, but they will often adjust it if they have other gigs in a given area and can schedule enough performances to make it all worthwhile. They might also lower their fee if a particular venue that they want to play does not have a budget that can handle their usual amount. While they usually get what they want or close to what they want, they are flexible.

When you are setting your fees, there are a number of things you have to remember. You

> ### ⭐ Tip from the Top
>
> Having your fans' e-mail addresses means that you can e-mail them when your CD comes out and ask them to request it at stores or on the radio. You can also e-mail them to remind them about upcoming shows and events.

Words from the Wise

Include an option for recipients to be deleted from your mailing list on each e-mail you send. Don't take it personally. Some people are just tired of being barraged by e-mail.

can always lower your fee, but once you set it, it's very difficult to raise it. If you give a club a specific fee because you want to play there, that is the fee they will expect to pay you the next time you appear. People often undervalue their talent because they worry that if they ask for what they think they're worth, they will not get it. One thing is for sure: If you don't ask for the big bucks, you'll never get them. If you think you're worth more, you have to ask for more. You might be pleasantly surprised.

Would your life be easier with an agent? It might be if he or she gets you good engagements. In reality, agents generally deal with a number of acts. Is it easier dealing with an agent? Sometimes. Do you need an agent? It certainly helps to have someone working for you.

Getting Exposure

To succeed in the industry, people need to know what you're doing. You need to set yourself apart. You need exposure. It's essential to your quest for success in your career. You can have the greatest CD in the world, but if no one knows about it, it probably isn't going anyplace. Similarly, you can have the best stage show, but unless people know about it, it's useless.

How do you get exposure? There are a variety of ways. Advertising, publicity, promotion, and marketing help. You need to catch the eye of people in the industry, catch the eye of the media, and catch the eye of fans. Sometimes you might need a professional. Publicists, press agents, and public relations counselors are all pros in garnering publicity and media attention and finding ways to bring your act to the attention of the public.

Can you do it yourself? It depends where you are in your career, what your skills are, and how much time you have to put into it. Publicity takes time and effort, but if you know the basics, you can try. If you have already put together your press kit/promo package, you're off to a good start. How was your act's bio? Did you feel comfortable writing that? If so, keep reading.

When you go to a professional publicist, press agent, or public relations counselor, you generally tell them your goal. They then will develop a plan of action. Depending on your goal, they might set up press conferences, send out a series of press releases, arrange for media interviews, send your press kits and CDs out, and so on. If you're not ready to hire a professional, make a commitment to yourself to work on a plan to get exposure for your act.

How do you do it? Let's say your goal is to make people aware of your new CD and let them know you're a major force in the entertainment industry. Here are some things you can try.

Tip from the Top

Unless you are signed exclusively with an agent, you don't have to rely on just one. The more agents you have working on your behalf, the more options for work you have.

◎ Develop a media list of local, regional, and national media outlets to send your press releases.

◎ Come up with interesting angle or hook for series of press releases on your act.
  ▫ Press release on how act was formed
  ▫ Press release announcing new CD
  ▫ Press release noting attention CD is receiving
  ▫ Press release about where act is performing
  ▫ Press release noting that story on act appeared in *Billboard*
  ▫ Press release on act playing for not-for-profit charity event
  ▫ Photo of act playing at charity event with photo caption

◎ Develop some sort of interesting angle or subject or platform for your act to focus on to create some buzz and garner media attention:
  ▫ Drinking and driving don't mix. Call a friend. (Public service.)
  ▫ Singing aloud eases stress. Come sing with us. (An interesting concept that would probably get some media exposure.)
  ▫ Stay in school. (Public service.)

◎ Call local, regional, and national (if you're ready) television and radio stations to determine what news, talk, and/or variety shows might feature your act.

◎ Send letters to television and radio show guest coordinators and producers asking about possibilities of appearances for act. Remember to mention your unique angle or platform to give you an edge.

⭐ Tip from the Top

Try to play benefits or fund-raisers. They are great for exposure, great for publicity, and get your name out to people who might not know about you. This, of course, is in addition to doing something to help a group trying to raise monies.

◎ Follow up your letters with phone calls.

◎ Call radio station program and music directors to make appointments to bring CDs.

◎ Call record stores or record departments to see if your act can perform a couple songs.

◎ Develop T-shirts and other promotional material and merchandise that you can give away or sell.

◎ Contact not-for-profit charity to offer entertainment gratis for one of their events or do a fund-raiser.

Keep doing things to create a buzz and get exposure. Get creative. The media can make or break your act. Develop a relationship with them. When someone does a story or reviews your act or your CD, write a note and thank them. Send them a T-shirt and other merchandise with your name and logo. Make sure the media always has passes to get into your shows even if you have to pay for tickets out of your own pocket.

If you're having a big show, you might take out some ads yourself in the local media. You might even partner with a business. There are a number of acts that have become really successful, for example, by partnering with local radio stations.

If you're just starting out, your local area is really important. This is where people know you and you can develop a large fan base. As you get more successful, you're going to move into larger markets and build a larger fan base. Fans are important. Treat them well. Without them, it's difficult to sustain your success.

Don't forget the Internet when looking for exposure. The World Wide Web enables you to have fans not only in your local area but on the other side of the world—even if you're just starting out.

I talked about having a Web site earlier in the book. The Internet is an interesting place. You can never tell who is looking. It might be a new fan, a potential manager, an A&R rep who heard of you, a possible booking contact, or a media person working on a story. If you want people to know about you, you need a Web site. Make it easy for people to find you. Don't make them search through obscure words that you know the meaning of but others might not. Your Web site should be where people can find out everything about you. Update your site with news about your act and keep it current so that people will come back.

Develop an e-mail list of people who visit your site. How? You might just have a section of your site where people can leave their e-mail address or you might have a guest book. Some artists also host giveaways on their Web site in order to entice people to leave their names and e-mail addresses. Certain states have rules on sweepstakes and giveaways, so check ahead of time to make sure your contest or promotion is legal.

Your Web site can do more than give you exposure. It can make you money. Don't forget e-commerce. Even if you aren't signed with a label, you can sell CDs and other merchandise via your site and reach the same people that a label does.

If all this seems more work than you can handle, find a friend or family member to help out or consider using a professional. Neglecting exposure and publicity and just hoping people will hear about you will more often than not hamper your career. Do your best to get your name out and get as much positive publicity and exposure as possible.

Your Recording Career

You're writing songs. You're performing live. Agents are calling. Your calendar is filling up with good dates. Things are going well, but you want to move to the next level. You want to be a recording artist. Let's go over some of the basics of getting signed by a label.

Your Demo

Do you need a demo? How professional does it have to be? Would should you put on it? Should it be on a cassette, a tape, or a CD?

Let's start with your demo. You need one if you are trying to get a recording contract, trying to get engagements, or trying to sell your songs. A demo alone won't *get* you a contract or an engagement or sell a song, but it can illustrate what you have to offer and your talents.

How professional does your demo have to be? The simple answer is as professional as possible. Should you go into debt to make your demo? No! Here's the deal. Chances are no label is going to use your demo as is to make your CD, so your goal is to illustrate your talent the best way you can. Make sure the sound quality is perfect.

Do you have to record it professionally? Your demo should sound professional, but that doesn't mean you need to have it professionally produced in a studio. If you can, it doesn't hurt, but it's not an absolute necessity. If you or a friend have good recording equipment at home, you might use that.

Should you use a cassette or a CD for your demo? Everyone has their own preference on this. Whichever you use, make sure your demo is labeled with your act's name, a contact name, and contact information. You should also list the songs that are included.

What should be on your demo? No more than three or four songs. Time is of the essence to label execs. They don't have time to listen to thirty minutes of your music. More is not better on a demo.

Listen to your demos *before* you send them out or bring them with you to an appointment. Here's a story of why.

At the beginning of my career in the industry I worked with an unknown solo artist. Like most other singers, he wanted a recording contract. He recorded four songs for a demo tape. Through networking, I managed to get an appointment with a major music mogul who promised to listen to the demo. As sometimes happens, there was a glitch in the timing getting the demos done. I had an appointment in New York City on Monday morning. Sunday afternoon, the demos still weren't done. I was promised that I'd have one in my hand by Sunday night. Sometime around 2:30 in the morning I finally received a demo tape.

Bright and early I left for my appointment, armed with the demo, the artist's bio, and a press kit. I walked in and was welcomed by the music mogul. After some chitchat, I handed over the tape, which, because I had received so late, I hadn't heard. He put the tape in, turned it on, and my heart dropped.

Two of the songs were playing in unison on top of each other. Something was very wrong. The big break I was lucky enough to get for this

---

Tip from the Coach

You might be able to get another opportunity, but you can never get back the opportunity you missed.

---

artist was quickly going down the drain. The music industry executive was very nice. He asked for another demo and told me these things happen on occasion. I gave him another tape and it sounded the same. On the third try, he said, "Why don't you come back when you have a good tape. Thanks for coming." I apologized for wasting his time and left. The chances of getting another appointment with him were minimal.

What did I learn? That no matter how rushed I was, never go into an appointment without checking to make sure everything that I had was perfect.

Should your demo be produced? You want your demo to sound good. If the guitars are warm, the drums have a deep beat, the musicianship is perfect, and the whole sound and mix are superb, will it get you a contract? Not unless the song, vocals, and music grab the attention of the person listening. And that is the crux of the situation.

So here's what you need to know. Your demo does not have to illustrate that you know someone who can produce a great demo. It has to show that you have star quality. It has to show that *you* have a hit song and/or you can be a top performer. If you can do both, fine. If not, go for grabbing the attention of the listener with your voice, your song, and your potential.

Finding A Label

You've made a demo. You have your press kit. You are ready. Now what? Let's begin with find-

> ## Words from the Wise
> Do your own quality control of your demos. Listen to them before you send them out. Make sure every demo is perfect.

ing a label? One thing you shouldn't do is get a list of labels and then haphazardly start sending your demo to every one of them. Why? Because labels generally specialize in certain genres of music, and not every label will represent the type of music you do. For example, sending your rap demo to a label whose main focus is country is a waste of time. Similarly, a label whose main focus is country probably wouldn't be interested in an artist whose primary music style is R&B. This doesn't mean that some labels don't crossover, because they do. The smart thing to do, however, is to find labels that have types of music similar to yours. You can then target the labels you want to reach.

What should you do with your demo tape? There are a number of options. To begin, you'll probably want to "shop your tape around." This means trying to find labels who will listen to your demo.

"So do we just send our demos to the label?" you ask.

You can, but it's probably not a good idea, because many labels don't accept unsolicited tapes.

"Why not?" you ask.

There are a few reasons. Number one, even labels that don't accept unsolicited tapes receive tons of them, sometimes hundreds a week. Listening to these tapes takes time that many A&R people just don't have. The truth is that just getting your demo to a label doesn't mean someone will necessarily listen to it. Labels that don't accept unsolicited tapes probably accept them from people they know and trust will send them demos that are worth listening to. Who are these people? Their friends, industry attorneys, publicists, club owners, radio people, managers, agents, and so on.

Remember we talked about how important networking was? Here's a good reason why: Your demo will get a lot more attention quicker if someone in the industry recommends it than if you send it yourself.

There's another reason labels don't like to get unsolicited demos from people they don't know: lawsuits. Years ago, some songwriters began to sue labels, claiming that their songs had been stolen by record companies. Once people sent demos to the label (even if they were sent unsolicited and never listened to), it illustrated that a label had the opportunity to steal their songs. Whether or not the songwriters won, the lawsuits were a nuisance. As a result, labels don't like to accept demos they haven't asked for or from people they don't know.

What happens when you send an unsolicited demo? At most of the larger labels, they will send it back with a letter explaining their policy regarding unsolicited material. This is not to say that no labels accept unsolicited material, but you should be aware that the larger ones usually don't.

Can you get around it? You can get around anything if you're creative and persistent. You might try calling the labels you're interested in sending your demos to and try to get permission to submit them.

First, try the straight approach. Decide which labels you're interested in pursuing and do some homework. Get the names of people in the A&R department. While the A&R director is in charge, you can bet that he or she is very busy and going to be hard to get on the phone.

Besides, once the director says no, you have no place to go. With that in mind, try to get the name of the A&R coordinator, the department administrative assistant, and the assistant director. Once armed with a name, make a call.

"Hi, Ms. Johnson, this is Roger Dylan. I don't want to take a lot of your time. My act has a demo that I think you'll like. Our music fits into the genre of (*fill in the name with the top current act that sounds the most like your music*) and we've developed a really huge fan base locally. Would it be possible to send you a copy along with a bio and our press kit?"

How will it play out? Here are some scenarios:

Ms. Johnson may say, "I'm sorry; we don't accept unsolicited material." In that case you'll reply, "Thanks for your time. Do you have any suggestions regarding who might present it for us?" If she says no, just thank her again and hang up.

Ms. Johnson may say, "All submissions have to come through your attorney."

Ms. Johnson may say, "You're right; we don't usually accept unsolicited material. Could you tell me more about your act and your music?" Be prepared. You don't want to lose an opportunity.

Ms. Johnson may say, "Tapes aren't sent to me; you'll have to send it Don Adams."

Ms. Johnson may say, "We don't normally accept unsolicited material, but yours sounds interesting. Why don't you send it to my attention?"

But what if you can't reach Ms. Johnson or any of the other A&R executives? Try a different method. Call and speak to a secretary or administrative assistant and see if they will give you the name and method of sending a demo. Method? Yes, labels often have a specific method they want you to use to send demos so they know that they aren't accepting unsolicited material. They might, for example, want you to put the person's name in a specific corner of the package.

What if you're not having any luck that way, either? Many label executives come in early or stay late to deal with people on the other side of the country. Take advantage of this by calling early before traditional office hours or later after traditional office hours when the executive's secretary probably won't be in and see if you can get through.

"What about voice mail?" you ask.

Off hours, most executives answer their own phone because they're waiting for calls.

"I'm not really good at selling on the phone," you say. "Is there any other way to get permission to send a demo?"

If you don't want to call or you want to try another approach, you can send a letter to the A&R departments of the labels in which you are interested. If this is the approach you're taking, make sure that you send the letter to specific names, not just a title. For example, Mr. Keo Smith, A&R Director, not just A&R Director. If you can get the name of the person in the A&R department in the area closest to your genre of music, even better. If your genre is country and Shannon Tubin is the assistant director of A&R in charge of country music, you would direct your letter to her instead of to Keo Smith.

To make your letter look as professional as possible, use stationery with your act's letterhead. If you don't have letterhead, you can cre-

> ### ⭐ Tip from the Top
> You sometimes have a better chance of response by sending a letter to an assistant, coordinator, or representative of a department instead of sending it to the president of a company or the director of a department.

ate some on your computer and then print it on high-quality paper.

The letter should tell who you are, explain a little about your act, and ask for permission to submit your demo and package. Here's an example to get you started.

Jeanne Phillips
Fortune Records
244 Any Road
Anytown, USA 12345

Dear Ms. Phillips:

AmTrax is a five-member, male, country-pop group that has been together for three years. We've been playing in clubs throughout the mid-west region and successfully selling out shows at 100+ seat clubs in both the Chicago and Indianapolis areas.

What makes AmTrax unique is every member of the group sings, plays at least three instruments, and writes material. Our shows are currently composed of 80 percent original material and 20 percent cover songs, which we've arranged to perform in our own style.

Four months ago, we recorded a CD of some of our original material, which we have been selling at our shows and in stores in our area. To date we have sold over 4500 copies.

I think our music would be a great addition to the roster at the Fortune label and would love to send you our demo and package for your review.

As I know you're busy, I've enclosed a stamped response card. I would appreciate it if you could just check the appropriate box with your answer and drop it in the mail.

Thanks for your consideration.

Sincerely,
Pat James

You can either have response cards professionally printed on a regular or oversized postcard or print them on your computer. Remember if you are using an oversized postcard to add appropriate postage.

Sample Response Card for Demo

Name of Company to Which You Sent Letter
(*type this in*)

[attach stamp here]

Your Act's Name
Contact Name
Address
City, State, Zip

(Reverse Side)

Thanks for responding to AmTrax!

_____Yes I would like to hear AmTrax. Please send me your demo.

_____Yes I would like to hear AmTrax live. Please send itinerary.

_____ We are not accepting material at this time. Contact again in a few months.

_____   _____
Name   Label Name

If you don't get permission, should you send your demo anyway? If a label definitely says not to, your demo will either be "returned to sender" or wind up sitting in a pile that probably won't get listened to, so you might want to rethink your plan. At almost every seminar I conduct, people tell me that no matter how bad the odds are of having their unsolicited demos listened to, they still want to send them. If you're truly determined to submit your tape or CD, even with the odds stacked against you and instructions from a label not send a demo, go ahead. After all, you never can tell.

Believe it or not, people have been discovered through their demos and songwriters have sent songs to A&R people who have then chosen them. While others might tell you not to even bother, here's my perspective. Other than the expense of sending your demo and your press kit, what does it cost? Nothing. What can the payoff be? A possible meeting, a contract, a dream come true.

Still, networking can be the most important element in getting your demo reviewed and getting your foot in the door. When you meet people in the industry, get their card. When you call or write to someone and ask to send your demo, remind him or her of where you met. For example:

Dear Ms. Stevens:
   It was great meeting you at our show at the Lion's Inn last week. I'm glad you enjoyed our act and our music. As promised, enclosed are a couple copies of our demo as well as our press kit. Thanks so much for offering to bring it to the attention of Bling Records. I'll be calling you next week. Thanks again.

                    Best regards,
                    (Your Name Here)

Solicited or unsolicited, what's the best way to send your demo? Send it with a cover letter indicating who you are, the name of the act, the type of music, and what's on the demo. Include your press kits, which will have the act's bio, photo, and any press clippings that might grab someone's attention. You also should include a stamped, self-addressed envelope. Why? It makes it easier for someone who is not interested to drop you a note. Why should you make it easier for them? Simple: Otherwise, you might not hear from them at all. For the same effort, you want to know who is *not* interested.

One of the questions everyone asks about sending out demos is "If I don't hear back from the label, how long should I wait until I call them?" That's a hard question to answer. It's dependent to a great extent on whether you sent your demo solicited or unsolicited.

Here's the good news. Generally, if a label is interested, you don't have to call them; they'll call you. Now here's the not so good news. If you sent your demo to a label unsolicited and you haven't heard from them after a period of time, they either haven't listened to it yet or they're not interested. If you absolutely feel you have to call, give it at least a few weeks. On the other hand, if you sent in a demo that was solicited, give it a couple of weeks and call. If you're told that they haven't listened to your demo yet, ask when would be a good time for you to check back. You sometimes have to keep following up. Be nice, but be persistent.

If you have a professional-sounding demo, it might be worth your while to send your demo to the trades. Many of them review new music. If you get a good review, you stand a decent chance of a label calling *you,* or at the very least you'll have an easier time getting through to them.

If you have management at this time, your management should handle this task instead of you or any of the members of your act. As we just noted, having someone in the industry make a call or forward your demo can make all the difference in the world. We're going to dis-

Words from the Wise
Whatever you do, don't call up a label and insist they make a decision *now* because you have another label interested in you. No one will believe you.

cuss attorneys, managers, and other people on your team in a little while.

Majors versus Indies

In the world of recording, there are labels known as the majors and then there are the indies. What are the major labels? Sony Music-BMG, EMI, Universal, and Warner Music Group are some good examples. Is that all? No, these are just the parent companies. Under the parent companies are other labels purchased by the majors and are now owned and distributed by the major labels.

What are the indies? They are the thousands of other record labels that are independent and not owned by the major music conglomerates. Indies are either distributed independently or in some cases through distribution agreements with the majors. There are large indies with staffs as well as small indies owned by people who just want to get their own CD out and are outsourcing what they can't do on their own.

What's the difference? Basically, major labels owned by major music conglomerates have major monies, major promotional channels, and major distribution channels. So, should you target independent labels? It's definitely worth considering. Why? To begin with, they are more accessible. While it's not impossible to get through to the major labels, it sometimes can be a challenge.

If you want to get through to indies, many times all you have to do is call their A&R

department and someone will talk to you and then they'll listen to your demo. Indies make their money by signing up-and-coming artists with potential. They then take the artists and help develop their careers. What does that mean to you? It means that at this very moment, an indie might be looking for someone just like you.

Consider how most independent labels work. Many successful indies have distribution deals with major labels. What does that mean to you? If you sign with an indie, you can bet that the major label distributing their music is listening to it. And if you start making noise in the industry, that major label just might want you on their label.

"But what if I'm already signed to the indie?" you ask.

Many of the distribution agreements indies have with major labels have an option written in that allows the major label to take an artist they want from the indie label and bring them over to their label. Basically, this means that if you sign to an indie, they are going to push you, promote you, and give you exposure. Then if your CD starts making noise, you stand a good chance of a major wanting to pick up your contract.

In many cases, indies will also give you more attention as an up-and-coming artist than a major will. One of the challenges facing many new acts is that the majors tend to put a lot of their effort into their established and megastar acts who are selling product already.

Keep in mind that every indie is not the same. Some are larger. Some have more resources. Some will put more into you and your career.

Does this mean you should forget the majors? Not at all.

Here's the deal. Shop your material around and see who wants to offer you a deal. Once they do, sit down and see which deal is the best for you. It might be with a major. It might be with an indie.

While there are a lot of pros with indies, there are also some cons. What are they? Depending on the size of the indie, they may have fewer resources, they may have more difficulty getting airplay, and they might not have the budget to produce expensive videos.

"But I want to be big," you say. "I want to be with the best."

That's perfectly understandable. Be aware, however, that there are a lot of acts out there who choose indies over majors.

Releasing Your Own CD

Can you release your own CD? Absolutely. It might not turn into a mega hit, but if you're playing a lot of gigs and have fans, people often like to buy your music. Before you move ahead on the project, remember that you're going to have to deal with some of the business that labels deal with. An attorney may help you with some of this.

If your songs aren't copyrighted yet, you'll have to do that as well as making sure all liner notes have the correct copyright notices. Songs may need to be registered with BMI or ASCAP depending on your affiliations. If the songs aren't yours, you're going to have to deal with mechanical licenses, which are agreements with the song's owner that grant you permission to record and sell your version. If you are using outside producers or musicians, you might need agreements for these as well. Of course, it goes without saying that all agreements should be signed prior to going into the studio.

You also need to find a good studio to record your material as well as companies to duplicate and package your CDs. Make sure you ask if the company will provide you with your own

Words from the Wise

Double check that the duplicator is giving you your own bar code, not a general company barcode. Otherwise, when your CD is scanned at a retail outlet, you will never be able to track sales. Why is this important? Because if you can show a label that your CD is selling, it's a good entrée for getting a contract.

bar code. This will identify your CD when it is sold in retail markets. A company called Sound Scan can register your CD and keeps track of data from scanned barcodes on CDs, cassettes, and records sold at retail outlets. Don't forget you are also going to need an artist to design your cover.

Think ahead to how and where you're going to distribute your CDs. Are you just going to sell them at gigs? What about on the Internet? Can you get your product into some local stores? Who is going to handle the publicity, promotion, and marketing?

Your Professional Support Team

You can have a lot of talent, but without people to help get you where you need to go, it's going to be a long, difficult road. Take a minute and think about all the successful people you know on the talent end of the music industry. Whether they're singers, musicians, recording artists, or touring artists, every one has a professional support team of some sort. Sometimes the team is smaller; sometimes it's larger, but it's a support team just the same.

What's a professional support team? In the music industry, your support team can include all the pros who help you with your career. Your support team in the music industry may include, among others:

- attorneys, to handle your legal needs
- personal manager, to handle your career
- business managers/accountants, to handle your financial affairs
- booking agents, to handle your booking
- publicists/press agents/public relations counselors, to handle your publicity
- tour coordinator/tour manager, to help coordinate and manage your affairs while on tour

Each person in your support team has his or her own specific job and each can help your career in some manner. While we've talked about some of these positions in earlier chapters, let's talk about some of them in more depth now.

Your Attorney

An attorney is essential to your success in the music industry. Whether you're a singer, musician, songwriter, or any other creative talent in the music industry, you're going to need one. And you don't just need any attorney. You need an attorney who specializes in entertainment or music industry law.

People at seminars often ask when they need an attorney. My answer is, as soon as you decide to go professional. Why? There are a number of reasons, but the main one is that an attorney specializing in the music industry can help you with your career.

What should you look for? Ethical, well-respected individuals who have contacts in the industry. Most important, the music industry is full of contracts. Music industry attorneys know what to look for in a contract. They know what should be there and what shouldn't be. They can protect you. You can have the most promising career in the world, but if you're not protected, you might wind up with nothing.

Additionally, your attorney should have experience negotiating contracts. Believe it or not, even a one-cent difference can mean a lot of money if you're selling millions of copies of a CD.

How do you find the best attorneys who specialize in the music industry? While you can find attorneys in directories or the Yellow Pages or in ads in the trade, word of mouth recommendations and referrals are your best bet.

Ask people in the industry who they are using. Are they happy with the individual, or are they complaining about him or her? You might also ask your own personal attorney for a recommendation. Before you ask why you can't just use your own attorney, let me answer the question. Unless your personal attorney is in the music industry, he or she does not have the experience and the contacts you need. No matter what anyone tells you, contracts are not all same.

What will you use your attorney for? Here's a list of a few things.

- recording contracts
- publishing contracts
- partnership agreements
- management contracts
- agency contracts
- merchandising deals

Words from the Wise

Even if your brother, sister, mother or father, wife or husband, neighbor or best friend offers to handle your legal needs for free, unless they specialize in the music or entertainment industry, politely thank them and nicely turn down the offer.

- incorporations
- performance agreements
- copyrights
- trademarks
- handling litigation
- sponsorship agreements

Your attorney might also have contacts with the labels, managers, agents, clubs, and so on and can help move your career in an upward direction. In some cases, especially at the beginning, there are attorneys who act as artist managers.

Personal Managers

A good personal manger will be your cheerleader. He or she will help mold your career, help push it in the right direction, and help *you* make the right decisions. Your manager helps you with the day-to-day running of your career. Your personal manager will be your chief advisor, someone who can speak on your behalf will help you network. Most of all, a good personal manager will believe in you and your act.

What else can a good personal manager do for you? If the individual is connected in the industry, he or she can help you find a recording deal, sponsorship opportunities, and other support personnel. He or she can also help you coordinate everyone else and everything else in your career.

When do you need a personal manager? That depends on where you are in your career and where you are going. A manager can be extremely effective, along with your attorney, when you're dealing with record labels, music publishers, and agents.

Can you continue to manage yourself? You can, but it is often difficult to successfully manage your act and still handle all the things you need to do on the talent end. If, however, you can't find management right away, make sure you and your act learn as much as possible about the business end of the industry.

What should you look for in a manager? Here are some desirable attributes.

- someone who believes in you and your act
- someone who is creative
- someone who is a self-starter
- someone you truly like
- someone you trust and is trustworthy
- someone who is honest
- someone who has a good reputation
- someone who is respected in the field
- someone who has contacts in the industry
- someone who can help you secure a record deal
- someone who can help you move ahead

How do you find a good manager? First of all, take your time. Think about it. Is there someone you might want as your manager? Do you see someone who is doing a great job for another act and you might want to approach? Would he or she be effective managing your act? If so, contact the individual. Managers often handle more than one act. If it's someone you know, approach him or her and simply ask. If it's someone you don't know, get their address and phone number and either give them a call or send a letter with your promo material, indicating that you are interested in discussing the situation.

What about a friend or family member? Can one of them manage your act? Anyone can manage your act. The question is who can do the best job? If your friend or family member is savvy, understands the music business, and is connected, it might work. If not, you might

> **Words from the Wise**
>
> Don't just sign a management contract to get a manager. Make sure you and your act are all comfortable with your choice.

want to think twice about it, but that's not to say that it never works. There are a number of artists who have friends or family members successfully manage their careers. Joe Simpson, for example, manages the careers of his two daughters, Jessica and Ashlee Simpson.

How else can you find a good manager? Consider having a showcase for potential managers. You also might want to advertise in some of the industry trades such as *Billboard.* You might also get lucky. A great manager might see your act and recognize your potential and approach you. Once you find a personal manager who you're comfortable with, your next step is negotiating and signing a personal management contract.

Generally, managers use a standard management contract that includes negotiated points, which have been agreed upon by both parties. Negotiating points might include the term of the contract, options, percentage paid to the manager, and areas of management.

It is essential to trust your manager because in many cases the manager will want the contract to state the he or she has power of attorney for your act. This means that manager has the power to sign contracts on behalf of your act. It also may mean that the manager can spend money on behalf of the act. A savvy attorney will list the specific areas of the artist's career where the manager has power of attorney and limit his or her authority to spend money over a certain amount without authorization.

The Inside Scoop

If you sign a management contract with a manager who works within a management company, you will most likely have a clause in your agreement called the "key man" or "key person" clause. This clause protects you in a number of situations including if the person who you signed with to be your manager leaves the company.

Personal managers are paid a percentage of the act's gross earnings ranging from 10 percent to 20 percent. Some managers believe so strongly in an act's talent that they may not take a percentage of the act's earnings until they get on their feet financially. They may also help an act with some of their expenses such as recording demos, developing press and promotion packages, taking professional photos, and/or promotion. The manager's hope is that that the act will make it big and that the risk and investment will pay off.

Business Manager

A business manager helps you manage your business affairs. He or she helps you make decisions on how to save money, spend money, and invest money. Specifically, your business manager may be responsible for paying your bills, doing your payroll, collecting income, and auditing your royalties. He or she will also handle tax planning. This is especially important because as a rule taxes are not taken out of your fees when you play at clubs, venues, or for other engagements. In some situations, especially if there is a complicated tax situation, the business manager will recommend a specialist.

When do you need a business manager? Generally, you don't have to worry about getting one until you are doing fairly well. You will, however, probably need to use an accountant until you get a business manager.

How do you find a good business manager? As with most other members of your team, ask for recommendations from friends and colleagues in the business.

What do you look for? You want an honest business manager who is familiar with the music and entertainment industry. While there are no formal requirements in most cases to be a business manager, accountants or CPAs would be your best bet.

You should be aware that business managers may be compensated in a number of ways ranging from a retainer to an hourly fee to a percentage of income. Which is better? That depends, but most industry professionals prefer paying an hourly fee.

Songwriters and Composers

A hit song can earn a tremendous of money, depending on how it's exploited. Let's take some time now to discuss your career as a songwriter or composer. You've written songs. You have confidence that they're good. What do you do with them now?

Words from the Wise

Always keep track of your monies. Know what is coming in and what is going out. Even if you use a business manager, make sure you are the one who has control over your monies. Some entertainers over the years have gone from being very wealthy to having nothing. In most of these cases, they indicated that one of the main problems was they didn't oversee their finances. If you want to be sure what is being spent, make sure you are the one signing all checks.

The number-one piece of advice is to register them for copyright protection. This not only protects you but the people to whom you are sending your material. Once that's done, you have a number of options depending on the direction you want your career to go.

You need to make a demo and pitch it in much the same manner as artists looking for a recording contract. Many artists write their own material, but others don't and need original songs for their CDs. Even artists who write their own material sometimes need the perfect tune, the one that will be a hit on the charts. Are you the songwriter who penned it? Perhaps, but you need to get it to the right people.

Perhaps you can "hear" an established act singing your song. What do you do? If you have access to the act, you might give them a demo and lyric sheet. If you don't have access to those people, consider contacting their management. You can find management names and contact information for most artists in directories such as the *Billboard's Annual Talent & Touring International Guide*. Write a letter introducing yourself and your music and ask for permission to send a tape and lyric sheets.

What else can you do? You might want to pitch your songs to publishers for their catalog. In turn, publishers pitch songs from their catalogs to producers, A&R personnel, record label executives, major and indie artists, advertising agencies, and production companies.

How do you make money as a songwriter? You might "work for hire," which means someone pays you to write a song. In this case, you don't usually retain any rights to the song. It belongs to the person who paid you. Certain labels also have songwriters on staff. The main way you're going to make money as a songwriter is through publishing agreements. Publishing is an important part of the music industry.

Let's start with the concept that you wrote the song and are the copyright holder and owner.

Basically, as the copyright holder and owner of a song, you have certain rights. These include, among others, the exclusive right to perform your song in public, the right to record it, the right to write down the music and lyrics and print them, and the right to use your music along with a visual image. No one else has these rights to your song, unless they pay you to gain them. When that occurs, you are in effect granting them a license. This is called publishing, and this is how as a songwriter you make money.

There are four main areas of publishing income:

Primary sources
◎ performance
◎ mechanical

Secondary sources
◎ print
◎ synchronization

Performance rights are the rights to perform your song in public. Performance royalties or performance license monies are paid when your song is performed or played in public or played on the radio, in elevators, in music services, or anywhere else. BMI, ASCAP, and SESAC are

The Inside Scoop

Writer's royalties should not be confused with recording royalties which artists receive when appearing on recordings. If an individual is the songwriter and performer on the CD, he or she will receive both writer and recording royalties.

the performance rights organizations that collect the monies from people, businesses, and organizations who play your music. This is often done through licensing agreements.

Mechanical rights are the rights to reproduce your song. Mechanical royalties are paid by the record label for the use of your song or songs on recordings. Each time someone makes a physical copy of your song on a CD, cassette, or record, you are paid a royalty.

A *print license* means that every time someone writes down or prints your song and publishes it, as the copyright holder and owner, you receive payment. This would include sheet music such as piano scores, music books, and so on.

A *synchronization license* means that every time your song is played along with a visual image, you are paid monies. This includes things such as background music used in television, films, and commercials, title songs for television, film soundtracks, and videos, and many other uses.

With all this money coming in from your songs, how do you collect it? How do you know who should pay what? Many songwriters contract with publishers. Their job is to collect the

---

Tip from the Top

As a songwriter you want to be affiliated with one of the three performance rights agencies, ASCAP, BMI, or SESAC. These organizations collect the royalties due to you for public performance of your songs.

---

monies owed to you from all publishing agreements and licenses. For them to do so, you generally have to assign your copyright to the publisher. While there are exceptions, the standard publishing agreement usually gives the publisher half of the revenues collected as a fee.

There are some songwriters who administer their own publishing by creating their own publishing companies. This can be very time consuming, but they also keep the extra revenue. Which option should you take? Only you can decide. It's important to understand when making this decision that in many circumstances, because publishers deal with licenses all the time, they often are more versed in the going rates.

Copyrights

If you are a songwriter or composer how important is protecting yourself in the industry? If you want to enjoy the fruits of your labor, it's very important. How do you protect yourself as a songwriter? You register your songs for copyright protection.

Technically, the minute you write a song down or put it on tape it is copyrighted. The problem is, however, without proof, it's often very difficult to prove. That's not to say it's impossible, but it is hard.

How do you register for copyright protection? It's simple. Contact the U.S. Copyright Office, get the forms, fill them in, and send them in with pay-

---

The Inside Scoop

Rates for mechanical royalties are set by the U.S. Copyright Office. Currently, mechanical rates are 7.1 cents per song. That means that if one of the songs you have written is on a CD that sells 100,000 units, you would have earned $7,100. If two of the songs were on that same CD that sold 100,000 units, you would have earned $14,200. Keep in mind that if the songs are used in other ways, you will earn additional monies as the copyright holder.

ment. At this time it's $45.00. Depending on your situation you may want to register your printed lyrics and music as well as the recorded version of your song embedded on a tape. If you have a number of songs to register, you might want to register them all on one tape. That way, while they're all registered, it will only cost one fee.

U.S. Copyright Office
Library of Congress
Washington, DC 20559
(202) 707-3000
http://www.copyright.gov

Trust the People You Work With

Here's something to think about: Trust the people you work with and only work with people you trust. Need a reason? Here's a true story of a man who I'm going to call Jack. I have changed his name to protect his identity.

Jack was the son of a successful singer, songwriter, and producer. He grew up in the music business. From the time he was a young boy, his father told him, "Don't even hum a song you hear in the house, outside of the family, until it's copyrighted. It's just too easy for people to hear a song and think it's theirs."

Jack started his career where his dad did, singing in church. As he grew into a young man, it was evident that he, too, was a talented singer, musician, and songwriter. By the time he was in his early 20s, Jack was on the road as the musical director and keyboard player of a well-known recording act.

It was not surprising that Jack made a lot of contacts and had a lot of friends in the industry. Jack and a two of his friends heard that a film producer they knew was working on a movie and looking for some music. One night the three friends got together at Jack's apartment and were discussing the film. While the other two

men had never written any music or lyrics, Jack had been writing for years.

As the three sat around talking about the film, Jack jotted down some possible lyrics and scoring for the music on a sheet of paper. It was a fun evening. The three were all laughing, talking, and partying.

As those evenings often go, sometime during the night, Jack passed out and his friends left. A couple days later, Jack went back on the road. He had called his friends a few times to discuss the film and ask if they had the lyrics and music he wrote, but for some reason they never hooked up.

And that would be the end of the story if a couple of years later, the movie didn't turn into a hit.

One day Jack turned on the radio. Guess what? The song Jack had written all those months before was now the title song of the movie. It was a hit, too. A little confused, Jack went to buy a copy of the single.

His name wasn't listed as the sole writer. As a matter of fact, his name wasn't listed as the writer at all. His two "friends" had taken the words and the music and copyrighted them under their names.

While Jack was understandably upset, at that point nothing could be done. With no proof, Jack lost out on fame and fortune.

What's the moral of the story? There are a few. Trust the people you do business with. When you're dealing with business, act professionally. Partying may have its place, but it is definitely not appropriate when you're dealing in business. As this story shows, it can be costly.

Protecting Yourself

I've given you a lot of advice in this book. I've covered a lot of different areas. Here is one of the most important things I have to tell you: As a creative talent, what you have to sell is *you.* You are the product. Whether you are a singer, musician, songwriter, producer, arranger, or any other person on the creative talent end of the music industry, if you don't protect yourself, you will have nothing! Do not get so caught up in what you want that you forget this fact.

If you take nothing else from this book, I hope you'll take this. I want you to protect yourself. Before you sign a contact, any contract, I want you not only to read it but know and understand what you're reading. If you don't understand something, no matter how small, ask. Don't be embarrassed, don't feel stupid, and don't feel like someone will laugh at you. Ask and get an explanation of what you don't understand. Clarify points.

If you're thinking that's what lawyers are for, the simple answer is yes. But that doesn't mean that you should leave your career to chance. Just because a lawyer reads over a contract doesn't mean you shouldn't too. Then ask him or her about points you don't understand.

At some point during your career, I can almost guarantee you that someone, whether it be a promoter, an agent, a manager, or a publisher, will give you something to sign and say to you something to the effect of: "You can read it over if you want, but it's a standard contract. You're really wasting your time."

Should you take their word? NO! Read everything. They probably are telling the truth, but perhaps their version of standard is not your version. Read every line.

I can also guarantee you sometime in your career someone will say to you one or more of the following:

◎ "We don't need a contract; we trust each other."
  ▫ You need a contract.
◎ "We're friends; we don't need a contract."
  ▫ A contract will assure you will stay friends.
◎ "It' a simple gig. Don't worry about a contract. All you have to do is show up, play, and you'll get paid."
  ▫ You will have little recourse if you don't get paid. You need a contract or an agreement of sorts.
◎ "A verbal contract is as good as a written one."
  ▫ Not really. You can produce a written contract. Even if you have a witness to what was said, a written contract is better.
◎ "A contract is only as good as the paper it's written on."
  ▫ While contracts can be broken, they are still contracts.
◎ "Let's just shake on it."
  ▫ You can shake on it, after you sign a contract.

Are you getting the idea? You need to protect yourself. Do you always need a complicated contract? No, a simple agreement can suffice sometimes, but you you should always have some sort of dated agreement signed by both parties stating what is expected of you (or your act), when it is expected, and what is expected in return. The best person to give you advice in this area is an attorney.

12

SUCCESS IS YOURS FOR THE TAKING

Do You Have What It Takes?

Do you have what it takes to be a successful professional?

"Well . . . I think so," you say.

You think so? That's not good enough. You have to know so! If you don't believe in yourself, no one else will.

"Okay," you say. "I get it. I *know* I can be successful."

That's good! Now what you have to remember is that no matter what comes your way, don't give up. The music industry is a great one in which to work. There may be stumbling blocks. You may have to take detours. There may even be times when you have to choose at a fork in the road. But it's worth it if you achieve your goals.

Whether you are dreaming of success in the talent area as a singer, musician, songwriter, producer, or arranger; whether you are dreaming of a career on the business end of the industry at a label, publisher, venue, magazine, newspaper, radio station, or school; always keep your eye on the prize. Whether you want to be in the forefront of the industry, the background, or somewhere in between, know that you can do it, as long as you don't give up.

Sometimes your dream may change. That's okay. As long as you are following *your* dreams,

not those of others, you usually are on the right road.

The music industry is huge. What is going to be your contribution? Are you going to be the one who writes the song? How about the one who publishes it? Will you be the one who sings or plays the music? How about the one who produces or records it?

Are you going give vocal lessons to singers or teach musicians how to play better? Is your job going to be at the record label, the music publisher, or the booking agency? Are you the one who is going to find the next big star or the next big song? Are you going to work on the sales and marketing end of the music industry?

Is your career going to be working in radio as a program director, music director, or disc jockey choosing and playing the music and helping make the hits? What about a career publicizing musical artists and helping catapult their careers? Are you going to be a music reviewer or music industry journalist? Are you going to work on the road? Are you going to manage an act, book them, or handle their legal affairs?

Where do you envision yourself? What do you see yourself doing? Seize your opportunity. It's there for you. Grab onto your dream to start the ball rolling.

I've talked to many people who are extremely successful in all facets of the music industry. One of the most interesting things about them is that most were *not* surprised at all that they were successful. As a matter of fact, they expected it.

I remember sitting backstage at a concert before a show talking to one of the singers in the act. We were discussing some of the other hot artists in the industry. The singer was telling me a story of another singer on the charts. "We knew he was going to be a star," he said about the other artist. "When he was still in school, he told everyone he was going to be one, and that's all he talked about."

"Doesn't everyone say that?" I asked.

"Sometimes they do," he continued, "But what made him different was he was specific about what he was going to do and when. He told everyone he was going to have a hit record before he graduated. [He hadn't even recorded anything at that time.] He started acting like a star and then dressing the part of a star. He went on and on about it so much that he almost had to be a star to save face. Funny thing was, he did have a hit before he graduated and he did turn into a huge star."

I know of at least three singers in the industry who told me that they chose outfits to wear to the Grammy's and American Music Awards the week they recorded their songs. Not only that; they wrote their acceptance speech. You know what? I later saw them pull that speech out and read it when they won.

Is it the planning and the work that creates the reality, or is it the dream that puts them on the road to success? I think it's a combination.

Have you picked out your Grammy outfit? Have you written your acceptance speech? Have you chosen the perfect suit you're going to wear when you are promoted to VP of A&R or legal affairs at the record label? Do you know what you're going to say?

If not, you should, at least in your mind. Why? Because if you claim something, you're often closer to making it happen. Over the years, I have heard many similar stories from people who have made it as very successful singers, musicians, songwriters, record company executives, publicists, journalists, and others. Was it that they knew what they wanted to do and focused on it more than others? Was it they had a premonition and things just worked out? Were they just lucky? Were they more talented than others? Was it visualization? Or was it that a positive attitude helped create a positive situation? No one really knows. The only thing that seems evident is that those who expect to be successful usually have a better chance of achieving it. Those who have a positive attitude usually have a better chance of positive things happening.

Tip from the Coach

Before writing my first book on the music industry, I mentioned to a number of people that I was looking for a publisher. Their response was always the same. "It is very difficult to get a publisher. Don't get your hopes up."

While my book wasn't yet written, I had already seen it in my mind. I knew what it would look like; I knew what it was going to say. I told everyone the same story. I was going to send out queries to publishers whose names started with *A* and go through the alphabet until I reached *Z* and find a publisher. The book would be a reality no matter what anyone thought. By the time I got to the Fs, I had sold my book idea. I wasn't surprised, because I not only knew it would happen; I expected it. That first book, *Career Opportunities In The Music Industry,* is now in its fifth edition.

We've covered visualization earlier in the book. Whether you believe this theory or not, one thing is for sure: It can't hurt. So plan your own personal Grammy party, plan your own celebration, plan for your own success, and then get ready for it to happen.

Creating a Career You Love

While working toward your perfect career, it's important to combine your goals with your life objectives. The trick to success in the music industry is not only following your interests but following your heart. If you're working toward your dream, going that extra mile, and doing that extra task, it won't be a chore. Obstacles won't be problems, just stepping-stones to get where you're going.

By now, you have read some (if not all) of this book. You've learned that there are certain things you need to do to stack the deck in your favor whether you want your success to be on the business or talent end of the industry.

You know how to get gigs. You know what to do with demos. You know how to find agents, managers, and how to deal with record labels. And you know how important an attorney can be to protecting you in your career in the music industry.

You've learned how to network and how to market yourself. You've learned some neat little tricks to get past the receptionist and get your foot in the door. You've learned that you need to find ways to stand out from the crowd. You've also learned that the music business is just that—a business—and you're ready to treat it as such.

Most of all, you've learned that it's essential to create a career you love. You've learned that you don't ever want to settle and wonder "what if?"

Creating the career you want and love is not always the easiest thing in the world to accomplish, but it is definitely worth it. To help you focus on what you want, you might find it helpful to create a personal mission statement.

Your Personal Mission Statement

There are many people who want to be in the music business. Some make it and some don't. I want you to be one who makes it. I want you to be one who succeeds. Throughout the book, I've tried to give you tips, tricks, and techniques that can help. I've tried to give you the inspiration and motivation to know you can do it. Here's one more that might make your journey easier.

Create your personal mission statement. Why? Because your mission statement can help you define your visions clearly. It will give you a path, a purpose, and something to follow. Most important, putting your mission statement in writing can help you bring your mission to fruition.

What's a mission statement? It's a statement declaring what your mission is in your life and your career. How do you do it? As with all the other exercises you've done, sit down, get comfortable, take out a pen and a piece of paper, and start writing. What is your mission?

Remember that your mission statement is for you. You're not writing it for your family, your friends, or your employer. It can be changed or modified at any time. Think about it for a moment. What do you want to do? Where do you want be? What are your dreams? What is your mission?

There is no one right way to write your mission statement. Some people like to write it in paragraph form. Others like to use bullets or numbers. It really doesn't matter, as long as you get it down in writing. The main thing to remember is to make your statement a clear and concise declaration of your long term mission.

Your mission statement might be one sentence, one paragraph, or even fill two or three pages. It's totally up to you. As long as your mission statement is clear, you're okay.

Here are some examples of simple mission statements.

- ◎ Singer
  - ▫ My mission is to use my skills and talent to create a career as a top recording and performing artist.
- ◎ Singer-songwriter
  - ▫ My mission is to use my skills and talent to write and publish songs recorded by other artists as well as creating a career as a top recording and performing artist myself.
- ◎ Music industry publicist-press agent
  - ▫ My mission is to work at a top music industry publicity firm as a press agent acquiring a large roster of chart-topping clients.
- ◎ Record label executive
  - ▫ My mission is to work at a top label in the A&R department and discover the next Madonna or Usher. I eventually want to become a record label president.
- ◎ Music producer
  - ▫ My mission is to find talented artists to work with and use my talents to produce creative, financially rewarding projects.
- ◎ Publisher
  - ▫ My mission is to learn as much as possible about the publishing business, start my own publishing company and sign a large catalog of successful songs.

Tip from the Coach

Put your personal mission statement on Post-it Notes and stick them up all around to keep you focused.

- ◎ Music journalist
  - ▫ My mission is to be working for a world-class publication writing about the music business.

What do you do with your mission statement? Use it! Review it to remember what you're working toward. Use it as motivation. Use it to help you move in the right direction.

You would be surprised how many successful people have their personal mission statement hanging on their wall or taped to their computer. I've seen several touring recording artists who even have their personal mission statement hanging on a mirror in their tour bus. Wherever you decide to place your mission statement, be sure to look at it daily so you can always keep it in mind.

Success Strategies

We have discussed marketing, promotion, and publicity. Used effectively, they can help your career tremendously. Here's what you have to remember! Don't wait for someone else to recognize your skills and talents; promote yourself. There are many keys to success in the music industry. Self-promotion is an important one.

Don't toot your own horn in an annoying or obnoxious manner, but make sure people notice you. You want to stand out in a positive way. Don't keep your accomplishments a secret. Instead, claim them proudly.

Buzz is very important in the music business. Start thinking like a publicist even if you're lucky enough to have one. Whether you're working on the business or talent end of the industry, you need to constantly promote yourself or no one will know you exist. While others may help, the responsibility really is on *you* to make your career work and make your career successful.

No matter where you are in your career, continue to look for opportunities of all kinds. Search out opportunities to move ahead in your career and then grab hold of them.

Also know that in your life and career, on occasion there may be doors that close. The trick here is not to let a door close without looking for the window of opportunity that is always there. If you see an opportunity, jump on it immediately.

Throughout the book we've discussed the importance of networking. Once you become successful, it's important to continue to network. Just because you have a contract with a label does not mean you don't want to meet other label executives. Just because you're signed with an agent doesn't mean you might not want to know another agent, and just because you have a job at label does not mean you might never want another job. You can never tell who knows who and what someone might need. There are always new opportunities ahead. If you don't keep networking you might miss some of them.

Don't be afraid to ask for help. If you know someone who can help in your career, ask. The worst they can say is no. The best that can happen is you might get some help. Of course, if you can help someone else do that as well.

The Inside Scoop
Don't procrastinate when an opportunity presents itself. Someone else is always on the lookout just like you, and you don't want to miss your chances.

Words from the Wise
Keep all professional conversations professional and positive. Don't complain. Don't whine. Don't be negative.

Always be prepared for success. It might be just around the corner. If you're a singer or musician, practice your craft and rehearse until you're perfect. Whether you're on the talent or business end of the industry, keep up with the trends, read the trades, and make sure you know what is happening in the industry today.

Whatever facet of the industry you're in, you are going to be selling yourself. It might be for a job, an engagement, negotiating for a recording contract, a management contract, to get some publicity, or a variety of other situations. Take a lesson from others who have made it to the top and prepare ahead of time. That way, when you're in a situation where you need to say something, you'll be ready. Come up with a pitch and practice it until you're comfortable.

Always be positive. Attitude is essential to your life and your professional success. Here's the deal. People want to be around other people who are positive. If there is a choice between two people with similar talents and skills and you have a better outlook than anyone else, a more positive type of personality and passion, you're going to be chosen.

Climbing the Career Ladder
Whatever part of the music industry you've chosen, most likely you're going to have to pay your dues. Now that you've done that, how do you climb the career ladder? How do you go from a job as an assistant to the vice president of a department or organization? How do you

go from an act that some people have heard of to the hottest act around?

There are many things you're going to have to do, but it can be done. We've covered a lot of them. Work hard, keep a positive attitude, and act professionally at all times. Stay abreast of the business, network, and hone your skills and talents so you can backup your claims of accomplishments.

Look for a mentor who can help you move your career in the right direction and propel you to the top of your field. Join trade associations, read the trades, take seminars, classes, workshops, and take part in other learning opportunities. Be the best at what you do.

Look at every opportunity with an open mind. When you're offered something, ask yourself:

◎ Is this what I want to be doing?
◎ Is this part of my plan for success?
◎ Is this opportunity a stepping-stone to advancing my career?

Remember that job progression in the music industry doesn't always follow a normal path. For example, a fairly new assistant working in the A&R department who finds the next big star may be promoted to the position of a manager or director of the department before someone with seniority.

The opening act at a concert in June might be the headliner by September if their new record hits the chart with a bullet and moves up to the top ten. There are countless stories of people who have been fans in the back of an arena one year, who are the headliners for that same band the next. That is one of the greatest things about a career in the music industry. You just never know.

You never know when your song is going to be recorded by a successful artist and become a mega hit crossing over to different genres of music. You never know when your act is going to record a song that becomes number one. And you never know when success will come your way. It can happen at any time.

It should be noted that success means different things to different people. There are many successful people in the music industry who are not mega stars yet they earn a high income and enjoy the creativity of being a performer whether it be a singer, musician, songwriter or on air personality.

Some singers and musicians back-up other acts either live or in recording sessions. Others experience success on a lower level but are successful just the same. Some artists travel throughout the country or the world on either a regional or national level performing in hotels, casinos, resorts, theaters, bars, clubs, and theme parks.

There are songwriters and composers who, while they haven't written a top-ten song, are earning very good livings writing jingles for commercials or music for other types of projects.

On-air personalities and disc jockeys move up the career ladder becoming better known, building larger followings, and moving up to bigger stations and other opportunities.

Risk Taking—Overcoming Your Fears

Everyone has a comfort zone from which they operate. What's a comfort zone? It's the area

> ### ⭐ Words from a Pro
> If you're starting to feel comfortable in your career or starting to feel bored, it's time to step out of your comfort zone and look for new challenges.

where you feel comfortable both physically and psychologically. Most of the time, you try to stay within this zone. It's predictable, it's safe, and you generally know what's coming.

Many people get jobs, stay in them for years, and then retire. They know what's expected of them. They know what they're going to be doing. They know what they're going to be getting. The problem is that it can get boring, there's little challenge, and your creativity can suffer. Stepping out of your comfort zone is especially important in the music business where creativity is essential. Wanting to step out of your comfort zone is often easier said than done, but every now and then you're going to have to push yourself.

Diana Ross, Lionel Ritchie, Dolly Parton, Cher, Beyoncé, and Justin Timerberlake were all part of successful groups before they stepped out of their comfort zone and became successful solo artists. Reba MacEntire was an extremely successful country singer before she decided to step out of her comfort zone and become a television star.

The key to career success in the music industry as well as your own personal growth is the willingness to step outside of your comfort zone. Throughout your career, you're going to be faced with decisions. Each decision can im-

Tip from the Top

Try to treat everyone from subordinates to superiors to colleagues the way you want to be treated—with respect and dignity. In addition to following the "golden rule" the way career progression sometimes works in the music industry, you can never tell if the people who are your subordinates today might be your superiors tomorrow.

pact your career. Be willing to take risks. Be willing to step out of your comfort zone.

Is it scary? Of course, but if you don't take risks you stand the chance of your career stagnating. You take the chance of missing wonderful opportunities.

Should you take a promotion? Should you stay at the same job? Should you go to a different company? Should you change managers? What songs are best for your new CD? Should you take a chance on the new bass player?

How do you make the right decision? Try to think about the pros and cons of your choices. Get the facts, think about them, and make your decision.

"What if I'm wrong?" you ask.

Here's the good news: Usually, you *will* make the right decision. If by chance you don't, it's generally not a life-and-death situation. If you stay at the same job and find you should have left, for example, all you need to do is look for a new job. If you change personal managers and you're not happy, either you can find a loophole or eventually your contract will end. Most things ultimately work out. Do the best you can and then go on.

If your career is stagnant, do something. Don't just stay where you are because of the fear of leaving your comfort zone and the fear of the unknown.

Words from the Wise

Whatever level you are at in your career in the talent end of the industry, always treat your fans well. They are ultimately the ones who can make your career. Fans buy your CDs, call the radio stations to request your music, come to your shows, and cheer you on.

Some Last Thoughts

No matter where you are in your career, don't stagnate. Always keep your career moving. Once you reach one of your goals, your journey isn't over. You have to keep moving.

Are you working at a label? Do you want to move up the career ladder? Keep working towards your goal. It can happen. A hit CD is great. A career as a successful recording artist is better. Keep trying.

Don't get caught up in a thought pattern that at least you're working in the industry and settle for less than what you want. Every goal you meet is another stepping-stone towards an even better career in music, whether your goal is to work in the business area, talent area, or somewhere in between.

While I would love to promise you that after reading this book your CD will go platinum, your act will be the top concert grosser of the year, your song will be recorded by the hottest act around, or you're going to be offered the job of president of one of the major labels, unfortunately I can't.

What I can tell you is that the advice in this book can help you move ahead and stack the deck in your favor in this very competitive business. I've given you the information. You have to put it into action.

Numerous factors are essential to your success in the music industry. To succeed in this industry, you need to be prepared. There's no question that preparation is necessary. Talent is critical as well. Being in the right place at the

> ## Tip from the Coach
> Persevere. The reason most people fail is because they gave up one day too soon.
> –Shelly Field

right time is essential, and good luck doesn't hurt.

Perseverance is vital to success in the music industry no matter what you want to do, what area of the industry you want to enter, and what career level you want to achieve. Do you want to know why most people don't find their perfect job in the music industry? It's because they gave up looking *before* they found it. Do you want to know why some people are on the brink of success, yet never really get there? It's because they gave up.

Do you want to know what single factor can increase your chances of success? It's perseverance! Don't give up.

Have fun reading this book. Use it to jump-start your career and inspire you to greater success and accomplishments. Draw on it to achieve your goals so you can have the career of your dreams in the music industry.

I can't wait to hear about your success stories. Be sure to let us know how this book has helped your career in music by logging on to http://www.shellyfield.com. I would also love to hear about any of your own tips or techniques for succeeding in the music business. You can never tell. Your successes might be part of our next edition.

APPENDIX I

TRADE ASSOCIATIONS, UNIONS, AND OTHER ORGANIZATIONS

Trade associations, unions, and other organizations can be valuable resources for career guidance as well as professional support. This listing includes many of the organizations related to the music industry. Names, addresses, phone numbers, Web sites, and e-mail addresses (where available) have been included to make it easier for you to obtain information. Check out Web sites to learn more about organizations and what they offer.

Academy of Country Music (ACM)
4100 W Alemeda
Burbank, CA 91505
(818) 842-8400
info@acmcountry.com
http://www.acmcountry.com

Acoustical Society of America (ASA)
2 Huntington Quadrangle
Melville, NY 11747
(516) 576-2360
asa@aip.org
http://asa.aip.org/index.html

Actor's Equity Association (AEA)
165 W. 46th Street
New York, NY 10036
equityjobsny@actorsequity.org
http://www.actorsequity.org

American Advertising Federation (AFA)
1101 Vermont Avenue NW
Washington, DC 20005
(202) 898-0089
aaf@aaf.org
http://www.aaf.org

American Bar Association (ABA)
750 N Lake Shore Drive
Chicago, IL 60611
(312) 988-5000
service@abanet.org
http://www.abanet.org

American Choral Directors Association (ACDA)
502 SW 38th Street
Lawton, OK 73505
(580) 355-8161
acda@acdaonline.org
http://www.acdaonline.org

American Composers Alliance (ACA)

73 Spring Street
New York, NY 10012
(212) 362-8900
info@composers.com
http://www.composers.com

American Federation of Musicians of the United States and Canada (AFM)

1501 Broadway
New York, NY 10036
(212) 869-1330
info@afm.org
http://www.afm.org

American Federation of Teachers (AFT)

555 New Jersey Avenue NW
Washington, DC 20001
(202) 879-4400
online@aft.org
http://www.aft.org

American Federation of Television and Radio Artists (AFTRA)

260 Madison Avenue
New York, NY 10016
(212) 532-0800
info@aftra.com
http://www.aftra.com

American Guild of Authors and Composers (AGAC; now called the Songwriters Guild)

1500 Harbor Boulevard
Weehawken, NJ 07086
(201) 867-7603
songwritersnj@aol.com

American Guild of Musical Artists (AGMA)

1430 Broadway
New York, NY 10018
(212) 265-3687
agma@musicalartists.org
http://www.musicalartists.org

American Guild of Variety Artists (AGVA)

363 7th Avenue
New York, NY 10001
(212) 675-1003

American Institute of Certified Public Accountants (AICAP)

Harborside Financial Center
201 Plaz Three
Jersey City, NJ 07311
(201) 938-3000
http://www.aicpa.org

American Marketing Association (AMA)

311 S Wacker Drive
Chicago, IL 60606
(312) 542-9000
info@ama.org
http://www.ama.org

American Music Conference (AMC)

5790 Armada Drive
Carlsbad, CA 92008
(760) 431-9124
sharonm@amc-music.org
http://www.amc-music.org

American Music Therapy Association (AMTA)

8455 Colesville Road
Silver Spring, MD 20910
(301) 589-3300
info@musictherapy.org
http://www.musictherapy.org

American Society of Composers, Authors and Publishers (ASCAP)
1 Lincoln Plaza
New York, NY 10023
(212) 621-6000
info@ascap.com
http://www.ascap.com

American Society of Music Arrangers and Composers (ASMAC)
PO Box 17840
Encino, CA 91416
(818) 994-4661
properimage2000@earthlink.net
http://www.asmac.org

American Symphony Orchestra League (ASOL)
33 West 60th Street
New York, NY 10023
(212) 262-5161
league@symphony.org
http://www.symphony.org

Association of Theatrical Press Agents and Managers (ATPAM)
1560 Broadway
New York, NY 10036
(212) 719-3666
info@atpam.com
http://www.atpam.com

Broadcast Music, Inc. (BMI)
320 W 57th Street
New York, NY 10019
(212) 586-2000
newyork@bmi.com
http://bmi.com

College Band Directors National Association (CBDNA)
c/o Richard L. Floyd
University of Texas
Box 8028
Austin, TX 78713
(512) 471-5883
rfloyd@mail.utexas.edu
http://www.cbdna.org/

Country Music Association (CMA)
1 Music Circle South
Nashville, TN 37203
(615) 244-2840
info@cmaworld.com
http://www.cmaworld.com

Electronic Industries Alliance (EIA)
2500 Wilson Boulevard
Arlington, VA 22201
(703) 907-7500
dmccurdy@eia.org
http://www.eia.org

Gospel Music Association (GMA)
1205 Division Street
Nashville, TN 37203
(615) 242-0303
info@gospelmusic.org
http://www.gospelmusic.org

Guitar and Accessories Marketing Association (GAMA)
c/o J&D Music Services, Ltd.
262 W. 38th Street
New York, NY 10018
(212) 302-0801
assnhdqs@earthlink.net
http://www.discoverguitar.com

International Alliance of Theatrical Stage Employees (IATSE)
1430 Broadway, 8th Floor
New York, NY 10018

International Brotherhood of Electrical Workers (IBEW)
1125 15th Street NW
Washington, DC 20005
(202) 833-7000
http://www.ibew.org/

International Conference of Symphony and Opera Musicians (ICSOM)
4 W 31st Street
New York, NY 10001
(212) 594-1636
rtl@icsom.org
http://www.icsom.org

Meet the Composer (MTC)
75 9th Avenue
New York, NY 10011
(212) 645-6949
hhitchens@meetthecomposer.org
http://www.meetthecomposer.org

Metropolitan Opera Association
Lincoln Center
New York, NY 10023
(212) 362-6000
metinfo@visionfoundry.com
http://www.metopera.org

Metropolitan Opera Guild (MOG)
70 Lincoln Center Plaza
New York, NY 10023
(212) 769-7000
http://www.metopera.org

Music Critics Association of North America (MCA)
7 Pine Court
Westfield, NJ 07090

Music Library Association (MLA)
8551 Research Way, Ste. 180
Middleton, WI 53562
(608) 836-5825
mla@aveditions.com

Music Publisher's Association of the United States (MPA)
PMB 246
1562 First Avenue
New York, NY 10028
(212) 327-4044
mpa-admin@mpa.org
http://www.mpa.org

Music Teachers National Association (MTNA)
441 Vine Street
Cincinnati, OH 45202
(888) 512-5278
mtnanet@mtna.org
http://www.mtna.org

Nashville Entertainment Association (NEA)
1105 16th Avenue South
PO Box 158029
Nashville, TN 37215
info@nea.net
http://www.nea.net

Nashville Songwriters Association International (NSAI)
1710 Roy Acuff Place
Nashville, TN 37203
(615) 256-3354
nsai@nashvillesongwriters.com
http://www.nashvillesongwriters.com

National Academy of Recording Arts and Sciences (NARAS)
3402 Pico Boulevard
Santa Monica, CA 90405

(310) 392-3777
info@grammyfoundation.org
http://www.grammy.com

National Academy of Television Arts and Sciences (NATAS)
5220 Lankershim Boulevard
North Hollywood, CA 91601
(818) 754-2810
todd@emmys.org
http://www.emmyonline.org

National Association for Campus Activities (NACA)
13 Harbison Way
Columbia, SC 29212
(803) 732-6222
webmaster@naca.org
http://www.naca.org

National Association of Broadcast Employees and Technicians (NABET)
501 3rd Street NW
Washington, DC 20001
(202) 434-1254
jclark@cwa-union.org
http://www.nabetcwa.org

National Association of Broadcasters (NAB)
1771 N Street NW
Washington, DC 20036
(202) 429-5494
nabstore@nab.org
http://www.nab.org/nabstore

National Association of Music Merchants (NAMM)
c/o Larry Lincoln
5790 Armada Drive
Carlsbad, CA 92008
(760) 438-8001

National Association of Recording Merchandisers (NARM)
9 Eves Drive
Marlton, NJ 08053
(856) 596-2221
rosum@narm.com
http://www.nram.org

National Association of Schools of Music (NASM)
11250 Roger Bacon Drive
Reston, VA 20190
(703) 437-0700
info@arts-accredit.org
http://www.arts-accredit.org

National Federation of Music Clubs (NFMC)
1336 N Delaware Street
Indianapolis, IN 46202
(317) 638-4003
nfmc@nfmcmusic.org
http://www.nfmc-music.org

National Music Publishers' Association (NMPA)
475 Park Avenue South
New York, NY 10016
(646) 742-1651
pr@nmpa.org
http://www.nmpa.org

National Opera Association (NOA)
PO Box 60869
Canyon, TX 79016
(806) 651-2857
http://www.noa.org

Opera America
1156 15th Street NW
Washington, DC 20005

(202) 293-4466
frontdesk@operaamerica.org
http://www.operaam.org

Piano Technicians Guild (PTG)
444 Forest Avenue
Kansas City, KS 66106
(913) 432-9975
info@ptg.org
http://www.ptg.org

Public Relations Society of America (PRSA)
33 Maiden Lane
New York, NY 10038
(212) 460-1400
http://www.prsa.com

Radio Advertising Bureau (RAB)
1320 Greenway Drive
Irving, TX 75038
(972) 753-6822
dareeder@rab.com
http://www.rab.com

Recording Industry Association of America (RIAA)
1330 Connecticut Avenue NW
Washington, DC 20036
(202) 775-0101
http://www.riaa.com

Screen Actors Guild
5757 Wilshire Boulevard
Los Angeles, CA 90036
(323) 954-1600
http://www.sag.org

Society of Professional Audio Recording Services (SPARS)
PO Box 770845
Memphis, TN 38177
(800) 771-7727
spars@spars.com
http://www.spars.com

Songwriters Guild
1500 Harbor Boulevard
Weehawken, NJ 07086
(201) 867-7603
songwritersnj@aol.com

Volunteer Lawyers for the Arts (VLA)
1 E. 53rd Street
New York, NY 10022
(212) 319-2787
(212) 752-6575 (fax)
epaul@vlany.org
http://www.vlany.com

APPENDIX II

MUSIC-RELATED WEB SITES

The World Wide Web is a premier resource for information, no matter what you need. Surfing the Web can help you locate almost anything you want from information to services and everything in between.

This listing contains an assortment of various music-related sites that may be of value to you in your career.

Use this list as a start. There are literally thousands of sites related to the music business and more emerging every day. This listing is for your information. The author is not responsible for any site content. Inclusion or exclusion in this listing does not signify any one site is endorsed or recommended over another by the author.

All Music Industry Contacts
http://www.allmusicindustrycontacts.com

A&R Worldwide
http://www.anrworld.com

ASCAP
http://www.ascap.com

Allied Artists
http://www.alliedartists.com

All Indies
http://www.allindies.com

All Media Guide
http://www.allmediaguide.com

Amazon.com
http://www.amazon.com

American Federation of Musicians
http://www.afm.org

American Music Showcase
http://www.americanmusicshowcase.com

ARTISTdirect
http://www.artistdirect.com

Association of Music Writers and Photographers
http://www.musicjournlists.com

BMI (Broadcast Music International)
http://www.bmi.org

Backstage World
http://www.backstageworld.com

Bandname.com
http://www.bandname.com

Bands 4 Bands
http://www.bands4bands.com

Bandsforlabels.com
http://www.bandsforlabels.com

Bandzoogle.com
http://www.banzoogle.com

Berklee Music
http://www.berkleemusic.com

Billboard
http://www.billboard.com

Blue Coupe
http://www.bluecoupe.com

CD Army
http://www.cdarmy.com

CD Replic8.com
http://www.cdreplic8.com

CDreview.com
http://www.cdreview.com

CDReviews.com
http://www.cdreviews.com

CD Street
http://www.cdstreet.com

CaféPress.com
http://www.cafepress.com

Cornerband.com
http://www.cornerband.com

CountryInterviewsOnline.net
http://www.countryinterviewsonline.net

Creative Musicians Coalition
http://www.aimcmc.com

Degyshop.com
http://www.degyshop.com

Demoshoppers.com
http://www.demoshoppers.com

Digital Club Network
http://www.digitalclubnetwork.com

Digital Music Company
http://www.audiosurge.com

Disc Jockey 101
http://www.discjockey101.com

Disc Makers
http://www.discmakers.com

Drummers World
http://www.drummersworld.org

Earbuzz.com
http://www.earbuzz.com

Entertainmentcareers.net
http://www.entertainmentcareers.net

Festival Finder
http://www.festivalfinder.com

Festival Network Online
http://www.festivalnet.com

Figgle.com
http://www.figgle.com

4 Front Media and Music
http://www.4frontmusic.com

Future of Music Coalition
http://www.futureofmusic.org

Gajoob
http://www.gajoob.com

Garageband
http://www.garageband.com

Getindie.com
http://www.getindie.com

Getsigned.com
http://www.getsigned.com

Harry Fox Agency, Inc.
http://www.harryfox.com

GigAmerica.com
http://www.gigamerica.com

Gigmasters.com
http://www.gigmasters.com

Global Music Project
http://www.globalmusicproject.org

Harmony-Central
http://www.harmony-central.com

H.E.A.R. (Hearing Education and Awareness For Rockers)
http://www.hearnet.com

Hit Quarters
http://www.hitquarters.com

Hot Jobs
http://www.hotjobs.com

House Concerts
http://www.houseconcerts.com

iMusicWorks
http://www.imusicworks.com

Independentbands.com
http://www.independentbands.com

Independent Distribution Network
http://www.idnmusic.com

Independent Music Network
http://www.imntv.com

Independent Online Distribution Alliance
http://www.iodalliance.com

Independent Songwriter
http://www.independent songwriter.com

Indiebiz.com
http://www.indiebiz.com

Indie Monkey
http://www.indiemonkey.com

Indie Music
http://www.indie-music.com

Indie Performer
http://www.indieperformer.com

Inside Sessions
http://www.insidesessions.com

Job Bank USA
http://www.jobbankusa.com

Job.com
http://www.job.com

Launch Media, Inc.
http://www.launch.com

Locals Online
http://www.localsonline.com

Lyrical Line
http://www.lyricalline.com

Lyrics.com
http://www.lyrics.com

Marketing Your Music
http://www.marketingyourmusic.com

MHZ Networks
http://www.mhznetworks.org

ModernRock.com
http://www.modernrock.com

Monster.com
http://www.monster.com

Muse's Muse Songwriting Resource
http://www.musemuse.com

Music Biz Advice
http://www.musicbizadvice.com

MusicContracts.com
http://www.musiccontracts.com

Musician.com
http://www.guitarcenter.com

Musician's Assistance Program
http://www.map200.org

Musicians.com
http://www.musicains.com

Musicians Contact Service
http://www.musicianscontact.com

Musicians National Referral
http://www.musicianreferral.com

Musiclink
http://www.musiclink.com

Music Office
http://www.musicoffice.com

Music Pages
http://www.musicpages.com

Music Player Network
http://www.musicplayer.com

Music Review
http://www.musreview.com

Musictoday
http://wwwmusictoday.com

MusicWire
http://www.musicwire.com

National Music Publishers Association
http://www.nmpa.org

New Music Times
http://www.nmtinc.com

Nolo.com
http://www.nolo.com

Nova Music Productions
http://www.novamusic.com

The Orchard
http://www.theorchard.com

Outersound
http://www.outersound.com

Performing Biz
http://www.performingbiz.com

Pitchfork Media
http://www.pictchforkmedia.com

Pollstar.com
http://www.pollstar.com

Poplife.net
http://www.poplife.net

PowerGig
http://www.powergig.com

Professional Musicians Referral
http://www.pmr-musicians.com

Radio and Records
http://www.radioandrecords.com

Record Store Review
http://www.recordstorereview.com

Rock & Roll Library
http://www.rocklibrary.com

Roots Music Report
http://www.rootsmusicreport.com

SESAC, Inc.
http://www.sesac.com

Shelly Field
http://www.shellyfield.com

sideRoad music group
http://www.sideroadmusic.com

Society of Singers, Inc.
http://www.singers.org

Song Quarters
http://www.songquarters.com

Songwriter Universe
http://www.songwriteruniverse.com

Sputnik7.com
http://www.sputnik7.com

StarPolish
http://www.starpolish.com

Stress Free Success
http://www.shellyfield.com

Studiofinder.com
http://www.studiofinder.com

Summit Artists
http://www.summitartists.com

Talkguitar
http://www.talkguitar.com

Taxi
http://www.taxi.com

Undercurrents, Inc.
http://www.undercurrents.com

Uniform Code Council
http://www.uc-council.org

USA Musician
http://www.usamusician.com

U.S. Copyright Office
http://www.copywright.gov

U.S. Patent and Trademark Office

http://www.uspto.gov

U.S. Small Business Administration (SBA)

http://www.sba.gov

Worldwide Internet Music Resources

http://www.music.indiana.edu/music_resources

BIBLIOGRAPHY

A. Books

There are thousands of books on all aspects of the music industry. Sometimes just reading about someone else's success inspires you, motivates you, or just helps you to come up with ideas to help you attain your own dreams.

Books can be a treasure trove of information if you want to learn about a particular aspect of a career or gain more knowledge about how something in the industry works.

The books listed below are separated into general categories. Subjects often overlap. Use this listing as a beginning. Check out your local library, bookstore, or online retailer for other books that might interest you about the industry.

Artist and Music Management

Davison, Marc. *All Area Access: A Personal Management Guide for the Unsigned Artist.* Milwaukee, WI: Hal Leonard Corporation, 1997.

Frascogna, Xavier M. *This Business of Artist Management.* New York: Watson-Guptill Publications, 2004.

Goodridge, Walt. *This Game of Hip Hop Artist Management.* New York: Passion Profit Company, 2004.

Marcone, Stephen. *Managing Your Band: Artist Management: The Ultimate Responsibility.* Wayne, NJ: HiMarks Publishing Company, 2003.

Music Managers Forum Staff. *The MMF Guide to Professional Music Management: Includes International Directory.* London: Sanctuary Publishing Limited, 2003.

Taylor, Joe, Jr. *Music Management for the Rest of Us.* Morrisville, NC: Lulu Press, 2004.

Bands

Bliesener, Mark. *Complete Idiot's Guide to Starting a Band.* New York: Penguin Group, 2004.

Taylor, Joe, Jr., and Robbins, Melissa. *Grow Your Band's Audience: Six Steps to Success for Independent Musicians.* Athens, GA: Taylor Creative Management, 2002.

Biographies and History: Musical Artists and Genres

Ariel Books Staff. *Elvis: The King of Rock'n Roll.* Kansas City, MO: Andrews McMeel Publishing, 2004.

Altschuler, Glenn C. *All Shook Up: How Rock 'n' Roll Changed America.* New York: Oxford University Press, 2004.

Berlinger, Joe. *Metallica. Some Kind of Monster.* New York: St. Martin's Press, 2004.

Blondie. *The Best of Blondie.* Milwaukee, WI: Hal Leonard Corporation, 2004.

Brackett, David. *The Pop, Rock, and Soul Reader: Histories and Debates.* New York: Oxford University Press, 2004.

Brett, David. *Elvis: The Hollywood Years.* London, England: Robinson Books, 2004.

Cashman, Lola. *Inside the Zoo with U2: My Life with the Biggest Rock Band.* London: John Blake Publishing, 2003.

Campbell, Garth. *Johnny Cash: He Walked the Line.* London: John Blake Publishing, 2003.

Cherry Lane Music Staff. *Steely Dan: Everything Must Go.* New York: Cherry Lane Books, 2003.

Coffey, Dennis. *Guitars, Bars and Motown Superstars.* Ann Arbor, MI: University of Michigan Press, 2004.

Coleman, Mark. *Playback: From the Victrola to Mp3, 100 Years of Music, Machines, and Money.* Cambridge, MA: Da Capo Press, 2005.

Collis, John. *Ike Turner: King of Rhythm.* London: Do-Not Press, 2004.

Cook, Richard. *Blue Note Records: The Biography.* Boston: Justin, Charles & Company Publishers, 2004.

Davis, Stephen. *Old Gods Almost Dead: The 40-Year Odyssey of the Rolling Stones.* Collingdale, PA: DIANE Publishing Company, 2004.

Dolenz, Micky. *I'm A Believer: My Life of Monkees, Music and Madness.* New York: Cooper Square Publishers, 2004.

Gittins, Ian. *The Stories Behind Every Song: Talking Heads.* Milwaukee, WI: Hal Leonard, 2004.

Gonzalez, Gabriela. *Backstage Pass.* New York: Harper Collins, 2004.

Graham, Bill. *Bill Graham Presents: My Life Inside Rock and Out.* Boulder, CO: Da Capo Press, 2004.

Gruen, Bob. *The Clash.* London: Vision On, 2004.

Hal Leonard Publications Staff. *Melissa Etheridge: Lucky.* Milwaukee, WI: Hal Leonard Corporation, 2004.

Hendricks, Tim. *The Mentor: The True Story of an Hourly Factory Employee who Became Financially Independent.* Nashville, TN: Music City Publishing, 2005.

Keogh, Pamela Clarke. *Elvis Presley: The Man, The Life, The Legend.* New York: Simon & Schuster, 2004.

Layden, Joe. *Home Before Daylight: My Life On the Road With the Grateful Dead.* New York: St. Martin's Press, 2004.

Lavigne, Avril. *Avril Lavigne-Under My Skin.* Milwaukee, WI: Hal Leonard Corporation, 2004.

Lewis, Dave. *Led Zeppelin: A Celebration 2.* Edmunds, UK: Bish Bash Books, 2004.

Markel, Rita J. *Jimi Hendrix.* Minneapolis: Carolrhoda Books, Inc., 2003.

Marsh, Dave. *Before I Get Old. The Story of the Who.* London: Plexus Publishing, 2003.

Martell, Nevin. *Dave Mathews Band: Music For People, Revised and Updated.* New York: Simon & Schuster, 2004.

McAdams, Tara. *The Elvis Presley Handbook.* London: MQ Publications, 2004.

Nugent, Shemane. *Married to a Rock Star.* Guilford, CT: Globe Pequot Press, 2004.

Parish, Steve. *Home Before Daylight: My Life with the Grateful Dead.* New York: St. Martin's Press, 2003.

Richie, Lionel. *Lionel Richie Anthology.* Hal Leonard Corporation: Milwaukee, WI: 2004.

Robinson, Peter. *Busted on Tour.* London: Virgin Books, 2004.

Ro, Ronin. *Bad Boy: The Influence of Sean "Puffy" Combs on the Music Industry.* New York: Simon & Schuster, 2002.

Rollins, Henry. *Get in the Van: On the Road with Black Flag.* Los Angeles: 21361, 2004.

Rubin, Dave. *Rockin' the Blues: The Best American and British Blues-Rock Guitarists: 1963–1973.* Milwaukee, WI: Hal Leonard Corporation, 2005.

Sandford, Christopher. *Mick Jagger. Rebel Knight.* New York: Music Sales Corporation, 2004.

Sawyers, June Skinner. *Racing in the Street: The Bruce Springsteen Reader.* New York: Penguin Group, 2004.

Sleazegrinde. *Gigs from Hell: True Stories from Rock and Roll's Frontline.* Manchester, UK: Headpress, 2004.

Starr, Ringo. *Postcards from the Boys.* San Francisco: Chronicle Books, 2004.

Thompson, Dave. *Red Hot Chilli Peppers: By the Way: The Biography.* London: Virgin Books, 2004.

———. *Turn It On Again: Peter Gabriel, Phil Collins, and Genesis.* San Francisco: Backbeat Books, 2004.

Tobler, John, and Andrew Doe. *Beach Boys: The Complete Guide Their Music.* Edmunds, UK: Bish Bash Books, 2004.

Wheeler, Jill. *Jessica Simpson.* Edina, MN: ABDO Publishing Company, 2004.

White, Charles. *The Life and Times of Little Richard. The Authorized Biography.* New York: Music Sales Corporation, 2004.

Wilson, Brian. *The Beatles: Ten Years That Shook the World.* New York: Dorling Kindersley Publishing, 2004.

Business

Aspatore Books. *Inside the Minds: CEOs and Presidents from Island Def Jam, Napster, LLC, EMI Music North Group and More Provide a Behind the Scenes Glimpse into Recording, Promotions and Entertainment: the Music Business.* Boston: Aspatore Books, 2004.

Grant, A. and Rene, Lo. *Music Business: It's all about the Music, Right?* Lincoln, NE: iUniverse, 2005.

Hall, Charles W. *Marketing in the Music Industry.* Boston: Pearson Custom Publishing, 2000.

Krasilovsky, M. William. *This Business of Music: The Definitive Guide to the Music Industry.* New York: Watson-Guptill Publications, 2003.

Prince, Dennis. *How to Sell Music, Collectibles, and Instruments on eBay . . . and Make a Fortune.* New York: McGraw-Hill, 2004.

Spellman, Peter. *The Musician's Internet: Online Strategies for Success in the Music Industry.* Milwaukee, WI: Hal Leonard Corporation, 2001.

Thall, Peter M. *What They'll Never Tell You About the Music Business: The Myths, Secrets, Lies & A Few Truths.* New York: VNU Business Media, 2002.

Williams, Alvin V., Jay King, and Ann Elizabeth Jones. *The Business of Music for the Gospel/Christian Industry.* Signal Mountain, TN: Waldenhouse Publishers, 2005.

Careers

Field, Shelly. *Career Opportunities in the Music Industry.* New York: Checkmark Books, 2004.

Field, Shelly. *Career Opportunities in Theater and the Performing Arts.* New York: Checkmark Books, 2006.

Contracts and Legal

Fera, Vito. *Contracts for the Music Industry.* Longwood, FL: NSP Publications, 2001.

Kellogg, John P. *Take Care of Your Music Business: The Legal and Business Information You Need to Grow in the Music Industry.* Denver: PJ's Publishing, 2001.

Platinum Millennium Publishing Staff. *Music Business and Entertainment Law Contracts: For Indie Recording Artist, Labels, Songwriters, Composers, Producers, Managers and All Others in the Record Industry.* Waterbury, CT: Platinum Millennium, 2004.

Platinum Millennium Publishing Staff. *101 Music Business Contracts – Updated Edition – Preprinted Binder / CD-ROM Set: Containing over 100 Contracts and Agreements for Recording Artist, Musicians, Record Companies, Managers, Songwriters, Labels, Producers, Indies and Any and All Others in the Music Industry: Entertainment Law at Its Best!* Waterbury, CT: Platinum Millennium, 2002.

Schulenberg, Richard. *Legal Aspects of the Music Industry.* Lakewood, NJ: Watson-Guptill Publications, 1999.

Wilson, Lee. *Making It in the Music Business: The Business and Legal Guide for Songwriters and Performers.* New York: Allworth Press, 2004.

Wilson, Lee. *The Copyright Guide: A Friendly Handbook for Protecting and Profiting from Copyrights.* New York: Allworth Press, 2003.

General

Blackwell, Roger and Stephan, Tina. *Brands That Rock: What Business Leaders Can Learn from the World of Rock and Roll.* Hoboken, NJ: John Wiley & Sons, 2003.

Heitman, William P. *Music's Broken Wings: Fifty Years of Aviation Accidents in the Music Industry.* Durham, NC: Dreamflyer Publications, 2003.

Parker, Nigel. *Music Business: A Professional Guide to Infrastructure, Practice and Law of the Industry.* Poole, UK: Palladian Law Publishing, Ltd., 2004.

Music Marketing and Public Relations

Baker, Bob. *Guerrilla Music Marketing Handbook: 201 Self-Promotion Ideas for Songwriters, Musicians & Bands.* St. Louis, MO: Spotlight Publications, 2002.

Summers, Jodi. *Making and Marketing Music.* New York: Allworth Press, 2004.

Field, Shelly. *Career Opportunities in Advertising and Public Relations.* New York: Facts On File, 2001.

Producing

Avalon, Moses. *Confessions of a Record Producer: How to Survive The Scams and Shams of the Music Business.* San Francisco: Backbeat Books, 2002.

Burgess, Richard James. *The Art of Music Production.* New York: Music Sales Corporation, 2004.

Granata, Charles. *Sessions with Sinatra: Frank Sinatra and The Art of Recording.* Chicago: Chicago Review Press, Inc., 2003.

Howard, David, N. *Sonic Alchemy: Visionary Music Producers and Their Maverick Recordings.* Milwaukee, WI: Hal Leonard Corporation, 2004.

Huber, Christian W. *Producing Your Own CDs. A Handbook.* New York: Music Sales Corporation, 2004.

King, Sahpreem A. *Gotta Get Signed: How to Become a Hip-Hop Producer.* New York: Music Sales Corporation, 2005.

Publishing

Howard, George. *Music Publishing 101.* Boston: Berklee Press, 2004.

Poe, Randy. *Music Publishing: A Songwriter's Guide.* Cincinnati: Writer's Digest, 1997.

Smith, Regina. *Music Publishing 101: Crash Course Made Simple and Easy.* No Walls Production & Publishing, 2000.

Recording

Albin, Zak. *The Poetics of Rock: Cutting Tracks, Making Records.* London: University of California Press, 2001.

Brooks, Tim. *Lost Sounds: Blacks and the Birth of the Recording Industry, 1890–1919.* Champaign, IL: University of Illinois Press, 2004.

Holzman, Keith. *The Complete Guide to Starting a Record Company.* Los Angeles: Solutions Unlimited, 2004.

Howard, George. *An Insider's Guide to the Record Industry.* Boston: Berklee Books, 2003.

Hull, Geoffrey, P. *The Recording Industry.* New York: Routledge, 2004.

Katz, Mark. *Capturing Sound: How Technology Has Changed Music.* Berkeley: University of California Press, 2004.

Morton, David. *Sound Recording: The Life Story of a Technology.* Westport, CT: Greenwood Publishing Group, 2004.

Ramone, Phil. *Making Records.* New York: Hyperion Press, 2003.

Schaefer, A. R. *Making a First Recording.* Bloomington, MN: Capstone Press Inc, 2003.

Spellman, Peter W. *Indie Power: A Business-Building Guide for Record Labels, Music Production Houses and Merchant Musicians.* Boston: Music Business Solutions, 2003.

Upton, Fred. *Recording Industry Marketing Practices: A Check-up: Congressional Hearing.* Collingdale, PA: DIANE Publishing, 2004.

Sales

Berman, Helen. *Ad Sales: Winning Secrets of the Magazine Pros.* Los Angeles: Berman Press, 2002.

Curran, Marc, W. *Sell Your Music: How to Profitably Sell Your Own Recordings On Line.* Simi Valley, CA: NMD Books, 2001.

Mulligan, Mark. *Music Retailing: Driving CD Sales with Competitive Pricing.* New York: Jupiter Research, 2004.

Warner, Charles and Buckman, Joseph. *Media Selling: Broadcast, Cable, Print and Interactive.* Ames, Iowa: Iowa State Press, 2004.

Songwriting

Bessler, Ian, ed. *2005 Songwriters Market.* Cincinnati: Writer's Digest Books, 2004.

Blume, Jason. *6 Steps to Songwriting Success: The Comprehensive Guide to Writing and Marketing Hit Songs.* New York: Watson-Guptill Publications, 2004.

DeMain, Bill. *In Their Own Words: Songwriters Talk about the Creative Process.* Westport, CT: Greenwood Publishing Group, 2004.

Dominick, Serene. *Burt Bacharach: Song By Song.* New York: Music Sales Corp, 2004.

Hirschehorn, Joel. *Complete Idot's Guide to Songwriting 2.* New York: Alpha Books, 2004.

Hooper, Caroline. *Learn Songwriting.* Tulsa, OK: EDC Publishing, 2004.

Karmen, Steve. *Who Killed the Jingle?* Milwaukee, WI: Hal Leonard Corporation, 2004.

Lee, Pincus. *The Songwriter's Success Manual.* Mattituck, NY: Amereon, Limited, 2004.

Hal Leonard Corp Staff. *Hip Hop and Rap Lyric Book.* Milwaukee, WI: Hal Leonard Corporation, 2003.

Rooksby, Rikky. *Melody: How to Write Great Tunes.* San Francisco: Backbeat Books, 2004.

Talent

Faulkner, Robert. *Hollywood Studio Musicians, Their Work and Careers in the Recording Industry.* Lanham, MD: University Press of America, 1985.

Martin, Bill. *Pro Secrets of Heavy Rock Singing.* London: Sanctuary Publishing, 2003.

Rodgers, Jeffrey Pepper. *The Complete Singer-Songwriter: A Troubadour's Guide to Writing, Performing, Recording and Business.* San Francisco: Backbeat Books, 2003.

Rudsenske, J Scott. *Music Business Made Simple: A Guide To Becoming A Recording Artist.* New York: Music Sales Corporation, 2004.

Touring

Gibson, Chris and Connell, John. *Music and Tourism: On the Road Again.* Cleavedon, UK: Channel View Publications, 2004.

Platinum Millennium Publishing Staff. *The Industry Yellow Pages: The Official Club and Venue Touring Directory, Listing over 1700 Music Clubs and Venues in the U.S. and Canada for Your Touring Band to Play at: Are You Ready for the Exposure That You Deserve?* Waterbury, CT: Platinum Millennium, 2003.

B. Periodicals, Publications, and Webzines

Magazines, newspapers, membership bulletins, and newsletters help keep you up to date with industry happenings and abreast of new trends. There are various periodicals geared towards different parts of the music industry. Use this listing as a beginning. Space limitations limit listing all periodicals.

Check out your local library, bookstore, or newsstand for additional titles of interest. Don't forget to look for Web versions of many popular music periodicals.

Acoustic Guitar Magazine
220 West End Avenue
San Rafael, CA 94901
(415) 485-6946
(415) 485-0831 (fax)
http://www.acousticguitar.com

Airplay Monitor
5055 Wilshire Boulevard
Los Angeles, CA 90036
(323) 525-2000
http://www.airplaymonitor.com

Alternate Music Press
PO Box 2643
Hollywood, CA 90078
(707) 313-7740 (fax)
http://www.alternatemusicpress.com

Alternative Press
6516 Detroit Avenue
Cleveland, OH 44102
(216) 631-1510
(216) 631-1016 (fax)
http://www.altpress.com

American Songwriters Magazine
50 Music Square West
Nashville, TN 37203
(615) 321-6096
(615) 327-6097 (fax)
http://www.americansongwriter.com

Amplifier
117 Park Drive
Boston, MA 02215
(617) 536-5295
http://www.amplifermagazine.com

Amusement Business
PO Box 24970
Nashville, TN 37202
(615) 321-4250
(615) 327-1574 (fax)
http://www.amusementbusiness.com

Bandclassifieds.com
PO Box 840
Northampton, MA 01061
http://www.bandclassifieds.com

Bass Player
2800 Campus Drive
San Mateo, CA 94403
(650) 513-4300
(650) 513-4642 (fax)
http://www.bassplayer.com

Big Takeover Magazine
249 Eldridge Street
New York, NY 10002
(212) 533-6057
http://www.bigtakeover.com

Billboard
770 Broadway
New York, NY 10003
(646) 654-4400
(646) 654-4681 (fax)
http://www.billboard.com

Billboard – Los Angeles
5055 Wilshire Boulevard
Los Angeles, CA 90036
(323) 525-2300
(323) 525-2394 (fax)
http://www.billboard.com

Billboard – Nashville
49 Music Square West
Nashville, TN 37203
(615) 321-4290
(615) 320-0454 (fax)
http://www.billboard.com

Blastitude
2101 North Mozart Street

Chicago, IL 60647
http://www.blastitutde.com

Blender
1040 Avenue of the Americas
New York, NY 10018
(212) 302-2626
(212) 302-9671 (fax)
http://www.blender.com

Blue Suede News
PO Box 25 East
Duvall, WA 98019
(425) 788-2776
http://www.bluesuedenews.com

BPM Culture Magazine
8517 Santa Monica Boulevard
West Hollywood, CA 90069
(800) 471-3291
(310) 360-71711 (fax)
http://www.djmixed.com

Broadcast and Cable
1705 DeSalles Street NW
Washington, DC 20036
(202) 659-2340
(202) 429-0651 (fax)
http://www.broadcastandcable.com

Buzzine
PO Box 18857
Encino, CA 91416
(818) 995-6133
(818) 995-6138 (fax)
http://www.buzzine.com

Caffeine Magazine
PO Box 4231-306
Woodland Hills, CA 91365

(323) 468-1250
(323) 465-0666 (fax)

Carebe News
15 West 39th Street
New York, NY 10018
(212) 944-1992
(212) 944-2089 (fax)
http://www.nycarebe.com

Chorus and Verse
1230 Celler Avenue
Clark, NJ 07066
http://www.chorusandverse.com

Circus Magazine
Six West 18th Street
New York, NY 10011
(212) 242-4902
(212) 242-5734 (fax)
http://www.circusmagazine.com

CMJ Network
151 West 25th Street
New York, NY 10001
(917) 606-1908
(917) 606-1914 (fax)
http://www.cmj.com

Country Weekly
118 16th Avenue South
Nashville, TN 37203
(615) 259-1111
(615) 259-1110 (fax)
http://www.countryweekly.com

Descarga
328 Flatbush Avenue
Brooklyn, NY 11238
(718) 693-2966
(718) 693-1316 (fax)
http://www.descarga.com

DIY Reporter
3662 Lowry Road
Los Angeles, CA 90027
(323) 665-8080
(323) 665-8068 (fax)
http://www.diyreporter.com

Downbeat Magazine
102 North Haven Road
Elmhurst, IL 60126
(800) 535-7496
http://www.downbeat.com

Expose
6167 Jervis Avenue
Newark, CA 94560
http://www.expose.com

Extreme Magazine
2316 Delaware Avenue
Buffalo, NY 14216
(716) 877-5777
http://www.extreme-magazine.com

Facility Magazine
4425 West Airport Freeway
Irving, TX 75062
(972) 255-8020
(972) 255-9582 (fax)

Fuse Magazine
4211 Hartwidk Village Place
Louisville, KY40241
http://www.fusemag.com

Global Rhythm
347 West 36th Street
New York, NY 10018
(212) 868-4359
http://www.gorhythm.com

Gritz Magazine
15 Wellington Avenue
Greenville, SC 29609
(864) 467-1699
http://www.gritz.net

Grooves
18 Eastwood Drive
Voorhees, NJ 08043
(732) 516-1946
http://www.groovesmag.com

Guitar Player
460 Park Avenue South
New York, NY 10016
(212) 378-0400
(212) 378-2149 (fax)
http://www.guitarplayer.com

Guitar World
1115 Broadway
New York, NY 10010
(212) 807-7100
http://www.guitarworld.com

Harp Magazine
8737 Colesville Road
Silver Springs, MD 20910
(301) 588-4114
(301) 588-5531 (fax)
http://www.harpmagazine.com

HM Magazine
6307 Cele Road
Pflugerville, TX 78660
(512) 989-7309
(512) 670-2764 (fax)
http://www.hmmagazine.com

Ice Magazine
PO Box 3043

Santa Monica, CA 90408
(310) 829-1291
(310) 829-2979 (fax)
http://www.icemagazine.com

Independent Musician Magazine
1067 Market Street
San Francisco, CA 94103
(415) 503-0340
http://www.immagazine.com

JAZZIZ Magazine
2650 North Military Trail
Fountain Square II Building
Boca Raton, FL 33431
(561) 893-6888
(561) 893-6687 (fax)
http://www.jazziz.com

JazzTimes
8737 Colesville Road
Silver Spring, MD 20910
(301) 588-4114
(301) 588-2009 (fax)
http://www.jazztimes.com

Juice Magazine
52 Market Street
Venice, CA 90291
(310) 399-5336
(310) 399-8687 (fax)
http://www.juicemagazine.com

Keyboard Magazine
2800 Campus Drive
San Mateo, CA 94403
(650) 513-4300
(650) 513-4642 (fax)
http://www.keyboardonline.com

Living Blues
PO Box 1848

301 Hill Hall
University, MS 38677
(662) 915-5742
(662) 915-7842 (fax)
http://www.livingblues.com

Magnet Magazine
1218 Chestnut Street
Philadelphia, PA 19107
(215) 413-8570
(215) 413-8569 (fax)
http://www.magnetmagazine.com

Maximum RockNRoll
PO Box 460760
San Francisco, CA 94146
(415) 923-9814
(415) 923-9617 (fax)
http://www.maximumrocknroll.com

Mix Magazine
6400 Hollis Street
Emeryville, CA 945008
(510) 653-3307
(510) 653-5142 (fax)
http://www.mixmagazine.com

MTV Magazine
1515 Broadway
New York, NY 10036
(212) 654-6336
(212) 654-4900 (fax)
http://www.mtv.com

Music Connection
4215 Coldwater Canyon
Studio City, CA 91604
(818) 755-0101
(818) 755-0102 (fax)
http://www.musicconnection.com

MusicDish.com
1814 Astoria Boulevard
Astoria, NY 11102
(718) 726-1938
http://www.musicdish.com

Music Monitor
107 East Aycock Street
Raleigh, NC 27608
(919) 821-9343
(919) 821-9343 (fax)
http://www.musicmonitor.com

Music Morsels
PO Box 2760
Aceworth, GA 30102
(678) 445-0006
(678) 494-9289 (fax)
http://www.serg.org.musicmorsels.htm

Music Row
1221 17th Avenue South
Nashville, TN 37212
(615) 321-3627
(615) 329-0852 (fax)
http://ww.musicrow.com

New Music Weekly
127 North Larchmont
Los Angeles, CA 90004
(323) 325-9997
http://www.newmusicweekly.com

No Depression
PO Box 213332
Seattle, WA 98103
http://www.nodepression.net

Outburn Magazine
PO Box 3187
Thousand Oaks, CA 91259

(805) 493-5861
http://www.outburn.com

Performer Magazine (Northwest)
285 Washington Street
Somerville, MA 02143
(617) 627-9200
(617) 627-9930 (fax)
http://www.performermag.com

Performer Magazine (Southeast)
449 ½ Moreland Avenue
Atlanta, GA 30307
(404) 582-0088
(404) 582-0089 (fax)
http://www.performermag.com

Performing Songwriter Magazine
PO Box 40931
Nashville, TN 37204
(615) 385-7786
(615) 385-5637 (fax)
http://www.performingsongwriter.com

Pitchfork Media
PO Box 60908
Chicago, IL 60660
http://www.pitchforkmedia.com

Pollstar
4697 West Jacqueline Avenue
Fresno, CA 93722
(209) 271-7900
(209) 271-7979 (fax)
http://www.pollstar.com

Recording Magazine
5412 Idlwild Trail
Bolder, CO 80301
(303) 516-9119
(303) 516-9118 (fax)
http://www.recordingmag.com

Resonance Magazine
PO Box 95620
Seattle, WA 98145
(206) 633-3500
(206) 633-0178 (fax)
http://www.resonancemag.com

Reviews Unlimited
6060 Arthur Avenue
St. Louis, MO 63139
(314) 645-3410
http://www.reviewsunlimited.com

Revolver
1115 Broadway
New York, NY 10010
(212) 807-7100
(212) 924-2352 (fax)
http://www.revolvermag.com

Rockgrl Magazine
7683 SE 27th Street
Mercer Island, WA 96040
(206) 275-4622
(206) 275-4624 (fax)
http://www.rockgrl.com

Rockpile
PO Box 258
Jenkintown, PA 19046
(215) 855-7625
(215) 885-7161 (fax)
http://www.rockpile.net

Rolling Stone
1290 Avenue of the Americas
New York, NY 10104
(212) 494-1616
(212) 484-1771 (fax)
http://www.rollingstone.com

Roots Music Report
350 North Guadalope Street
San Marcos, TX 78666
(877) 532-2225
http://www.rootsmusicreport.com

Skyscraper Magazine
PO Box 4432
Boulder, CO 80306
(303) 544-9858
http://www.skyscrapermagazine.com

Songwriter Universe
11684 Ventura Boulevard
Studio City, CA 91604
http://www.songwriteruniverse.com

Soundcheck Magazine
389 Main Street
Malden, MA 02148
(781) 388-7749
(781) 388-1817 (fax)

The Source
215 Park Avenue South
New York, NY 10003
(212) 253-7300
(212) 253-9344 (fax)
http://www.thesource.com

Spin
205 Lexington Avenue
New York, NY 10016

(212) 231-7400
(212) 231-7300 (fax)
http://www.spin.com

Tracks Magazine
460 North Orlando Avenue
Winter Park, FL 32789
(407) 628-4802
(407) 628-7061 (fax)
http://www.tracksmusic.com

URB Music
2410 Hyperion Avenue
Los Angeles, CA 90027
(323) 315-1700
(323) 315-1799 (fax)
http://www.urb.com

Unsigned The Magazine
PO Box 165116
Irving, TX 75016
(469) 583-2516
http://www.unsignedthemagazine.com

Vibe
215 Lexington Avenue
New York, NY 10016
(212) 448-7300
(212) 448-7400 (fax)
http://www.vibe.com

INDEX

interests, resume component 110–111
Internet and exposure 217
Internet Service Provider (ISP) 132
internships 63, 89
interviews
    environments 166–168
    follow-up 174
    getting 159–165
    media 215
    process 165
      what to bring 165
      what to wear 165–166
    questions
      from interviewer 168–171
      from you 171
    salary and compensation 171–172
    thank-you notes 173–174
    tips for 68, 172–173
    vacation and personal days for 86
inventory and self-assessment 64–65
ISP. *See* Internet Service Provider

J

Jagger, Mick 21
jingles 238
job search strategies 84–103
job
    v. career 13
    hotlines 89
    using to create career 84
job market
    hidden 87, 90–92
    open 87–89
journal. *See* action journal
journalists 16, 236

K

Kelloggs 175
Keys, Alicia 21

L

labels. *See also* independent labels
    finding 218–223
    getting noticed by 214
    getting signed by 217–223
    major v. independent 223–224
lawyers 16, 83, 158, 225–226
learning tools in the workplace 190–192
leisure time skills 68
letters of recommendation 60, 114–115, 154, 165
libraries and open job market 88

lists, making 202–203
locations, geographic 16, 26, 39, 77–79
logo 129
long-term goals 32–33, 42
Los Angeles, CA 39, 77, 79, 88, 159, 202

M

MacEntire, Reba 239
Madonna 204
magazines 207, 258–264
mailing lists 211
mailing/shipping resume 162
major v. independent label 223–224
Making It in Music seminars 11, 124
management books 253
management contract 227–228
managers 148, 157, 225. *See also* business managers;
    personal managers
market, determining 39, 61
marketing yourself 16, 134
    becoming an expert 184–168
    contacts, making and using 156–157
    finding a mentor/advocate 157–158
    five Ps of 176–177
    getting gigs 209
    importance of 175–176
    like a pro 180–184
    meeting the right people 145–148
    networking basics 148–156
    new opportunities 188–190
    on the phone 134–144
    putting together your package 177–180
    other strategies 186–188
    visibility and 180–184
    who you know 144–145
McDonalds 175
mechanical rights 229, 230
media
    people 158, 183, 216
    possibilities lists 60, 216
mentor, finding 157
meet and greet 96, 97
Millennium Music Conference 146
mission statement, personal 235–236
Monster.com 89
morals in the workplace 199–200
mugs to get call back 143
musicians 15, 157, 238. *See also* talent end, success on
music industry
    breaking into 206–207
    career. *See* career, music industry
    contacts. *See* contacts, music industry